PROTECTION
of
FOREIGN INTERESTS

✦

A Study in Diplomatic
and Consular Practice

✦

By WILLIAM McHENRY FRANKLIN

SPECIAL PROJECTS DIVISION, DEPARTMENT OF STATE

GREENWOOD PRESS, PUBLISHERS
NEW YORK

Originally printed
by the U.S. Government Printing Office

First Greenwood Reprinting 1969

Library of Congress Catalogue Card Number 69-13898

ACKNOWLEDGMENTS

The author takes this opportunity to express his appreciation to Mr. Albert E. Clattenburg, Jr., Chief of the Special Projects Division, and Mr. E. Wilder Spaulding, Chief of the Division of Publications, for their constant assistance and encouragement in the preparation of this study.   Mr. E. Tomlin Bailey, Assistant Chief of the Special Projects Division, read the entire work in manuscript and improved it with constructive suggestions.   Mr. Dayle C. McDonough, now American Consul General at Glasgow, aided the author in matters pertaining to the history and interpretation of the *Foreign Service Regulations*. To Mr. James C. Henderson, American Consul at Guadalajara, the author is indebted for the comprehensive collection of current papers on the subject which Mr. Henderson compiled in the course of his tour of duty in the Special Division (now the Special Projects Division) during the early part of the recent war.

WILLIAM M. FRANKLIN

DEPARTMENT OF STATE,
  June 5, 1946.

CONTENTS

INTRODUCTION

IT IS a recognized fact that the basic aim of every power in maintaining a diplomatic and consular service is the protection of the interests of that particular power in foreign lands. In order that there may be no misunderstanding on this score, the diplomatic and consular regulations of most states lay emphasis on the fact that the principal duty of the diplomatic or consular officer is to protect or safeguard the interests of his state and its nationals abroad. Referring to the duties of an American Foreign Service officer, the Department of State has said that "he protects generally the interests of the United States in accordance with international law and protects, advises, and otherwise assists Americans resident or traveling abroad for business or other purposes".[1] In the protection of nationals and their interests abroad the prevailing rule has been squarely based on what Secretary of State Hamilton Fish felicitously termed "the correlative rights of allegiance and protection".[2]

In view of this accepted thesis it is significant that the *Foreign Service Regulations of the United States* also provide that "diplomatic and consular officers may, upon request, assume temporarily the protection of *foreign* interests".[3] This

---

[1] Department of State, *The American Foreign Service* (Government Printing Office, Washington, 1942), p. 3.

[2] The Secretary of State (Fish) to the Minister to Japan (De Long), no. 108, Sept. 19, 1871, MS., Japan, Instructions, vol. 1.

All citations indicated by the abbreviation "MS." are manuscripts of the Department of State. The National Archives is the depositary of Department of State documents dated prior to 1930.

[3] Department of State, *Foreign Service Regulations,* chap. XII, sec. 4 (the edition revised to 1946 is meant, unless otherwise indicated). Italics in the text are by the present writer.

1

extraordinary provision, so contrary to the prevailing premises of diplomatic and consular representation, acquires additional significance when it is noted that similar provisions
are to be found in the diplomatic and consular regulations of
many other states and that they reflect, not an occasional
variation from the prevailing rule (as one might suppose),
but a time-honored international practice which Secretary
of State William Jennings Bryan referred to as "a matter of
constant, indeed almost daily, occurrence, in peace as well
as in war".[4]   The most spectacular examples of the practice
are those which occur in time of war when a neutral state
undertakes to protect the interests of one belligerent within
the territory of another.   During the present century this
practice has been so generally followed and its possibilities for
indirect communication between belligerents so extensively
exploited as to constitute in effect an important modification
of the traditional "severance of relations" between states at
war.   It has furnished a striking indication of the cohesive
tendencies of modern society even in the midst of hostilities.
Less widely known, but equally significant and far more
numerous, are the instances in time of peace when the diplomatic or consular officers of one power have been called upon
to extend their protection in one form or another to the interests of a foreign state within the territory of a third power.
Since the essentials of the practice are the same in peace or
war, the present work will draw no arbitrary distinction between these two conditions and will cite examples from the
protection of either belligerent or non-belligerent foreign
interests wherever appropriate to the development of the
subject.

Since the terminology of the practice has not always been

---

[4] The Secretary of State (Bryan) to the Vice Consul at Nogales
(Simpich), no. 386, Mar. 2, 1914, MS., file 312.52/80, cited in Green
Haywood Hackworth, *Digest of International Law* (Government
Printing Office, Washington, 1942), vol. IV, p. 494.

either clear or consistent, a word of clarification is necessary at this point. For many years the practice has been variously referred to as "good offices", "representation", or "protection".[5] In former days "good offices" was used most widely as the generic term for the practice as a whole and the digests of Moore and Hackworth cite examples of the practice under this heading.[6] Unfortunately the term "good offices" has been burdened with several other meanings in diplomatic usage and even in this particular sense it has been employed in recent American practice only to indicate the most informal and occasional type of protection of foreign interests.[7] During the present century the word "representation" has been increasingly used as the generic term, but this usage has made for confusion whenever it was desired to distinguish between the peculiar characteristics of the representation of foreign interests as opposed to the normal representation of the interests of a state by its own diplomatic and consular officers. In emphasizing this important distinction Secretaries of State have frequently had to point out that in the so-called representation of foreign interests the American diplomatic or consular officer does not actually *represent* the foreign government in question; that he does not become its official *representative;* and that no *representative* office of any sort attaches to his activities in behalf of the foreign government.[8] The type of ambiguity which has resulted from this usage of the term "representation" may be seen from the following statement which appeared in a circular instruction

---

[5] Professor Borchard has used the additional variant, "delegated protection"; see Edwin M. Borchard, *The Diplomatic Protection of Citizens Abroad* (The Banks Law Publishing Company, New York, 1927), p. 471.

[6] John Bassett Moore, *A Digest of International Law* (Government Printing Office, Washington, 1906), vol. IV, pp. 584 ff.; Hackworth, *op. cit.,* vol. IV, pp. 485 ff.

[7] See *post,* p. 175.

[8] See Hackworth, *op. cit.,* vol. IV, p. 487.

of 1921: *"Representation* of foreign interests usually ceases upon the direction of the *unrepresented* government . . ."[9] In order to avoid such ambiguities the latest edition of the *Foreign Service Regulations* employs as the generic term for the practice the word "protection", which had often been used in official correspondence as a synonym for either "good offices" or "representation". This is the usage followed throughout the present work, except in portions quoted verbatim where either "good offices" or "representation" may have been used in the original text.

The protection of foreign interests always involves three states, customarily designated as the protected power, the protecting power, and the local power, i.e. the power within whose territory the protection is exercised. In this connection the words "state" and "power" will, for convenience, be employed interchangeably; while the expression "local government" or "local authorities" will be used to indicate the national governmental authorities of the local power rather than the authorities of a particular city or province. It must be emphasized that the protection of foreign interests, as the phrase is technically used, concerns a relationship between sovereign states and does not refer in any sense to a protectorate or a situation involving dependent areas. Likewise it does not refer to intervention on behalf of foreigners in their own states. It is used exclusively to designate the protection of the interests of state "X" by the diplomatic and consular officers of state "Y" within the territory of state "Z".

This trilateral relationship obviously involves three points of view. In the present study we shall approach the problem primarily from the point of view of the protecting power, although frequent references will be made to those policies of local states and protected states which have influenced the practice. The United States has had a rich experience in

---

[9] MS., General Instructions Consular, no. 177, Mar. 14, 1921. Italics by the present writer.

all three positions.   As an outstanding neutral, the United States was the logical choice as a protecting power for many countries embroiled in European or Asiatic wars.   As a major belligerent in the greatest wars of this century, the United States Government has had to arrange for neutral countries to protect its far-flung interests in enemy territory.   At the same time it has had to permit and control the protection by other neutrals of the extensive interests of enemy powers within its own borders.   In time of peace the prestige of the United States and the extent of its diplomatic and consular representation throughout the world have made it natural for other states to request that an American Foreign Service officer take charge of their interests in some part of the globe where, for one reason or another, they temporarily lacked a representative of their own.   It is upon this rich experience of the United States that we have principally drawn in the present study, although foreign sources have not been entirely neglected.   Actually, however, the trilateral character of every instance of protection of foreign interests inevitably has produced a remarkable degree of international uniformity in the practice.   Certain national variations have occurred from time to time and will be noted at the appropriate points, but as a general rule it is safe to conclude that the experience of the United States on the subject faithfully reflects the international practice as a whole.

In its clearly recognizable modern form the practice of protecting foreign interests is less than a hundred years old yet, oddly enough, a century ago it was regarded as a time-honored procedure, rather than an innovation.   This peculiarity is attributable to the fact that while the protection of foreign interests, as we know it today, took shape very quickly in the mid-nineteenth century in response to new circumstances and the needs of the time, it was merely a new application or combination of three older practices or concepts long recognized in the diplomatic world.   For this reason it is

necessary for us to examine in chapter I of this work the
origins of the practice and to trace certain of the lines of
thought and action which produced the modern practice and
which still influence its characteristics. In order that the
reader may become acquainted with the variety of circumstances in which protection of foreign interests has taken
place we shall survey briefly in chapters II and III most of
the outstanding instances from 1867 to 1945 in which the
United States has served as a protecting power. Chapter IV
will state and analyze the ten basic principles which have
emerged from this experience. In chapters V and VI we
shall discuss certain administrative procedures generally followed in connection with this practice and the specific duties
of the diplomatic or consular officer who is placed in charge
of foreign interests. In order that the work may be as pertinent and helpful as possible these last three chapters will
deal extensively with the experiences of World War II, which
will be only briefly treated at the end of the chronological
survey in chapter III.

CHAPTER I

ORIGINS OF THE PRACTICE

IN ITS modern form the practice of extending protection in special circumstances to the nationals abroad of another state dates only from the middle of the nineteenth century. During the 1850's and 1860's the practice took shape with remarkable rapidity and by the 1870's it had become an accepted technique in the conduct of international relations. In that development the United States played an important part, but to understand the significance of the practice, as well as the reasons for its appearance at that particular time, it is necessary to examine briefly three older practices in the intercourse of states which contained most of the elements and concepts which entered into the modern practice of protecting foreign interests. Those earlier practices are the exercise of extraterritoriality, the employment of foreigners in representation abroad, and the use of personal good offices by diplomatic and consular officials.

1. EXTRATERRITORIALITY

Before the age of modern nationalism the granting of protection in certain circumstances to foreign subjects and their property was a not uncommon practice among the sovereigns of Europe. Community of religion, race, or language, as well as the enhancement of royal prestige, and occasionally the replenishing of princely exchequers, appear at various times to have been the impelling motive for the practice. Since sovereignty was then regarded as personal rather than territorial (*L'État c'est moi*), extraterritorial rights of protection were often claimed, particularly in non-Christian

7

countries.[1] Frequently these extraterritorial rights involved the protection not only of the nationals or subjects of the sovereign claiming them but also of other persons or groups seeking his protection. Thus, for instance, as early as the thirteenth century the Venetian Resident at Constantinople (the Bailo) at the instance of his Government was accorded the protection and jurisdiction not only over Venetians but also over Armenians and Jews in that city.[2]

Subsequently, under the regime of the Capitulations in the Ottoman Empire various European sovereigns were granted the privilege of extending their protection not merely to their own subjects but also to "other Christians" or other persons claiming the protection of their respective flags. Even before the first Capitulation of 1535 France had claimed the right to exercise such protection and in the treaty of 1581 between Henri III and Sultan Amurat the first article (capitula) specifically guaranteed that French protection should continue for "the Venetians, Genovese, English, Ragusans and all those who have gone under the name and banner of France".[3] In the treaty of 1604 between Henri the Great and Achmet I, this provision was repeated with the additional clarification that these foreign subjects who came under French protection would obey the French consuls in the ports of the Ottoman Empire.[4] From other articles of this treaty and subsequent ones between France and the Ottoman Empire it appears that protection by the French consuls gave to these foreign merchants doing business under the French flag certain real advantages in

---

[1] Frank E. Hinckley, *American Consular Jurisdiction in the Orient* (Lowdermilk & Co., Washington, 1906), pp. 16–17.

[2] Presumably the Christian Armenians received this protection free of charge, but history has recorded that the Jews were required to pay "des sommes très fortes". See Alex de Miltitz, *Manuel des Consuls* (A. Asher, London, 1838), livre II, p. 436.

[3] *Ibid.*, livre III, p. 106.

[4] *Ibid.*, p. 112.

the form of extensive exemption from Ottoman jurisdiction and considerable French assistance in matters affecting legacies, contracts, lawsuits, and criminal actions. It is interesting to note that this pre-eminent position which France occupied for many years in the protection of European Christians throughout the Ottoman Empire resulted from the fact that French protection was extended at a time when the other European nations had not yet concluded treaties of peace and friendship with the Porte and did not accredit ambassadors to the Sultan. Thus as early as the sixteenth century the protection of the interests of non-nationals was predicated on the absence of protection by their own sovereigns, a circumstance which we shall have occasion to note as one of the basic prerequisites of the modern practice of protecting foreign interests.[5]

In subsequent centuries the privileges granted to the French were claimed by other European powers and by the United States in various treaties with the Porte containing the "most-favored-nation" clause, and the practice of according protection to Westerners within the Ottoman Empire ceased to be a French monopoly and developed rapidly into an almost competitive system in which European and American diplomatic and consular officers granted protection on a wholesale scale to Christians and native protégés, with little regard for nationality.[6] The basis of this practice with respect to Westerners in Turkey was well described in an instruction from John W. Foster, Secretary of State, to the American Minister at Constantinople in 1892:

A very important and useful feature of the status of foreigners in Turkey is the solidarity among them. Foreigners have for centuries been classed under the generic name of Franks. Their rights and

---

[5] Cf. *post,* p. 116.

[6] It should be noted that in this study we are concerned not with the protection extended to natives against their own sovereign but with the protection extended by one Western power to the nationals of another Western power within the Mohammedan world.

privileges are analogous, and the protection of the representatives of one great power has been not infrequently extended to the citizens resident in Turkey of another.   The files of your legation will afford many instances of recourse to the good offices of British consuls in Turkish dominions for the protection of our citizens in quarters where no consular representation of the United States has been established.   This friendly aid is cheerfully given whenever sought.   The exercise of such protection is an inherent Frankish right, and resort to Frankish protection is in like manner the prerogative of every Frank.   Indeed, the rule in Turkey recognizes the right of any Frank to be enrolled in the protected list of any Frankish consulate, whether of his own nationality or not.[7]

As a matter of policy, however, the United States Government was among the earliest to discourage the indiscriminate granting of protection.   As early as 1833 Secretary of State Livingston instructed the American consuls at Tangier, Tripoli, and Tunis as follows:

Some misunderstanding having arisen at the consulates on the coast of Africa in relation to the extent of the protection which ought to be afforded to individuals under the flag of the United States, I am instructed by the President to inform you that such protection is to be afforded to none but American citizens, and the persons actually in the service of the consul, and not to them, if they have been guilty of any crime involving a breach of the peace, proved to the satisfaction of the consul, and for which he can not inflict a punishment satisfactory to the Government.[8]

The practice of mutual protection among Westerners in the Near East continued, however, for many years and was the subject of repeated correspondence between the Department of State and the American representatives in those areas.   A general consular instruction of 1855 contained the following interesting paragraphs on the subject:

By the laws of Turkey and other Eastern nations, the consulates therein may receive under their protection strangers and sojourners whose religion and social manners do not assimilate with the religion and manners of those countries.

---

[7] Moore, *op. cit.*, vol. IV, p. 585.
[8] *Ibid.*, vol. II, p. 727.

The individuals who are thus protected become thereby clothed, for the time being, with the nationality of the protecting consulate. Usage, if not positive stipulation, recognizes and sanctions the rights acquired by this connection. Consuls of the United States are, however, instructed that, while it is expected that the same rights and privileges will be accorded to them in regard to protecting persons not citizens of the United States as may be enjoyed by the consuls of other nations, who have no special treaty stipulation on the subject, they are to exercise this right with much discretion.[9]

The limitation of the practice was stressed from a slightly different point of view in the following instruction of 1860 to the American Minister to Turkey:

Upon the policy which leads several of the great European powers to take under their protection certain religious sects in Turkey, I do not deem it necessary to express an opinion, but it is one certainly in which we can never participate. This Government undertakes to protect neither Protestant nor Catholic, neither Greek nor Armenian, but only *American citizens;* and this Department can not but think that, if the person or the property of any American citizen had been imperiled, you would have occupied higher and stronger ground in appealing for the necessary protection for a citizen of the United States in that character alone, than in confounding him in a general protection afforded to any sect whatever.[10]

In 1872 the Department of State refused to except a Syrian merchant at Beirut from "the rule which for some time past has been adopted, restricting the protection of this Government to persons in the Turkish dominions, other than citizens of the United States, to those foreigners who may be in the actual service of our diplomatic and consular officers in that quarter".[11]

During the latter portion of the nineteenth century the European powers likewise began to curtail the indiscriminate

---

[9] Department of State, *General Instructions to the Consuls and Commercial Agents of the United States* (A. O. P. Nicholson, Washington, 1855), pp. 116–117.

[10] Moore, *op. cit.,* vol. II, p. 737. Italics by the present writer.

[11] *Ibid.,* p. 738.

granting of protection to foreigners by their diplomatic and consular officers within the Ottoman Empire and the practice finally terminated with the recent abrogation of the Capitulations. Its persistence, however, for more than three centuries produced attitudes and techniques which were found applicable to other situations in the intercourse of states outside the realm of the Capitulations. For purposes of later comparison certain characteristics of foreign protection under the Capitulations are worth noting at this point:

(a) The general protection of Westerners regardless of nationality by the diplomatic and consular representatives in the Levant of various European powers (particularly France in the early days) was predicated on the absence, or inadequate extent, of representation within the Turkish Empire of those European states whose subjects sought foreign protection.

(b) The protection was based on the consent of the local sovereign, expressed and repeatedly confirmed in the treaties known as Capitulations.

(c) A feeling of Christian humanitarianism and of common opposition to the arbitrary imposition of power on the individual, regardless of his nationality, was discernible in the practice.

(d) The protection of foreigners under the Capitulations did not take the form of an official protection by one European power of the interests of another European power. It was essentially a bilateral arrangement between the local power (the Ottoman Empire) and the protecting power, which in turn dealt with its foreign protégés of various nationalities on an individual basis and customarily without reference to their respective home governments or sovereigns.

(e) Although the United States Government frequently relied upon British consular officials to protect Americans in those parts of the Turkish dominions in which there were no

American consuls, the United States Government opposed the indiscriminate granting of its own protection to foreigners and particularly to religious sects without regard for the nationality of the members thereof.

It is interesting to note that the extraterritorial privileges granted to various Western powers in China and Japan, contrary to customary practice in the Levant, never extended to the nationals of non-treaty powers nor were they capable of being exercised by a foreign consul temporarily in charge of the interests of a treaty power.[12] On the other hand many incidents in the history of the expansion of Western influence in the Far East indicate that despite imperialist rivalries there was a strong undercurrent of feeling among Occidentals that "blood was thicker than water", as Commodore Tatnall expressed it in justifying his unauthorized assistance to British subjects in China.[13] Furthermore various European powers not infrequently extended a measure of protection to missionaries of certain Christian sects in the Far East as well as in the Levant even when the missionaries themselves were of another nationality than that of the power extending the protection. Thus for a considerable period France was recognized as the chief protector of all Roman Catholics in the Far East as well as in the Levant, while Tsarist Russia traditionally maintained a right to protect members of the Orthodox Church, regardless of their nationality.[14] Great Britain and Germany from time to time have exerted diplomatic and moral pressure in the defense of the "great faiths which are so closely connected with their national history".[15]

---

[12] Hinckley, *op. cit.,* pp. 57, 89.

[13] John Holladay Latané, *A History of American Foreign Policy* (Doubleday, Doran and Company, New York, 1934), p. 345.

[14] The exercise of this "right" in Turkey was one of the contributing causes of the Crimean War. See J. A. R. Marriot, *The Eastern Question* (Clarendon Press, Oxford, 1917), pp. 229–236.

[15] Hinckley, *op. cit.,* p. 109.

Akin to the concept of extraterritoriality is the time-honored principle of the inviolability of diplomatic premises.[16] While this inviolability to local jurisdiction derived from the personal immunity of the diplomatic officer, there was a marked tendency during the nineteenth century to regard the inviolability of the premises as continuing even after the outbreak of war and the departure of the diplomat whose personal immunity was the cause and justification for the inviolability of the property necessary to the discharge of his official functions.[17]   From this trend in thought and practice there arose the natural presumption that a diplomat departing from his post upon severance of relations or before the arrival of his successor had a right to expect that his official property (particularly the archives) would be respected by the local power and that in order to insure the observance of this right he was entitled to place these properties under seal and to entrust them to the protection of one of his colleagues representing a "friendly" or neutral power. Whether such continuing inviolability may be claimed as a matter of right is open to question, but in practice it has long been accorded and in more recent times it has even been extended by analogy to consular as well as diplomatic premises.[18]

---

[16] Such premises, of course, are not actually extraterritorial, however much their inviolability may be respected. Cf. Charles Cheney Hyde, *International Law*, 2d rev. ed. (Little, Brown and Company, Boston, 1945), vol. II, pp. 1285–1286; Amos Shartle Hershey, *Diplomatic Agents and Immunities* (Government Printing Office, Washington, 1919), pp. 167–180.

[17] Thomas J. Lawrence, *The Principles of International Law*, 7th ed. (Heath and Company, New York, 1923), p. 400; Sir Ernest M. Satow, *A Guide to Diplomatic Practice*, 3d ed. (Longmans, Green and Company, London, 1932), p. 166; L. Oppenheim, *International Law*, 6th ed. (Longmans, Green and Company, New York), vol. II, p. 244; also the Legal Adviser (Hackworth) to the Acting Secretary (Welles), Feb. 10, 1942, and Acting Secretary Welles to President Roosevelt, Mar. 14, 1942, MS., file 701.0011/420.

[18] Hyde, *op. cit.*, vol. II, pp. 1328–1329.

Upon the inviolability of diplomatic premises has been based the granting of asylum therein to persons wanted by the local authorities.   While asylum has generally been extended to nationals of the local power, it is interesting to note that it has occasionally been granted to nationals of other powers as well, thus constituting a limited form of protection of foreign interests on a purely humanitarian basis.[19]   Although the modern practice of protecting foreign interests no longer includes the granting of asylum to protected nationals as a customary function, the connection between the two ideas may be seen in the fact that the American Minister to France, who was in charge of German interests during the Franco-Prussian War, had no hesitation in granting asylum within the American Legation to a German subject who claimed to have been abused by the French.[20]

2. EMPLOYMENT OF FOREIGNERS AS OFFICIALS

The idea of employing foreigners to supplement a sovereign's own diplomatic and consular representation abroad has been traced back to very early times.   The *proxenos* of the ancient Greeks was customarily a notable citizen who voluntarily served as a sort of honorary consular officer to protect within his own nation the interests of a foreign state.[21] Before the rise of modern nationalism this concept found many applications, some of which are by no means obsolete even today.   Professional diplomats and consuls, like soldiers

---

[19] See Moore, *op. cit.*, vol. II, "Asylum", pp. 755–845; Hackworth, *op. cit.*, vol. II, pp. 634, 636, 637, 642.

[20] The object of Minister Washburne's exceptional hospitality turned out to be a common thief!   See E. B. Washburne, *Recollections of a Minister to France* (Charles Scribner's Sons, New York, 1887), vol. I, p. 243.   A summary of Minister Washburne's activities will be found *post*, p. 41.

[21] G. Bie Ravndal, *The Origins of the Capitulations and of the Consular Institution* (Government Printing Office, Washington, 1921), pp. 57–58.

of fortune, were frequently found in the service of sovereigns of a nationality foreign to their own, and, although such situations were often beclouded by feudal relationships, they actually involved a protection of foreign interests on the part of the officer, or, from the point of view of the sovereign, the employment of a foreigner as an official agent in his own diplomatic or consular service.

A few examples will indicate the extent and nature of this practice. During the early sixteenth century the same consul served both Catalonian and French merchants at Alexandria.[22] The eminent Grotius, a Dutchman by birth, was appointed in 1632 as the Ambassador of Sweden to the Court of France. On two occasions in the early eighteenth century the King of Spain was represented at London by envoys of Irish birth, one of whom was a member of the peerage. In 1798 Benjamin Thompson, born in New Hampshire, was appointed by the Elector of Bavaria as his Minister Plenipotentiary to Great Britain.[23] In 1796–1797 the Marquis del Campo represented both the King of Spain and the Duke of Parma at Paris.[24] During the same period the position of Swedish Consul at Salonica was occupied by the Dutch Consul with the approval of the Estates-General of Holland.[25] From 1815 to 1834 Pozzo di Borgo, a naturalized Russian of Corsican birth, served as Russian Ambassador to France.[26] The extent of this practice in the late eighteenth century may be gathered from the fact that in 1763, out of twenty-seven Austrian consular posts in the Levant only ten were actually

---

[22] Miltitz, *op. cit.,* livre II, p. 431.

[23] Satow, *op. cit.,* vol. I, pp. 193, 213.

[24] Paul Pradier-Fodéré, *Traité de droit international public* (A. Duran, Paris, 1887), vol. III, p. 56.

[25] Jac. Wertheim, *Manuel des consuls des Pays-Bas* (Binger Frères, Amsterdam, 1861), pp. 35–36.

[26] Satow, *op. cit.,* p. 213.

filled by Austrian consuls, the others being entrusted for reasons of economy to the consuls of various "friendly powers".[27]

As a small and impecunious nation the young United States could ill afford to dispense with the employment of aliens in its foreign service, despite the resolution passed by the Continental Congress on March 16, 1784, which declared it to be "inconsistent with the interest of the United States to appoint any person not a citizen thereof, to the office of Minister, chargé d'affaires, Consul, vice-consul, or to any other civil department in a foreign country".[28] While foreign citizens or subjects were never appointed as American ministers, they were frequently named to positions as high as consul and sometimes acted as chargé d'affaires. The rising tide of nationalist sentiment beginning in the second quarter of the nineteenth century brought forth bitter criticism of this practice. Typical of the growing attitude on this subject was the blunt remark of the American Minister at Constantinople in 1849, who, in reporting to the Department on the difficulty of finding a suitable American for the post of Consul at that port, added the following remark:

. . . and I should be loath to give it to an Englishman: for an Englishman is thorough English and not a proper representative of our interests where they come into conflict or competition with those of his own country.[29]

In presenting to the House of Representatives a bill for the reorganization of the diplomatic and consular service in Jan-

---

[27] Josef Ritter von Malfatti, *Handbuch des Oesterreichisch-Ungarischen Consularwesens* (Wilhelm Braumüller, 1879).

[28] Graham H. Stuart, *American Diplomatic and Consular Practice* (Appleton-Century Company, New York, 1936), p. 167. *Journals of the Continental Congress, 1774–1789* (Government Printing Office, Washington, 1928), vol. XXVI (1784), p. 144.

[29] The Minister to Turkey (Carr) to the Secretary of State (Clayton), no. 23, Mar. 23, 1849, MS., Turkey, Despatches, vol. 11.

uary 1855, Representative Perkins of Louisiana spoke as follows as this subject:

One reform of this bill, which operates equally upon diplomatists and consuls, to which I especially invite the attention of the House, is, that heretofore there has been nothing to prevent the Executive from commissioning to act as a foreign agent of this government, the citizen of another government.   A person, for instance, in the employ of Austria— an Austrian subject—may not only hold the commission of this government in Vienna, and discharge the duties of American consul, but, in the absence of our minister there, actually represents us at that court. In point of fact this happened in 1849, at the very time we were sending a special and confidential minister to recognize the independence of Hungary.   The majority of those in our consular service were at one time foreigners, and armed with power to tax, to almost an indefinite extent, American commerce and American citizens in a manner most injurious to our interests.   .   .   .[30]

Despite these sentiments it was not until well into the present century that the employment of any but American citizens as officers in the United States Foreign Service became really exceptional.[31]

Although private American citizens might accept appointment as consular or even diplomatic officers of foreign governments,[32] the Constitution of the United States (foreshadowing the spirit of the nationalist era) had forbidden

---

[30] *The Diplomatic System of the United States,* a speech of the Hon. John Perkins, Jr. (A. O. P. Nicholson, Washington, 1855), pp. 18–19; also Stuart, *op. cit.,* p. 172.

[31] Tracy Hollingsworth Lay, *The Foreign Service of the United States* (Prentice-Hall, New York, 1925), p. 21; National Civil Reform League (Richard H. Dana, President), *Report on the Foreign Service* (New York, 1919), p. 66.   The American Foreign Service still includes a few consular agents of foreign nationality.

[32] The most outstanding example was that of Anson Burlingame, who resigned as American Minister to China in order to accept from the Chinese Government the post of special ambassador to the United States and certain European powers.   See John W. Foster, *The Practice of Diplomacy* (Houghton Mifflin Company, Cambridge, 1906), p. 49.

any officer of the United States from accepting without the consent of Congress "any present, Emolument, Office, or Title, of any kind whatever, from any King, Prince, or foreign State." [33]   During the early nineteenth century similar provisions appear to have been enacted by most European powers and thereafter it became increasingly rare for the diplomatic or consular officer *de carrière* of one state to be employed in a similar capacity by another government. [34]   Public opinion obviously tended to agree with M. Pradier-Fodéré, who condemned the practice of employing foreign officials as "vicieux" and maintained that it was better not to be represented at all than to be represented inadequately. [35]   The practice, however, had certain real advantages in economy and convenience, and these advantages, by coincidence, became quite apparent at the very time when national legislation was being enacted against the practice.   With the opening up of trade and travel in previously isolated parts of the globe during the mid-nineteenth century, it became increasingly necessary for every nation to enlarge its diplomatic and consular representation, although the needs of these posts did not always justify the full-time appointment of a regular diplomatic or consular official.   To a certain extent this situation was met by the commissioning of foreign private citizens resident in those areas where additional representation was desired.   When this procedure was not considered feasible or desirable, attempts were made to obtain permission

[33] Constitution of the United States, art. I, sec. 9.

[34] Cf. Fernand Labori and Emile Schaffhauser, "Agent diplomatique", *Répertoire encyclopédique du droit français* (Soubiron, Toulouse, 1889), pp. 281 ff.   In Great Britain the approval of the Secretary of State for Foreign Affairs is required for acceptance of such an appointment; in Switzerland, of the Federal Council; in Sweden, of the Minister of Foreign Affairs.   See *General Instructions to His Majesty's Consular Officers* (1923), chap. V, sec. 6; *Règlement consulaire suisse* (1923), art. 33; *Royal Ordinance concerning the Consular Service of Sweden* (Norstedt and Söner, Stockholm, 1909), art. 15.

[35] Pradier-Fodéré, *op. cit.*, vol. III, p. 58.

for foreign diplomatic or consular officers already on the spot to take charge of the interests of the unrepresented state.

Thus in 1870 the Peruvian Government requested that the American Ministers to China and Japan be authorized "to act as the Ministers of Peru with those Governments respectively". In response to this request Secretary Fish did not raise the question of constitutionality but merely instructed the Ministers in question to attend to any matters entrusted to their charge by the Government of Peru, in so far as this could be done "compatibly with other instructions from this Department".[36] In the following year the King of Hawaii commissioned Minister De Long as his Envoy Extraordinary and Minister Plenipotentiary to the Japanese Government for the purpose of negotiating a treaty. When apprised of this fact, the Secretary of State promptly referred the question to the Attorney General who replied as follows:

I find no authority pertinent to the question which you informally submitted to me on the 17th instant, to wit, whether an American minister to one foreign power can accept a diplomatic commission to the same power from another foreign power, except the opinion of Attorney-General Cushing that the marshal of the United States for the southern district of Florida is prohibited from holding the office of commercial agent of France, without the consent of Congress, by the last clause of section nine, article one, of the Constitution. (6 Opins., 409.)

A minister plenipotentiary from this Government to a foreign power certainly holds an office of profit and trust under the United States. A similar commission from a third power gives him an office under such power, and this the Constitution forbids him to accept.

Unquestionably, a minister of the United States abroad is not prohibited by the Constitution from rendering a friendly service to a foreign power, even that of negotiating a treaty for it, provided he does not become an officer of that power. But whatever difficulties may grow out of the vagueness with which this term is defined in the books, it is clear that the acceptance of a formal commission as minister plenipotentiary creates an official relation between the individual thus commissioned and the government which in this way accredits him as its representative.

---

[36] The Secretary of State (Fish) to the Minister to Japan (De Long), Apr. 13, 1870, MS., Japan, Instructions, vol. 1.

Valid treaties have been negotiated by uncommissioned persons, for it is the ratification and not the original authority of the negotiator which gives validity to a treaty. But the character of a minister plenipotentiary is known to the law of nations and to the Constitution of the United States (Art. I, section 2) as an office, and no person without the consent of Congress can properly accept it while holding an office of profit or trust under the United States.[37]

In accordance with this opinion the Secretary instructed Minister De Long that he was not at liberty to accept the position conferred on him by the King of Hawaii. At the same time he was informed that there was no objection to the exercise of his good offices in behalf of the Hawaiian Government in so far as this could be done consistently with the ruling of the Attorney General.[38]

Here then was the solution to the dilemma. As a temporary measure it would be permissible for a diplomatic or consular official to extend his good offices on behalf of a foreign power, even though he might not be permitted to accept a commission as an officer of that power. The arrangement accorded well with the needs of the time, and since the concept of personal good offices was nothing new in the diplomatic world, the procedure seemed to be no startling innovation. In subsequent chapters we shall see, however, that the idea of actually commissioning foreigners to act as diplomatic or consular officials persisted tenaciously for many years and rendered it constantly necessary to clarify the peculiar position of an officer authorized to protect foreign interests through the exercise of his good offices.

3. PERSONAL GOOD OFFICES

The term "good offices" has come to have a variety of meanings or connotations in diplomatic usage, but in its most

---

[37] *Opinions of the Attorneys General* (Government Printing Office, Washington, 1873), vol. XIII, pp. 537–538.

[38] The Secretary of State (Fish) to the Minister to Japan (De Long), Dec. 21, 1871, MS., Japan, Instructions, vol. 1.

basic and original form the expression referred to the time-honored prerogative of a diplomat or consul to intervene unofficially with the local authorities in order to obtain a favor for one of his nationals in a private matter.[39]   As Secretary Hay expressed it, "it corresponds to the French term *officieux,* or the Spanish *oficioso,* and means the unofficial advocacy of interests which the agent may properly represent, but which it may not be convenient to present and discuss on a full diplomatic footing".[40]   In this sense good offices are by no means obsolete, although the term is not so frequently employed in this connection as it once was.

Examples from the past century indicate that personal good offices were employed by diplomats and consuls on a variety of matters, all of which had some intrinsic merit but were not of sufficient importance to be treated as "affairs of state".   For instance, good offices were employed to obtain permission for an American archeologist to conduct researches in Palestine, to obtain a safe-conduct for the family of an American citizen in Verdun during the Franco-Prussian War, and to recommend to various foreign governments certain private claims of American nationals.[41]   In all such

[39] Baron Ferdinand de Cussy, "Bons offices", *Dictionnaire du diplomate et du consul* (Brockhaus, Leipzig, 1846), p. 90; Baron Charles de Martens, *Le Guide diplomatique* (Gavelot Jeune, Paris, 1854), vol. I, p. 179. With "good offices" as a form of mediation we are not concerned in this study. For recent American usage of the term to describe a strictly limited type of protection of foreign interests, see *post,* p. 175. For "good offices" as a synonym for protection of foreign interests in general, see *ante,* p. 3.

[40] Moore, *op. cit.,* vol. VII, p. 3.

[41] The Secretary of State (Fish) to the Minister to Turkey (Morris), July 30, 1869, MS., Turkey, Instructions, vol. 2; the Secretary of State (Fish) to the Minister to France (Washburne), no. 173, Sept. 22, 1870, MS., France, Instructions, vol. 18; the Secretary of State (Hay) to the Minister to Bolivia (Sorsby), no. 31, May 12, 1903, MS., Bolivia, Instructions, vol. 2; see also Borchard, *op. cit.,* pp. 440–441.

cases, including those in which good offices were suggested by the Department, the actual decision to take such action was left to the discretion of the officer in the field. Such good offices were regarded as his personal prerogative, and many cases of the sort were doubtless never referred to the home government by the diplomat or consul concerned.

Personal good offices were not always limited to compatriots of the diplomatic or consular officer. It has already been noted that in the late eighteenth and early nineteenth century British consuls in the Levant often employed their good offices on behalf of American citizens in areas where there was no American consul.[42] Doubtless many a diplomat and consul in other less-frequented parts of the world had had occasion now and then to assist unofficially a deserving foreigner who had no representative of his own to whom to appeal; but since such good offices were considered strictly a personal prerogative of the officer, such incidents were not likely to appear in official correspondence. During the mid-nineteenth century, however, it appears that such incidents were becoming increasingly frequent, as a result of the tremendous expansion of trade and travel which far outstripped the increase in diplomatic and consular posts throughout the world.[43] One of the first of such incidents of official record involving Americans outside of the Levant appears to have occurred in 1854 when a group of seven impoverished Americans straggled into the office of the British Vice Consul at Islay on the southern coast of Peru and begged his assistance on grounds of humanity. These men had lost everything in their search for gold in the interior of the country and were typical of the destitute adventurers of all nationalities whom

---

[42] *Ante,* p. 10.

[43] Particularly in the Far East it appears that the small group of official representatives took a lively interest in the welfare of all Westerners traveling or residing in the area. See, for example, the Minister Resident in Japan (Harris) to the Secretary of State, no. 8, Feb. 13, 1861, MS., Japan, Despatches, vol. 3.

the gold rush of 1849 had left on the west and north coasts of South America. The British Vice Consul advanced them about $150 out of his own pocket and arranged for their passage on the next ship to Callao. When he subsequently requested reimbursement from the American Government, he was informed by the American Minister at Lima that, while his kindness was greatly appreciated, there were no funds available for such purposes.[44]

In the same year a revolution took place in Peru, which resulted in a number of claims by Americans and other resident aliens against the Peruvian Government. The American Minister, who, incidentally, had provided asylum for the wife of the leader of the successful faction, was besieged with requests to press these private claims, and it was probably in that connection that he was appealed to for protection by a Mexican citizen at Lima. Mr. Clay promptly inquired of the Department of State "as to how far Ministers of the United States should use their friendly offices with the Government to which they are accredited, in favor of foreigners, whose nation is not represented by a Diplomatic Agent or Consul." [45] To this inquiry Mr. Marcy replied guardedly:

. . . any good offices which a minister may undertake to render under such circumstances must be entirely of a personal character, or such as may be demanded by humanity or the pressing urgency of the case; but in rendering such services the minister must exercise very great prudence, lest he give offence to the government near which he resides, or compromise his own immunities by seeming to interfere with the administration of the internal affairs of that government.[46]

Significant in this reply is the cautious fear of overstepping the diplomatic proprieties and the insistence that the exercise of good offices was exclusively a personal affair of the Min-

---

[44] The Minister to Peru (Clay) to the Secretary of State (Marcy), no. 233, Nov. 22, 1854, MS., Peru, Despatches, vol. 11.

[45] *Id.* to *id.*, no. 232, *loc. cit.*

[46] Mr. Marcy to Mr. Clay, Nov. 23, 1854, MS., Peru, Instructions, vol. 15; also cited in Moore, *op. cit.*, vol. IV, p. 586.

ister for which the Department could assume no responsibility whatever. It does not appear from Mr. Clay's despatches that there was any further correspondence regarding this subject and it may be assumed that after receiving Mr. Marcy's word of caution he hesitated to take energetic action in a matter concerning which he had no official authorization and for which he might be held severely accountable if it produced embarrassing complications.

In 1859, however, a revolution in Mexico produced a quite different reaction in the Department of State to the question of good offices. When the Miramon Government revoked the exequatur of the American Consul at Mexico City, the Americans at that place appealed for protection to the British Minister, who declined to exercise his good offices in their behalf. This action provoked the following angry protest from Secretary of State Cass, which was transmitted through the American Minister at London:

In countries in a state of revolution, and during periods of public excitement, it is the practice of modern times for the foreign representatives residing there to interpose by the exertion of their influence for the protection of the citizens of friendly powers, exposed to injury or danger, and left without any minister of their own country to watch over them. It is a commendable procedure, humane indeed, to which it is difficult to discover any well-founded objection.

. . . The President would not hesitate to visit with marks of his displeasure any American Minister who should have it in his power to afford protection to the persons or property of the citizens of a friendly nation, placed in peril by revolutionary commotions, and having no national representative to appeal to, and should fail to exert his influence in their behalf.[47]

This instruction, while reflecting the growing importance of the subject, appears to have overstated the case to a certain extent. It is unlikely that the President would have actually visited "with marks of his displeasure" any American minister or consul who hesitated to assume the personal respons-

[47] *Loc. cit.*

ibility of protecting other foreigners in the country to which he was assigned. Up to this time such matters had been left almost entirely to the discretion of the officer himself, and it is indicative of the personal, as opposed to the official, nature of the practice that in the Peruvian incident of 1854 and the Mexican incident of 1859 the appeal for assistance was made by private persons direct to the officer whose help was sought. The increasing number of such instances, however, was inevitably bringing the matter of good offices to official notice. During the 1860's, for instance, it was decided that the United States Government would reimburse any British Consul in the Near East who incurred expenses in exercising his good offices on behalf of Americans, provided that these good offices had been officially requested or approved by the American Minister to Turkey or the nearest American Consul.[48]

Early in 1866 there occurred a vacancy in the American consular post at Venice, in connection with which the American Minister at Vienna wrote as follows to the Department of State:

. . . Moreover as the vacancy has now existed for a considerable time it is to be supposed that the matter has already engaged the attention of the Department and that a new consul may be expected to arrive at any moment. I have therefore instructed Mr. Thayer [Consul at Trieste] to notify those who may for the present wish to export goods from Venice to the United States to apply to a consul of a friendly nation for authentification of invoices and have suggested the British consul.

I am aware that this does not conform to the letter of the law but it seems to me in accordance with its spirit, as for all practical purposes there is no United States Consul in the "country" in which Venice is situated.

Deferring entirely to your better judgment I beg thus to indicate the course provisionally adopted, and to call your attention to the case.[49]

---

[48] The Secretary of State (Seward) to the Minister to Turkey (Morris), no. 179, Apr. 7, 1868, MS., Turkey, Instructions, vol. 2.

[49] The Minister to Austria (Motley) to the Secretary of State (Seward), no. 154, Mar. 27, 1866, MS., Austria, Despatches, vol. 7.

The Department's reply indicated that a new consul for Venice had already been appointed and that in the interim Mr. Thayer should certify the invoices from Venice. "This course", Mr. Seward added, "is deemed preferable to the one suggested by you." [50] There were, however, precedents for the procedure suggested as an interim measure by Mr. Motley. In 1849 the Danish Minister of Foreign Affairs was authorized by his Government to entrust temporarily the Danish Legation at Constantinople to the Chargé d'Affaires of Sweden-Norway. [51] It is not clear whether this transfer took the form of an appeal for good offices or was in the nature of an actual commissioning of the Swedish Chargé as an official of Denmark; but the event aroused so little interest at the time that it was not reported to the Department by either the American Minister or the American Consul then in the Turkish capital. During the Crimean War the Austrian representative at Constantinople had extended his good offices on behalf of Russian subjects, [52] and during the so-called Seven Weeks' War of 1866 the representative of Sweden-Norway extended his protection over Italians in Austria, although his activities in this connection appear to have been brief and nominal. [53]

It may seem surprising that the good offices of neutral diplomats had not been more widely requested or extended during the eighteenth and early nineteenth centuries for the protection of the nationals of states at war. The principal explanation for this circumstance appears in the fact that before the middle of the last century it was not uncommon for the consular officers of belligerents to remain at their

[50] Mr. Seward to Mr. Motley, no. 177, Apr. 21, 1866, MS., Austria, Instructions, vol. 1.

[51] Pradier-Fodéré, *op. cit.,* vol. III, p. 56.

[52] The Minister to Turkey (Morris) to the Secretary of State (Seward), no. 288, Jan. 4, 1869, MS., Turkey, Despatches, vol. 20.

[53] Alfred Escher, *Der Schutz der Staatsangehörigen im Ausland durch fremde Gesandtschaften und Konsulate* (dissertation, Zürich), (Saarländer and Company, Aarau, 1928), p. 73.

posts and to render such assistance as might be necessary to their compatriots who for one reason or another did not avail themselves of the opportunity (which was generally granted prior to the Franco-Prussian War) for return to their respective homelands.   In this connection it may be noted that during the early years of the conflict between Napoleon and Tsar Alexander, French consuls continued without official interference to perform the functions of their office in Russia and it was not until the invasion of Russia in 1812 that the Tsar ordered their departure and that of the consuls of other powers allied to France.[54]   During the American War of 1812 the American consuls at London and Liverpool remained at their posts while the departing British Minister informed Secretary of State Monroe that he was leaving behind him a Secretary of Legation, a steward, and several domestics, all of whom he had "perfect confidence" would be "considered under the protection of the Laws of Nations".[55] During the entire Crimean War consular relations remained unbroken by agreement between Russia and England, while in 1864 Prussian and Danish consuls remained at their posts despite the war between their sovereigns.[56]   During the Mexican War of 1848, however, American consuls had their exequaturs revoked and were expelled from Mexico shortly after the departure of the American Minister.   The Consul at Mexico City took the most valuable papers of the Legation and Consulate with him and left the remainder, packed in trunks and boxes, in the custody of an American citizen remaining in that city.   The entire procedure was quite informal, largely because of the Consul's confident expectation when leaving Mexico City that he would simply go to Vera Cruz and promptly return to the Mexican capital with the

---

[54] Pierre Bouffanais, *Les Consuls en temps de guerre et de troubles* (Loviton and Company, Paris, 1933), p. 27.

[55] The British Minister (Foster) to the Secretary of State (Monroe), June 21, 1812, MS., Notes from Great Britain, vol. 7.

[56] Bouffanais, *op. cit.*, p. 26.

advancing United States Army.[57]   During the rupture of
diplomatic relations between Great Britain and Brazil in
1863 the British Minister entrusted his archives to the British Consul at Rio de Janeiro, who remained at his post.[58]

The expulsion of enemy consuls and the imposition of
stringent measures on enemy aliens does not appear to have
become customary practice until the Franco-Prussian War of
1870–1871, and it was during this conflict that there occurred the first outstanding example of neutral protection of
belligerent interests, i.e. the protection by the United States
of German interests in France.[59]   Three years prior to this
time, however, the good offices of the American Consul at
Mexico City had been officially requested by several European governments on behalf of their interests in Mexico.
With this incident the extension of good offices on behalf of
foreigners ceased to be regarded as the personal prerogative
of the individual officer in the field and became a matter of
official concern.   The exercise of these good offices continued
to be in the nature of a semi-official activity on the part of
the individual diplomat or consul, but the practice as a whole
was henceforth to be recognized as a matter for official negotiation between the interested governments.

---

[57] Only his own ill health occasioned a delay in this plan; see
Consul John Black to Secretary Buchanan, Aug. 3, 1848, MS., Mexico,
Consular Letters, vol. 9.

[58] Bouffanais, op. cit., p. 26.

[59] Post, p. 39.

CHAPTER II

THE FORMATIVE PERIOD, 1867–1899

IT IS the purpose of this chapter and the one which immediately follows to give the reader an idea of the general nature and extent of the practice of protecting foreign interests and an impression of the great variety of circumstances in which this practice has been applied by the United States. In order that the development of the practice through the years may be made apparent, the material has been arranged in the form of a chronological survey from 1867 to 1945, the present chapter dealing with the period up to 1899 and chapter III presenting the continuation of the story up to the conclusion of World War II. This division of chapters by the turn of the century is more than a matter of convenience—it is a reflection of the fact that the most rapid and significant growth of the practice took place during the formative years from 1867 to 1899, while the later developments represent for the most part an expansion and variation on the theme already well marked by the beginning of the twentieth century.

The incidents described in these two chapters do not constitute a complete tabulation of every instance in which the United States has extended its protection over foreign interests in third countries. The present list, however, includes all the outstanding examples of the practice, together with a considerable number of incidents which, although of minor importance *per se,* were not without effect either positively or negatively on the development of the practice. The descriptive material in these two chapters will be presented with a minimum of explanatory comment.   In succeeding chapters we shall approach the subject analytically, discussing in detail the basic principles, administrative procedures, and specific duties which have evolved from the practice.   In this connection we shall have opportunity to compare the experience of the United States with that of other nations which have engaged from time to time in the protection of foreign interests in third countries.

1. EUROPEANS IN MEXICO, 1867–1876

Shortly after the execution of Emperor Maximilian in June 1867 the Governments of France, Italy, Belgium, Austria, and Prussia, which had supported Maximilian's regime, decided to withdraw their representatives from Mexico.   Before their departure these representatives appealed to Marcus Otterbourg, the American Consul in charge of the American Legation at Mexico City, for his assistance and protection. The note from the French Minister to Mr. Otterbourg, which was similar, *mutatis mutandis,* to the notes addressed to him by the other departing diplomats, read as follows:

MEXICO, *July* 12, 1867.

MR. CONSUL: The Emperor Napoleon having determined to recall his agents from Mexico, and my intention being to leave as soon as possible for Vera Cruz, I have the honor to request you to take the subjects of his Majesty temporarily under the protection of the government of the United States, which you so ably represent.

According to the verbal agreement with you, I send six boxes, containing the archives of my legation, together with the proof of the burning of all political documents for the years 1860, 1861, 1862, 1863, 1864, 1865, 1866 and 1867, up to this date.

You will please draw up a certificate of deposit of the last-mentioned document, so that its existence may be proved without doubt in any emergency.   I will call at your office any time you may fix to sign that certificate.

The relations that exist between France and the United States are sufficiently cordial to induce us to hope the measure will be approved by our governments.

As the French are numerous in this city, to save you labor I can send two clerks from my office to aid you. Under your direction, those clerks can draw up the same certificates they made out under me.

Accept [etc.]   ALPHONSE DANO [1]

The following was the reply of Mr. Otterbourg, who had just been raised to the rank of Minister:

MEXICO, *July* 24, 1867.

I have to acknowledge the receipt of your excellency's note in which you request me, in view of your early departure for Vera Cruz, to extend to French subjects in Mexico the protection of the government of the United States.

The cordial relations existing between the United States and France, and the assurance derived from different conversations with the Mexican authorities that the rights of foreigners in person and property would be respected, enable me to accept the office of mediator between those authorities and French subjects, whenever, under circumstances equal to those in which it should be exerted in favor of citizens of the United States, my mediation might be invoked by the subjects of France.

In regard to the clerks, whose assistance you propose, on account of the large French population in Mexico, I beg that you will leave me at liberty to call for their services should at any time it become necessary.

The archives of the French legation, deposited the 11th instant in the consulate of the United States, for which I enclose a receipt, are transferred to the legation, and the official certificate of original deposit and transfer shall be, as you desire, transmitted to your excellency.

Copies, not only of these documents but also of your excellency's communication, shall, in deference to your request for protection to French subjects, be forwarded to the Department of State at Washington.

I avail myself [etc.]   MARCUS OTTERBOURG [2]

Meanwhile, the French and Prussian representatives at Washington had, on instructions from their Governments, ap-

---

[1] *Papers Relating to the Foreign Relations of the United States, with the Annual Message of the President,* 1867 (Government Printing Office, Washington), part II, p. 443.

[2] *Ibid.,* p. 442.

proached Secretary of State Seward with the request that
the American Minister at Mexico City be authorized to take
charge of the interests of the French and Prussian subjects in
Mexico.   The significant portions of Mr. Seward's instructions to Mr. Otterbourg, dated August 10, 1867, were as
follows:

Under these circumstances the United States, in conformity with a
political custom which has long obtained and is sanctioned by and
has regard to the general interests of civilization, have consented to allow
its diplomatic and consular representatives in Mexico to take charge of
the interests of subjects of those states in Mexico, and of any other states
whose governments are found in the same condition of non-representa-
tion in that republic.   This can only be done, however, with the consent and acquiescence of the government of Mexico; and no proceedings will be taken by United States representatives in behalf of subjects
of such foreign states different from the course prescribed by this government, for its representatives, for the protection of the interests of
citizens of the United States.

You will seek an opportunity to communicate the contents of this
instruction to the government of the republic and ask an expression of
its views thereupon.[3]

The Mexican Foreign Minister replied to Mr. Otterbourg's
note respecting his assumption of the protection of French
and Belgian subjects in the following vein:

MEXICO, *September* 7, 1867.

You stated in your note that in consideration of the cordial relations
existing between the United States, France, and Belgium, and the assurances derived from various conversations that you had held with
the Mexican authorities that the persons and property of foreigners
would be respected, you did not feel any impropriety in accepting the
office of mediator between said authorities and the French and Belgian
subjects who may invoke such mediation, under the same circumstances
in which it could be exercised in favor of citizens of the United States.

As I have before had the honor to manifest to you verbally, the
government of Mexico, desiring to avoid all danger of disturbance of
its friendly relations with the United States, feels that it would be better

---

[3] *Ibid.,* p. 447.

that you should not interpose any mediation of an official character in the instances in which the subjects of France and Belgium might desire to promote their interests.   But should you wish to interpose your good offices privately, the government will attend to them with all possible consideration.

In short, foreigners resident in Mexico who have no representatives of their governments have been and are under the protection of the Mexican authorities, and to them they can recur with the confidence they have enjoyed, and they will enjoy the guarantees that the laws of the republic concede.[4]

To Edward L. Plumb, who succeeded Mr. Otterbourg as Chargé d'Affaires, Mr. Seward sent the following instructions:

You will respect the wishes of the government of Mexico in this matter, and will lend your good offices to the subjects of France and Belgium in that country under the instructions heretofore given you, in such manner, whether public and official or private and unofficial, as shall be most acceptable to the government of the republic.

The substance of this instruction will be communicated by this department to the governments of France and Belgium respectively for their information.[5]

When the United States representative proposed taking over the protection of Italian, Austrian, and German interests as well, the Mexican Foreign Minister, Lerdo de Tejada, repeated his earlier position and clarified it even further in the following terms:

The government of the republic holds in the highest estimation its good and friendly relations with the United States, earnestly desiring to avoid every danger of any difference occurring between them.

For this grave reason, as I made known to Mr. Otterbourg, the government has felt a difficulty about the representatives of the United States in Mexico taking in charge the interests of the subjects of other nations.

Although they have no direct representation, the government provides with especial care that they be protected by the Mexican authorities, and enjoy the guarantees which the laws of the republic concede to

---

[4] *Ibid.*, p. 463.

[5] *Ibid.*, p. 466.

them. The efficient protection they receive has been the cause that they make no complaints under these circumstances.[6]

Referring to this communication, Mr. Seward instructed Mr. Plumb to allay the fears of the Mexican Government in the following words:

November 19, 1867.

. . . It is manifest to the government that all the European states, now unrepresented in Mexico, must come very quickly to such recognition of the republic as its dignity and interest require, and as is desired most earnestly by the United States. The interposition of good offices, in the meantime, which they ask from the United States, is to be exercised in such a manner as will facilitate instead of hindering that important object. At the same time nothing is further from our desire than in any way to cause embarrassment to the government of Mexico, nor are any apprehensions entertained by me that any misunderstanding will arise between us and the Mexican government from such unofficial good offices.

You will please make the contents of this despatch known to Mr. Lerdo de Tejada. . . .[7]

Contrary to Mr. Seward's expectation, it was not until the consolidation of the Diaz regime in 1876 that most of the European powers renewed their diplomatic relations with Mexico. During the intervening years successive American Ministers at Mexico City were called upon from time to time to exercise their good offices on behalf of the governments of eight different nations, namely, Great Britain, France, Austria, Belgium, Switzerland, Russia, Sweden, and Japan.[8] The nature of these duties varied widely. Immediately after the execution of Maximilian the good offices of Mr. Plumb were called upon to obtain the release of various European notables who had been closely associated with the ill-fated Emperor. He was successful in obtaining the release of M. Eloin of

---

[6] *Ibid.,* p. 468.

[7] *Ibid.,* p. 480.

[8] John W. Foster, *Diplomatic Memoirs* (Houghton Mifflin Company, Boston, 1909), vol. I, p. 31.

Belgium and Prince Salm-Salm of Prussia.[9]   In handling the more routine aspects of French protection he was assisted by M. Farine, the Chief Clerk of the French Legation, who remained at his post even after the withdrawal of the French Minister.[10]   This anomalous situation induced the French Government to undertake direct communication with Mr. Plumb regarding French interests, but the latter very properly referred the matter to the Department of State, which in turn informed the French Government that the desirable channel for such communications would be via the Department in Washington.[11]

John W. Foster, the American Minister to Mexico during the latter part of the period in question, has given us the following interesting account of his activities in behalf of foreign nationals in Mexico:

Because of the absence of representatives of the leading European Powers, there was thrown upon the Legation of the United States a large amount of unofficial duties.   I was called upon from time to time to exercise my good offices with the Mexican Government, by eight different countries, to wit, Great Britain, France, Austria, Belgium, Switzerland, Russia, Sweden and Japan.   And as it became necessary for the Mexican Government also at times to communicate with some of these countries, my good offices were invoked by it for such purpose.

I was asked most frequently to act in behalf of British interests.   The first note I addressed to the Mexican Foreign Office was in behalf of a British mercantile and banking house, which was seeking to establish a large claim for damages caused by the acts of the Mexican authorities. British bankers, merchants, and mining companies were established throughout the Republic, and during my entire term of service I was repeatedly called upon to interpose in their behalf.

My relations with the British residents were quite intimate and cordial, they regarding me as their *de facto* Minister, and the London Foreign Office made frequent expressions of appreciation of my service, which it would have put into the form of decorations; but that, happily

[9] *Foreign Relations,* 1867 (Government Printing Office, Washington), part II, pp. 474–475.

[10] *Ibid.,* p. 469.

[11] *Ibid.,* pp. 464, 480.

for the good of our foreign service, is not permitted by our Government. From the other Governments named, I also received repeated expressions of thanks for the good offices rendered to their subjects and their interests.

The French population of Mexico was more numerous than the British, but was not of such a character in its business relations as to require so much of my time, although I was frequently called upon for my good offices, as in the case of the French Sisters of Charity, related in the next chapter. These Sisters before their departure sent a delegation to the Legation to express their thanks for my interposition. . . .

All the monastic orders and religious communities had some time before been broken up and their members forced to leave the country or go into other occupations, with the exception of the Sisters of Charity, who had been tolerated because of their humane work in the hospitals and other charities. But now that the Laws of Reform had with so much pomp been incorporated in the Constitution, the Government felt that consistency required that its provisions should be impartially enforced, and orders were issued that the Sisters of Charity should cease their vocation or leave the country. I was instructed by the Secretary of State, at the request of the French Government (there being no French Minister in Mexico) to intervene in behalf of the French members of the order, who constituted the majority, to secure a postponement of their departure. This I readily accomplished, as the Government granted them whatever reasonable time they desired. But the orders of the Government caused the adherents of the Church to break forth into new demonstrations of indignation. The opposition manifested itself most prominently in what were termed the "protests of the ladies," documents which were drawn up with the ostensible object of expressing sorrow for the departure of the Sisters of Charity, but whose real purpose and effect were to attack and denounce the existing Government and weaken its influence with the people.[12]

2. GREEK INTERESTS IN TURKEY, 1868

In December 1868 the Greek Minister at Constantinople withdrew from Turkish territory as a result of the rupture of relations between Greece and Turkey in consequence of the uprising in Crete. The Greek Minister requested E. Joy Morris, the American Minister at Constantinople, to extend

---

[12] Foster, *op. cit.*, pp. 31, 50–51.

his protection over the 60,000 Hellenic subjects who were confronted with expulsion from Turkey. On the understanding that his efforts were to be strictly humanitarian and in no way political, Mr. Morris agreed to the Greek Minister's request, subject, of course, to the approval of the Department of State.[13] Secretary Seward replied to Mr. Morris' despatch as follows:

During the suspension of diplomatic relations between Turkey and Greece, you may informally lend your good offices to either government for communicating with the other, in no case, however, committing or compromising the United States. You will adhere to my former instructions concerning protection and asylum in Turkey, so as to avoid entangling complications, and you will fully report every proceeding on your part.[14]

Mr. Morris had but one "proceeding" to report, i.e. his interview of December 25 with Safvet Pasha, Turkish Minister of Foreign Affairs. On this occasion Mr. Morris alluded to the Greek Minister's request and explained his own humanitarian concept of the protective functions which he was prepared to assume. The Turkish Foreign Minister expressed some reservations about the non-political character of such activities and stated that he could not approve Mr. Morris' position as protector of Greeks in Turkey until the matter had been referred to the Grand Vizier. On the following day Mr. Morris received his reply: a polite but categorical "No" on the part of the Porte. The American Minister promptly informed the Greek Minister that he would not undertake to exercise even his most informal good offices in behalf of Greeks in Turkey in view of this refusal of the Turkish authorities to give their assent thereto.[15]

---

[13] The Minister to Turkey (Morris) to the Secretary of State (Seward), no. 282, Dec. 23, 1868, MS., Turkey, Despatches, vol. 20.

[14] Mr. Seward to Mr. Morris, no. 202, Dec. 31, 1868, cited in Moore, *op. cit.*, vol. IV, pp. 586–587.

[15] Mr. Morris to Mr. Seward, no. 288, Jan. 4, 1869, MS., Turkey, Despatches, vol. 20.

3. THE FRANCO-PRUSSIAN WAR, 1870–1871

Upon the outbreak of war between France and the North German Confederation in 1870 the North German Government requested that the United States Government authorize the American Minister at Paris, E. B. Washburne, to use his good offices for the protection of North Germans in France. Secretary of State Hamilton Fish promptly informed Mr. Washburne of this request by telegraph and added the following instruction: "President directs you to notify the Duke de Gramont of this request, and say that if the French Government consents thereto, the United States will extend to North Germans same care which they extended to subjects of the Emperor in Mexico." [16]   The request was promptly granted by the French Government, which also acceded to the subsequent extension of American protection over the nationals of Saxony, Hesse, Saxe-Coburg and Gotha.   After the departure of most of the diplomatic corps during the siege of Paris, Mr. Washburne was also entrusted with the protection of the nationals in Paris of Colombia, Portugal, Uruguay, the Dominican Republic, Ecuador, Chile, Paraguay, and Venezuela.

As President Grant said in his annual message to Congress, "the charge was an onerous one, requiring constant and severe labor, as well as the exercise of patience, prudence and good judgment." [17]   It was by far the most elaborate extension up to that time of American protection over foreign interests both belligerent and neutral and it exerted very considerable influence on the subsequent development of the practice. According to Mr. Washburne there had never before been "a case of the kind where so many interests, and where so many people had been concerned".   As far as he was aware, no particular rules had ever been laid down for such a situation and he felt himself "obliged to grope in the dark", fearing that if he avoided Scylla he "might be wrecked on

---

[16] Moore, *op. cit.,* vol. IV, p. 600; *Foreign Relations,* 1870, p. 65.

[17] *Foreign Relations,* 1870, p. 3.

Charybdis".[18]   His work, however, was eminently satisfactory and won for him the praise of the President, the Secretary of State, and the Government of the North German Confederation.

Washburne's protection of German interests was characterized from the outset by energetic action and a very liberal interpretation of his good offices.   He stored in the United States Legation the most valuable of the German archives at Paris, and he raised the American flag over the German Embassy, which he placed under the charge of two young Americans then in Paris.   The fifty thousand thalers which the German Government placed at his disposal for aid to Germans in Paris he deposited not in his own name but in the name of the "Minister of the United States, charged with the protection of the subjects of the North German Confederation in France, pending the existing war between France and Prussia". [19]   Travel documents for Germans he signed in the same manner.

Most interesting of all was the lively debate in which he engaged with the Duke de Gramont respecting the merits of the French decree which prevented the departure from France of Germans of military age.   In Washburne's opinion this regulation "violated all the well-established principles of public law", and should not be given "even an implied assent".[20]   On his own initiative and without awaiting instructions from the Department of State or an expression of the views of the German Government, he proceeded to inform the French Foreign Minister by means of a formal note that the French Government was not acting in accord with the prevailing international practice which allowed enemy nationals a reasonable period of time in which to de-

[18] E. B. Washburne, *Recollections of a Minister to France* (Scribner's Sons, New York, 1887), vol. I, pp. 43–44.

[19] *Ibid.*, pp. 39, 70.

[20] *Ibid.*, p. 45.

part for their homeland or for neutral territory.[21]   Considering the reply of the Duke de Gramont quite unsatisfactory, Mr. Washburne wrote a sharp rejoinder and continued his protests when the French Government suddenly reversed itself and ordered the expulsion of the Germans *en masse*.

Mr. Washburne's own account gives such an excellent picture of these difficulties and of the general nature of his protective functions that it deserves being repeated here *in extenso:*

When I took upon myself the protection of the German subjects in France, I had but a faint idea of what the undertaking was going to involve, for I had not supposed it possible that I should be charged with the care and with the superintendence of more than thirty thousand people expelled from their homes on so short a notice.   From the time of the breaking out of the war, and so soon as it became known that the Germans had been placed under my protection, it could be well imagined, considering so large a German population, what would take place.   The legation began to be crowded from day to day by persons desiring protection, advice, information and assistance.   Many were thrown into prison charged with being "Prussian spies," many were under arrest as dangerous persons, and the lives and property of others were threatened in their neighborhoods.   My good offices were sought for, and cheerfully rendered, in all such cases, and I believe I never failed to accomplish all I undertook in such emergencies.   The first extraordinary order of the French government, prohibiting all such Germans from leaving France who might by any possibility owe military service, and about which I had so long a correspondence with the Duke de Gramont, created great alarm among a large number of them, who were extremely anxious to get away.   The practical operation of that order prevented any German from leaving French territory without special authority to that end first had and obtained from the Minister of the Interior, and all applications for such authority had to be made through me.   Subsequently all that was changed, and the expulsion of the Germans decreed *en masse,* and it was required that I should vise the passports or give a *laissez-passer* to every German in France.   I esti-

---

[21] His action was subsequently approved and commended by the Secretary of State, Hamilton Fish.   See Mr. Fish to Mr. Washburne, no. 162, Sept. 13, 1870, MS., France, Instructions, vol. 18.

mated that the number of Germans placed under my piotection, and who were expelled from France, amounted to thirty thousand. I made that estimate from the number of vises and passports which I gave out, and that number, as recorded in the legation, amounted to eight thousand nine hundred. In the rush and hurry of business, there was no record made in many cases. It was entirely safe to say that the whole number of vises and passports going through the legation amounted to not less than nine thousand; the larger number of these passports included husband, wife and children, and it was a moderate estimate to say that there was an average of three and one-third persons to each passport, which would make thirty thousand souls, according to such calculation. I issued cards which, by an arrangement that I had made with the railroad company, entitled the holder to a railroad ticket from Paris, through Belgium, to the German frontier, for nine thousand three hundred and thirty-two persons, and pecuniary assistance to a smaller number. That involved an examination of each person as to his or her want of the necessary means to get out of the country; for my instructions were not to make advances to people who had the means of paying their own expenses. I was under the necessity of sending two or three persons from the legation to the railroad depot every night, in order to see that the holders of the cards received their railroad tickets and were properly sent off.

It was about the middle of August when the expulsion of the Germans from France began to be rigidly enforced, and when I received the credit of fifty thousand thalers from the Prussian government to assist them. From that time to the middle of September, when the Northern Railroad was cut, we were literally overwhelmed by these poor people, seeking vises or passports, and the means of getting away. For days, and I may even say for weeks, the street was completely blocked by them, awaiting their turns to be attended to. On one day, more than five hundred had gathered in front of the legation before seven o'clock in the morning; and on some days there were not less than twenty-five hundred to three thousand persons in waiting. It took a police force of six men to keep the crowd in their turn. With such an amount of work so suddenly thrown upon the legation, I found it almost impossible to get the necessary help to assist me, though I was authorized by the State Department to employ what force I should deem necessary. I was fortunate in being able to procure the services of the Secretaries of the Saxon and Darmstadt legations, and of the clerk of the Prussian Consul-General in Paris, all of whom proved invaluable from their knowledge of both the French and German languages. I had also the benefit of the services of Mr. Nicholas Fish, the son of the Secretary of State, and the Honorable George Eustis, whom I have heretofore mentioned, and by several other friends, who were kind enough to lend me a helping hand.   Some days there were no less than eleven persons engaged at the legation, but with all the force we had, it was impossible to keep up with the demands upon us.   In view of this extra work and the increased price of living, I recommended to the State Department that, with the consent of Congress, certain extra allowances should be paid to my secretaries and other persons connected with the legation. All such amounts were cheerfully allowed by the State Department, with the approbation of Congress.

There were at this time a large number of Germans in Paris who were under my protection.   Considering the large German population in the city prior to the breaking out of the war, it was not a matter of wonder that a good many were found still in the city, when all communication was cut off.   When it became evident that the city was to be besieged, I redoubled my exertions to get these unfortunate people away.   Deprived of all work, their little resources exhausted, with the intense hostility of the French people toward them—bad as their condition was, it was to become infinitely worse in case of a siege.   Many were imprisoned for vagabondage and many were detained charged with being spies, dangerous persons, etc.

As I have stated, upon my application to Gambetta he concerted with the Count de Keratry, the Prefect of Police, for their discharge *en masse* and for sending them, at the expense of the French government to the Belgian frontier.   But after all, quite a number still remained.   Many were too old and infirm to leave.   Some were sick, some were children left behind, who had been put out to service; but perhaps the largest number were, as I have said, female domestics, most of whom had been persuaded by their employers to remain, under pledges of protection. Not a day passed that there was not some new application for assistance.

In view of the duties which had been imposed upon me, in virtue of the functions with which I had been charged, in respect to the *nationaux* of the countries I have named, it would have been almost too much to expect that I could discharge them in a manner entirely satisfactory to both the belligerent powers and to my own government.   My position was sometimes very embarrassing.   None of the writers on public law, so far as I had been able to find, had laid down any rule to be observed, or referred in any manner to what was proper to be done by the representative of a belligerent power, remaining in the country of the enemy, in a state of war.   I had, therefore, to grope almost entirely in the dark. I did not, however, shrink from my duty or labor.   During two months I had occupied from twelve to eighteen hours daily in my work.   When the pressure for the departure of the Germans was the greatest, I went myself to the railroad depot at night, after working all day at my legation, and remained till midnight to superintend their departure and to seek out and provide for cases of extreme destitution, that had not been made known.   It was a satisfaction for me to know that, with the means which had been so generously placed at my disposal by the Prussian government, I had been able to relieve a vast amount of suffering and misery.   It was pleasant for me to know that no complaint of any German ever reached the legation of a failure on my part to do everything that could properly be done by me in respect to the protection, advice or assistance.   On the other hand, all classes signified to me their thankfulness and gratitude for what I had been able to do for them.[22]

4. PROTECTION OF SWISS CITIZENS, 1871 AND AFTER

In May 1871 President Schenk of Switzerland spoke to Horace Rublee, the American Minister at Bern, about a matter which had been of concern to him for some time.   For years the Swiss Federal Council had made it a practice to request various foreign governments to extend their protection to Swiss citizens having occasional need of such protection in countries where the Swiss Confederation did not maintain a diplomatic or consular representation of its own.   Such incidents were becoming increasingly frequent and in order to avoid the inevitable delays of official correspondence respecting each case, he had recently persuaded the German Government (which protected a number of Swiss citizens abroad) to issue a general authorization permitting German diplomatic and consular officers to extend such protection when requested by Swiss citizens without waiting for an official request from the Swiss Government and an official approval from Berlin.   The President wondered if a similar general instruction might be issued by the United States Government to its diplomats and consuls, since many Swiss might desire American protection in similar circumstances.[23]

---

[22] Washburne, *op. cit.*, pp. 227–231.

[23] The Minister to Switzerland (Rublee) to the Secretary of State (Fish), no. 46, May 19, 1871, MS., Switzerland, Despatches, vol. 8.

The ensuing correspondence on this matter, which continued intermittently until 1887, throws a flood of light on the development of the practice of protecting foreign interests. As we shall see, the unexpectedly embarrassing, yet amusing, complications which resulted from this simple request were to result in a more careful examination of the practice of protecting foreign interests than had yet been given to the subject on either side of the Atlantic.

The response of the Department of State to President Schenk's request was favorable and the following circular instruction was issued to American diplomatic and consular officers:

Circular No. 11   WASHINGTON, *June* 16, 1871.

GENTLEMEN: His Excellency, the President of the Swiss Confederation, has expressed to this Department through the Minister of the United States accredited to that government, a wish that you would severally extend your protection to Swiss citizens who may desire it and who may be sojourning at places where there are no diplomatic or consular representatives of that republic.

This Government has, on more than one occasion, upon the request of friendly powers, given to its diplomatic and consular representatives permission to take upon themselves, with the consent of the government within whose jurisdiction they reside, the function of representing those powers at places where the latter had no such officers. It has understood this to amount simply to the granting of the services of our agents, with their own consent, to meet what has ordinarily been a fortuitous and temporary exigency of the friendly government. When this function is accepted, the diplomatic or consular officer becomes the agent of the foreign government as to the duties he may perform for its citizens or subjects; he becomes responsible to it for his discharge of those duties; and that government is alone responsible for his acts in relation thereto.

With this understanding of the obligations, you are authorized, with the consent of the authorities of the country or place where you officially reside, to extend such protection to Swiss citizens whenever it may be required or needed. It is expected, however, that, in complying with this authority, you will exercise due discretion, and will be careful not to give just cause of offense in any quarter.[24]

---

[24] *Foreign Relations,* 1871, pp. 28-29.

While the wording of this circular may have been correct in principle, it produced the unfortunate impression in the minds of a number of the officers to whom it was addressed that they were, as "agents", to become official representatives of the Swiss Government to which, as the circular stated, they were "responsible".[25] This impression was so wide-spread and so productive of international complications that the Swiss Government could not refrain from bringing it to the attention of the American authorities, despite the danger of appearing ungrateful for favors too freely granted. The Swiss note was a carefully drafted document the importance of which warrants the repetition at this point of the complete text in translation.

Since the Government of the United States, responding with a kindness which we have already had occasion to acknowledge to a request of the Federal Council, sent a circular to all its diplomatic and consular officials authorizing them upon request to take under their protection Swiss citizens residing in countries where the Confederation has no representatives, certain misunderstandings have arisen in the interpretation of this instruction by a number of consuls, which, although not serious, require clarification in the interest of the two parties concerned.

It appears that certain American diplomatic and consular representatives have not fully understood the circular which was addressed to them and the aim which the Federal Council had in mind in requesting that in certain circumstances its nationals might receive their friendly protection. They have apparently felt that they were being requested to charge themselves with Swiss consular representation, as officers of the Federal Council, and that the latter was at one stroke creating Swiss consulates in all localities where none exist at present by placing them under the direction of the consuls of the United States. This interpretation has not actually been expressed by any one of them, but it alone is able to account for the various requests which they have made to the Federal Council on this subject, which we would like to take the liberty of citing as illustrations.

The American Consul at Warsaw requested under date of July 17,

---

[25] During the period in question the expression "agent" or "diplomatic agent" was frequently used to indicate an official representative. For detailed analysis of the principles involved in this matter see *post*, p. 137.

1871 that the Federal Council send him the laws, diplomas, documents, flags and coats of arms [*écussons*] which the Consulate required. On October 27 he asked for a certificate of appointment which [he indicated] was indispensable for obtaining his exequatur as Swiss Consul from the Russian Government.

The Legation of the United States in Peru stated in a communication of August 28, 1871 that it had already assumed the duties of its new charge and inquired whether the Federal Government [of Switzerland] had made arrangements for defraying its chancellery expenses, etc.

The American consulate at Bucharest stated on the 3rd of October that it was willing to accept the position of agent and said that it had already obtained the authorization of the Roumanian Government. Documents, instructions, etc., were requested.

The American Legation at Quito announced on August 22 that its protection would henceforth extend to all Swiss then residing in the Republic of Ecuador or who might subsequently establish residence there. It was made clear that while it would assume the responsibility for administration in this matter, the Federal Government [of Switzerland] would be ultimately responsible for its actions.

Further examples might be cited but these will suffice to indicate both with what great kindness the aforementioned officials have put themselves and their services at the disposition of the Federal Council and, on the other hand, the extent to which the original intentions of the Council have been rather exceeded. In order to explain our point of view as clearly as possible, let us review the question from the outset.

Up to the present the Federal Council has allowed to every Swiss citizen residing in a country where the Confederation does not have diplomatic or consular officials complete freedom to place himself under the protection of any foreign consulate which, by virtue of language or other personal or local circumstances, appeared most suited to meet his needs. Thus at present Swiss citizens may be found under the protection of American, German, French, Italian, Belgian, Dutch, English, Russian and other consuls. In certain countries, even in certain cities, one Swiss may be protected by a certain consulate while another one of his compatriots will be registered with the consulate of another nation. The conditions governing the acquisition of this protection are quite varied: for French consulates, for example, it is only necessary to obtain the personal consent of the consul; for others, particularly for American consulates, it is necessary to have a special authorization from the consul's government, which must be sought through diplomatic channels. In order to avoid the delays which this official correspondence entails, the Federal Council has long desired that the governments which have this special requirement would be so good as to give their representatives a general authorization permitting them without further formalities to extend the protection which might on occasion be requested of them.

A request of this sort made to the Federal Council by a Swiss residing in one of the Central American countries, together with the instruction issued by the Chancellor of the German Empire, permitting German consuls to extend their protection to Swiss citizens who so requested, furnished an appropriate occasion for us to express our desire on this subject to the United States Government, since many Swiss citizens may prefer to place themselves under American protection. By note of June 29, Mr. Minister, you communicated to us the reply of your government and indicated that the latter had sent a circular to all of its diplomatic and consular officers in countries where Switzerland has no representation, authorizing them to take under their protection those Swiss citizens who might request it.

We have had the honor to indicate in preceding paragraphs how this circular has been interpreted by a certain number of consuls to which it was addressed, and we have taken the liberty of stating our impression that our intentions have been exceeded by certain of those officials, to whom none-the-less we are indebted. If the intention of the Federal Council had been to establish Swiss Consulates wherever they have not so far existed and to place them under the administration of consuls of the United States, we would have addressed ourselves to the persons concerned and if they had been willing to accept our offer, we would then have sought the superior authorization of the Government of the United States. We would then have informed the governments of the localities in which these consulates were to be established and would have requested the issuance of their "exequatur."

What we desire is simply that the United States Government, like the government of Germany, might extend its general authorization to cover what up to this time it has permitted its consuls to do in each particular case on request of the Federal Council.

It is unnecessary to point out at great length that the present state of affairs might result in embarrassment and complications for both the United States Government and the Swiss Government, and that it is important to avoid such contingency.

With this aim in mind we have explained our point of view to all the Ministers and Consuls who have written to us in the above sense. It seems to us, however, that it would be appropriate if the American Government would inform its Consuls that the instruction which was sent to them refers only to countries in which the Swiss Confederation has no diplomatic or consular representation, and applies only to those Swiss citizens who may ask to be placed under the protection of the American Consuls.

In the hope that you will be so kind, Mr. Minister, as to explain the foregoing to your Government and to inform us in due course of the decision reached in this matter, we extend the assurances of our distinguished consideration.[26]

In response to this note the Secretary of State attempted to rectify the "misapprehensions" of certain American diplomatic and consular officers by issuing the following circular instruction on December 15:

Information has reached this Department that the purpose of its Circular No. 11 of the 16th of June last, relative to the protection of citizens of Switzerland, may, in some instances, have been misunderstood. You are consequently informed that you were not, for that purpose, expected to become a diplomatic or consular officer for that republic, which is prohibited by the Constitution to officers of the United States who are citizens. The intention was that you should merely use your good offices in behalf of any Swiss in your vicinity who might request them in the absence of a diplomatic or consular representative of Switzerland, and with the consent of the authorities where you reside.[27]

This instruction clarified the immediate difficulties and served as a basis for the protection which American officers extended to Swiss citizens for more than a decade thereafter. By virtue of this general authorization it is probable that many specific acts of protection took place which were never referred to the Department. We know, however, that during 1872 the American Minister to China extended protection to Swiss citizens in that country.[28] During the Russo-Turkish War the protection of Swiss citizens was specifically mentioned in a circular instruction issued on June 28, 1877.[29]

[26] Mr. Rublee to Mr. Fish, no. 75, Bern, Nov. 24, 1871, enclosure 1, MS., Switzerland, Despatches, vol. 9; translation by the present writer.

[27] *Foreign Relations,* 1872, p. 5.

[28] Mr. Rublee to Mr. Fish, no. 108, Oct. 22, 1872, MS., Switzerland, Despatches, vol. 9.

[29] Moore, *op. cit.,* vol. IV, p. 595.

By March 1882 a sufficient number of such cases had arisen to warrant the issuance of another circular authorizing American diplomatic and consular officers to draw on the Department for any expenses incurred in the protection of Swiss citizens.[30]   In the following year, however, it was held that the acting American Consul General at Havana could not be reimbursed by the United States Government for expenses which he had incurred in paying relief money to a destitute Swiss citizen in Cuba, since such financial assistance was not authorized to American citizens (except seamen) in similar circumstances.[31]   In the same year the American Consul at Guayaquil employed his good offices with success in behalf of Swiss citizens who had been called up for military service in Ecuador.[32]   During the latter part of 1883 the American Minister to Chile endeavored to use his good offices in presenting claims of Swiss citizens against Chile, but the Chilean Government refused to allow any presentation of claims through the good offices of any foreign government, "except upon the basis of a formal agreement".[33]   In the following year the United States Government tried to include these Swiss claims in the terms of a convention respecting the claims of American citizens, but again the Chilean Government maintained its "inalterable rule to admit no claim presented by other nations".[34]   Despite this rule the United States Government agreed in 1885 to make another effort to assist Switzerland in this matter by forwarding the Swiss claims to the Chilean Government through the American

---

[30] *Loc. cit.*

[31] The Acting Secretary of State to the Acting Consul General at Havana (Springer), no. 101, Nov. 6, 1883, MS., Instructions to Consuls, vol. 108.

[32] The Secretary of State (Freylinghuysen) to the Swiss Minister (Frey) Dec. 26, 1883; *id.* to *id.*, Mar. 8, 1884, and Apr. 19, 1884, MS., Notes to Switzerland, vol. I, pp. 59, 66, 70.

[33] *Id.* to *id.*, Dec. 18, 1883, *ibid.*, p. 58.

[34] *Id.* to *id.*, Dec. 11, 1884, *ibid.*, p. 91.

Minister at Santiago.   Secretary of State Bayard added that "It must be understood, however, that Mr. Roberts would act in such cases, in no sense as the representative of the Swiss Government, but merely as an Agent for the purpose of handing over, without any endorsement or approval on his part, the papers evidencing such claims to the Government of Chile".[35]   In the same year Swiss claims against Colombia were presented by the American Minister at Bogotá, acting "merely as the Agent to hand over the papers without endorsement, and not as the agent of Switzerland".[36]

While the Swiss Government was duly appreciative of the services thus rendered in its behalf and for the benefit of Swiss citizens by diplomatic and consular officers of the United States, it could not fail to note that the protection granted by the United States was much more unofficial and considerably less effective than that granted to Swiss citizens by certain other powers, particularly Germany.   In 1871 the Swiss Government had had to reject the "too official" representation of its interests by certain American officers; by 1887 the Swiss Government had become convinced that its interests required a more official protection than they had been receiving during the intervening years from the American diplomatic and consular representatives.   This point of view was expressed in a note from the Swiss Minister, Colonel Frey, to Secretary of State Bayard, of which the significant portion was as follows:

The President of the Confederation has instructed the undersigned to convey to you his warmest thanks for the readiness with which you have been pleased to comply with our wishes in this matter, and to avail himself, at the same time, of this occasion to express to you the thanks of the federal council for the valuable services which have been rendered since 1871 by your representatives to Swiss citizens.   The undersigned

[35] The Secretary of State (Bayard) to the Swiss Minister (Frey), June 13, 1885, *ibid.*, p. 103.

[36] The Acting Secretary (Porter) to the Swiss Chargé d'Affaires (Kloss), Aug. 11, 1885, *ibid.*, pp. 107–108.

assures you that the federal council fully appreciates the good will and the friendly sentiments which have been manifested by the United States Government in this matter.

With regard to the scope of the protection hereafter to be extended to our citizens by your representatives, I have, however, the honor, in obedience to the instructions of the President of the Confederation, to remark that the views expressed by you on this subject do not appear to accord in all respects with those of the federal council, nor, as we think, with the position taken in relation to this matter by the United States Government in the year 1871.

In the opinion of the President of the Confederation, protégés should be treated in all respects as if they were citizens of the protecting country. A Swiss, by placing himself under the protection of the United States, becomes assimilated, in the opinion of the President of the Confederation, while he is under that protection, to a citizen of the United States; his character as a Swiss is for the time being not to be considered, and, so far as the foreign state is concerned, he is covered by the United States flag. Diplomatic protection, if it is to have any real meaning, must not be conditional or limited; it must be more than an unofficial mediation in behalf of such claims for indemnity as may arise; otherwise it would be of no avail when most needed—that is to say, at the time when the violated rights of the protégé are to be asserted.

This view of the scope of the protection to be afforded by no means involves any direct intercourse of the federal council with the diplomatic or consular officers of the protecting state, and there consequently seems to be no ground for the assumption that those officers by protecting Swiss citizens assume the role of officers of the Swiss Confederation. It might rather be assumed that a contrary state of things took place, since a Swiss, who places himself under foreign protection, loses, to a certain extent, the outward characteristics of his nationality.[37]

In reply Mr. Bayard stated that he could not accept the principle of "assimilation" under which a protected foreign national would receive the same protection as a citizen of the United States, cited a number of examples indicating that the protection granted by the United States had always been

---

[37] The Swiss Minister (Frey) to the Secretary of State (Bayard), Apr. 15, 1887, *Foreign Relations,* 1887, p. 1074; also cited in Moore, *op. cit.,* vol. IV, p. 494.

limited to exercise of good offices, and concluded with the following sentence:

It is evident that anything further than this, on behalf of other nations, might involve this government in great complications with the government to which the protecting minister or consul was accredited, and on which, as regarded our own affairs, we had no disputed claims, and might eventually be of as little benefit to the Swiss nation as to the United States.[38]

On this informal basis (which the Swiss perforce accepted) protection has been extended to Swiss citizens by American representatives on many occasions, the most recent of which occurred in Afghanistan in 1943.[39]

5. JAPANESE IN HAWAII, 1871–1885

On the 26th of September 1871 Henry A. Peirce, the Minister Resident of the United States in the Hawaiian Islands, received an extraordinary letter written in Japanese and addressed to "His Excellency, H. A. Pairs". Along with the original came a copy in English translation which read as follows:

TOKEI, JAPAN, *the 5th–7th Month*
4th Year Meigi

YOUR EXCELLENCY: We have the honor to address your Excellency that, although the term for labor of the Japanese at Hawaiian islands has expired on the 5th month of this year (corresponding with July, 1871) and the Japanese ought to return to this Empire on that time, the certain Japanese made us an application stating their wishes to stay in that islands for labor and we allowed this application and gave the licenses for it.

---

[38] The Secretary of State (Bayard) to the Swiss Chargé d'Affaires (Kloss), July 1, 1887, *Foreign Relations*, 1887, p. 1076.

[39] See Moore, *op. cit.*, vol. IV, pp. 597–598; Hackworth, *op. cit.*, vol. IV, p. 490; Assistant Secretary of State (Long) to the Minister to Switzerland (Harrison), no. 1595, Nov. 7, 1942; and Secretary of State (Hull) to the Legation at Kabul, telegram no. 80, July 27, 1943, MS., file 704.5490H/2–4.

When Wooeno Kwantokunokami made the contract for the Japanese in Hawaiian islands, Your Excellency took many trouble for managing the matter and signed the contract, we therefore write this to Your Excellency and beg respectfully to give your attention to the Japanese remained in that islands.

With respect and consideration [40]

MIYAMOTO OKADZA
Shiogo for Foreign Affairs.

Mr. Peirce's reply was couched in the following language:

LEGATION OF THE UNITED STATES OF AMERICA
HONOLULU, Sept. 30[h] 1871.

His Excellency MIYAMOTO OKADZA,
    Shiogo for Foreign Affairs,
        YEDO, JAPAN.

SIR, I have the honor to acknowledge the receipt on the 26[h] inst. of your despatch to this Legation, of date Tokei, Japan the 5th – 7th month – 4th year Meigi, which relates to Japanese subjects here, the contracts for whose labor expired in July last, and who were by agreement, then to be conveyed back to Japan, but which was not carried into effect in consequence of the recent permission given to them by the Japan Government to remain in this country. And in view of the part taken by me in effecting an amicable arrangement of the whole matter, your Excellency requests me to give my attention (to the protection of the Japanese now in this country).

On ascertaining that Mr. Wodehouse, Her B. Majesty's Commissioner and Consul Gen'l here, was in receipt of a similar letter as the above named; we called on the Hawaiian Minister of Foreign Affairs and had joint consultation on the subject of your request. The matter was arranged to the satisfaction of the Minister, of Mr. Wodehouse and myself. In giving my consent to act in the capacity your Excellency has requested, it is to be understood, that it is only by the approval of my Government, to be hereafter made known, and only for a time sufficiently long to enable the Japan Gov't to appoint a proper official agent of its own to take charge of the interests of Japanese subjects residing in this Country.

I am credibly informed that your people here are very contented and in a healthy condition— earning high wages as free labourers in the various capacities they are adapted to.

---

[40] The Minister to Hawaii (Peirce) to the Secretary of State (Fish), no. 122, Oct. 2, 1871, enclosure 1, MS., Hawaii, Despatches, vol. 14.

The Hawaiian Gov't on the 27ᵗʰ inst. caused the National Standard of Japan to be displayed and saluted with 21 guns, in honor of the Empire of Japan and in commemoration of the treaty lately effected by and between the two Countries.

With great consideration and high respect, I have the honor to be Your Excellency's Most Obdt Serv't.[41]

> HENRY A. PEIRCE
> Minister Resident
> of the U. S. A. Hawaiian Islands.

In acknowledging the receipt of Minister Peirce's despatch respecting this correspondence Secretary Fish stated: "In the absence of any official Agent of Japan to that country you are authorized to extend your good offices for their protection." [42] Apparently this arrangement achieved a certain degree of standing recognition with the years, for in 1880 the Japanese Government transmitted through the Department of State certain documents addressed to the King of Hawaii.   In forwarding these papers to the American Minister at Honolulu, Secretary of State Evarts explained that "The steps thus taken by Japan, in communicating with the authorities of H. M. at Honolulu, is owing, as Mr. Inouye explained to Mr. Bingham, to there being no Diplomatic Agent of Hawaii in Japan, and the good offices of this government having been availed of before, under similar circumstances." [43]   Although the files of the Department of State do not indicate any noteworthy examples of protective activities by American Ministers at Honolulu on behalf of Japanese subjects, it appears that the United States Government served as the channel of communication between the Japanese and Hawaiian Governments until 1885, when the Japanese appointed J. O. Carter as Japanese Commercial Agent at Honolulu.   In the

---

[41] *Ibid.,* enclosure 2.

[42] Mr. Fish to Mr. Peirce, no. 54, Nov. 18, 1871, MS., Hawaii, Instructions, vol. 2, pp. 219–220.

[43] The Secretary of State (Evarts) to the Minister to Hawaii (Comly), no. 84, Dec. 10, 1880, *ibid.,* pp. 383–384.

following year a Japanese Consulate was established in that city.[44]

6. GERMANS IN GUATEMALA, 1874

In May 1874 the German Consul at Guatemala, Friedrich Augener, was obliged to return home before the arrival of his successor. He therefore approached George Williamson, the American Minister to Guatemala, with the request that he "watch over the interests of the German subjects [in Guatemala] during the interval mentioned." Mr. William-son consented so to do, but promptly reported the incident to the Department. The reply of Secretary of State Hamilton Fish revealed that the Department had given very careful consideration to the matter:

SIR: Your No. 154, dated at Guatemala May 17, is accompanied by a copy of correspondence with Mr. Friedrich Augener, Consul of Germany, and with the Minister of Foreign Affairs, in regard to the extension of protection to German subjects in Guatemala until the arrival of the gentleman who is to assume the charge of that Consulate.

Mr. Augener's note to you says that you have "consented to watch over the interests of the German subjects during the interval mentioned, etc." In your letter to the Minister of Foreign Affairs referring to Mr. Augener's request, you speak of it as a "request that the citizens of his country in Guatemala may be taken under the protection of (your) this Legation,"—while the Minister of Foreign Affairs considers that you have been "desired to take charge of the German subjects residing, etc."

The nature of the duties which you are to assume with regard to these German residents in Guatemala is best defined in the expression used by Mr. Augener in his request addressed to you. It is understood to amount to the granting, during the interval referred to, to such Germans as may have occasion to seek your aid, and with the consent of the Government of Guatemala, of your good services in their behalf. In the discharge of such duties as may devolve upon you, in this relation, you are to be responsible to the Government of Germany, and that Government and not the Government of the United States is responsible for your acts relative thereto.

---

[44] *Almanach de Gotha,* 1885, 1886, "Hawaii".

In view of the probability that there was not sufficient time to consult your Government and obtain its assent before answering the request made of you, your acceptance of the charge as above explained, is approved.[45]

As it turned out, however, these careful instructions proved entirely unnecessary, since Mr. Williamson did not have one single occasion to exercise his good offices in behalf of German interests during the four months preceding the arrival of Mr. Doeding, the new German Consul.[46]

7. ITALIANS ON WEST COAST OF SOUTH AMERICA, 1880

The protection of foreign interests, as we have defined it and as it has generally been exercised, is a diplomatic and consular function.   On occasion, however, protection has been extended to foreigners by military and naval officers of the United States in the course of their activities in defense of American lives and property in troubled areas.   While this type of protection by armed force is more in the nature of interposition, it has occasionally taken place in circumstances resembling the diplomatic and consular protection of foreign interests, as will be seen from the following letter of 1880 from the Secretary of State to the Secretary of the Navy:

I have the honor to inform you that Prince Camporeale, the Chargé d'Affaires ad interim of His Majesty the King of Italy near this Government, has, in a personal conference, brought to my notice the fact that Italian subjects residing or sojourning on the West Coast of South America may be exposed to danger and injuries during the present hostilities in that region between the Chileans and the Peruvians and the Bolivians; and has at the same time stated to me that his government would esteem it a deep obligation, as well as an evidence of the

---

[45] The Secretary of State (Fish) to the Minister to the Central American States (Williamson), no. 83, June 18, 1874, MS., Costa Rica, vol. 17, p. 179; also cited in Moore, *op. cit.*, vol. IV, pp. 588–589.

[46] Mr. Williamson to Mr. Fish, no. 208, Aug. 10, 1874, MS., Central America, vol. 6.

strong and long continued friendship between the United States and Italy, if the naval vessels of the United States cruising in the Pacific could be instructed, by telegraph, to furnish such aid as they may properly be enabled to render to Italian subjects and interests within the sphere of hostilities, in the absence of vessels of their own nation on the spot, in case of emergency. The Italian Government promises reciprocal instructions to its naval commanders with respect to American citizens and protecting their interests in like circumstances.

It has afforded me pleasure to assure Prince Camporeale that the friendly proposal which he was directed by his government to make would be at once brought to your favorable notice. Awaiting the favor of your reply in order that I may be able to give prompt information of its tenor to the Italian Chargé d'Affaires, I have the honor, et cetera.[47]

The Secretary of the Navy replied, in part, as follows:

In view of the amicable relations existing between the government of the United States and that of Italy, and the desire on our part that they should remain unchanged, I have this day, by telegraph, instructed Rear Admiral Thomas H. Stevens, commanding our Pacific Squadron, in accordance with the desire of Prince Camporeale, directing him to issue orders to that effect to all the vessels composing the Squadron.[48]

It does not appear that the files of the Department of State contain any further correspondence on this subject which would indicate the extent to which Rear Admiral Stevens had occasion to extend his protection to the Italian subjects in question.[49]

8. CHINESE IN CERTAIN AMERICAN REPUBLICS, 1885 AND AFTER

On August 26, 1885 the American Consul General at Panamá was instructed to use the same type of good offices

---

[47] The Secretary of State (Evarts) to the Secretary of the Navy (Thompson), Oct. 18, 1880, MS., Domestic Letters, vol. 34, p. 649.

[48] Mr. Thompson to Mr. Evarts, Oct. 19, 1880, MS., Miscellaneous Letters, 1880, part I.

[49] During the civil war in Chile in 1891 "the British Government, on the request of that of Germany, directed that the protection of British ships of war in Chilean waters be extended to German subjects." (Moore, *op. cit.*, vol. IV, p. 592.)

for the protection of Chinese subjects on the Isthmus as were covered by the rules laid down in the Department's circular instruction for the exercise of good offices on behalf of Swiss citizens, "it being distinctly understood that the United States consular officer should not thereby become a consular officer of the Chinese Government, and that the consent of the Colombian Government should first be obtained." [50]

The strictly informal protection thus granted to Chinese subjects in Panama was extended in subsequent years to Chinese in other American republics.[51] In 1894 the Chinese Minister at Washington approached Secretary of State Gresham about the matter, as a result of which the Secretary sent the following instruction to the American Minister to Guatemala:

Referring to your No. 114, of the 26th ultimo, I have to enclose a copy of a note from the Chinese minister, of the 16th instant, concerning the petition addressed to him by Chinese subjects residing in Guatemala.

He asks, in consequence of the absence of any treaty relations with that Republic permitting Chinese to appoint consular representatives therein, that you may be allowed to exercise your good offices in behalf of the Chinese subjects living in Guatemala.

This is not an unusual request, and the good offices of the diplomatic and consular representatives of the United States have been employed for the protection of Chinese elsewhere, as well as other foreigners. The interests of our own people in parts of Turkey, where no United States consular officer resided, have been looked after by British consular officers.

In the present instance your efforts are to be confined to the friendly intervention in case of need for the protection of the Chinese in their person and property from unjust and harsh treatment. You are not to hold any representative character or function as respects the Chinese Government, and are to act informally. Before taking any steps in

---

[50] *Ibid.*, p. 596.

[51] Consular good offices were also extended to Chinese in Hawaii in 1892; see the Secretary of State (Foster) to the American Minister to Hawaii (Stevens), no. 54, Sept. 8, 1892, and no. 55, Sept. 22, MS., Hawaii, Instructions, vol. 3, pp. 152–153.

the matter, however, you should represent to the Guatemalan Government the wish of the Chinese minister, and the willingness of your government to accede thereto, as herein indicated, provided the assent of the Guatemalan authorities is entirely favorable. The decision of that Government upon the subject should be reported to the Department.[52]

The Guatemalan authorities did accede to the request but as a formality and courtesy they felt that an official request should come to them from the Chinese Government or its representative in Washington. In January 1896 a sealed note from the Chinese Minister at Washington was duly transmitted and delivered to the Guatemalan Government by the American Minister.[53] In 1894 the United States Government agreed to extend its good offices to Chinese subjects in Costa Rica, but the Costa Rican authorities declined to grant their consent, on the ground "that the number of Chinese there was small, and that the immigration of Chinese was forbidden by law".[54]

In 1896 American good offices for Chinese subjects were extended to Nicaragua and Salvador with the consent of the governments concerned. The note from the Chinese Minister at Washington requesting the extension of American good offices reveals an interesting aspect of that historical relationship, to which reference was made in chapter I, between the practice of employing foreigners as diplomatic or consular officials and the practice of seeking third-party protection:

SIR: I have the honor to state that upon my receipt in June, 1894, of a petition from the Chinese residents in Bluefields, Nicaragua, proposing the appointment of Mr. Ferdinand Beer, an American citizen, as a consular representative of China there, I addressed a note to your Department, asking its good offices in obtaining information regarding the character and standing of the said Mr. Beer, which it did in due course by transmitting to me copy of a note from the United States Minister

---

[52] *Foreign Relations,* 1896, p. 377.

[53] *Ibid.,* p. 378.

[54] Moore, *op. cit.,* vol. IV, p. 590.

to Nicaragua, speaking favorably of that gentleman. It would have been a matter of gratification to me to bring about the appointment of Mr. Beer as a consular agent of China, but the non-existence of treaty relations between China and Nicaragua precluded the possibility of taking such a step. As there are diplomatic and consular represent-atives of the United States in Nicaragua—and taking for a precedent the case of Guatemala, where the United States Minister, by courtesy of his Government toward that of China, is permitted to exercise his good offices on behalf of Chinese residing in that Republic—I am led again to invoke the friendly offices of the United States Government, by which the ministers and consuls of the United States may be invested with the proper authority to afford protection to those Chinese who may reside in that country, and to ask that you will kindly direct the honorable minister to obtain the assent of the Nicaraguan Government to the proposed arrangement. . . .[55]

In connection with the protection of Chinese in Nicaragua and Salvador, Secretary of State Olney suggested that the American Minister, who was accredited to both countries, might work out a certificate in consultation with the Nica-raguan and Salvadoran authorities along the following lines:

I, _____ (Minister or Consul), of the United States of America, certify that _____ claims to be a subject of the Emperor of China, resident in (Salvador/ Nicaragua) and that upon proving his status as such Chinese subject he is under the protection of the Government of the United States and entitled to the good offices of the diplomatic and consular officers thereof in case of need, in pursuance of an understand-ing between the Governments of (Salvador/ Nicaragua) and China to that end.[56]

This informal exercise of good offices for Chinese in various republics of Central America spread during the present cen-tury to various other countries in South America and the Caribbean area. It appears that in most instances the use of certificates similar to the one above mentioned was recom-mended by the Department.[57] With reference to the pro-

---

[55] *Foreign Relations,* 1897, pp. 94–95.
[56] *Ibid.,* pp. 96, 425–426; Moore, *op. cit.,* vol. IV, pp. 590–591.
[57] See Hackworth, *op. cit.,* vol. IV, p. 489.

tection of Chinese subjects in Guatemala in 1903 the American Minister was instructed to employ his good offices "to secure for them the same degree of protection from tort" as he "could demand of right for an American citizen similarly circumstanced".[58]   He was not, however, to present claims of Chinese to the Guatemalan Government.   In an instruction to the Consul General at Guayaquil in 1909 the Department further explained the nature of this protection as follows:

This Government desires its representatives to endeavor to protect Chinese from oppression and injustice, but in using their good offices in accordance with the Department's instructions American officials should remember that this Government cannot lend its support to Chinese who may desire to use such influence to strengthen their position in factional quarrels nor can it permit them to invoke the threat of American interference in the settlement of private differences.[59]

Like the intermittent protection of Swiss citizens, the protection of Chinese nationals by American diplomatic and consular officers has continued up to the present time.   In 1941 good offices for Chinese citizens were extended in Colombia, Dominican Republic, Ecuador, Haiti, Honduras, and Venezuela.   With the subsequent expansion of the Chinese foreign service this list has been reduced to Colombia, Ecuador, and Haiti.[60]

9. SINO-JAPANESE WAR, 1894–1895

Upon the outbreak of the Sino-Japanese War in July 1894, the American Chargé d'Affaires at Peking, Charles Denby, Jr., sent the following telegram to the Secretary of State:

Have received a telegram from the United States minister in Japan with reference to taking Japanese citizens under the protection of the

---

[58] *Foreign Relations,* 1903, p. 573.

[59] Hackworth, *op. cit.,* vol. IV, p. 490.

[60] *Foreign Service Regulations,* January 1941, chap. XII, sec. 3; Circular Instruction, Apr. 30, 1945, serial number 362, file 704.0000/4–3045.

United States in case of war.   Chinese Government has given consent and asks the United States to protect Chinese in Japan.   A reply is requested.[61]

In reply Secretary Gresham sent the following telegram to Mr. Denby and, *mutatis mutandis,* to Mr. Dun, the American Minister to Japan:

China acceding, you may act as custodian Japanese legation and afford friendly offices for the protection Japanese subjects in China, either directly or through consuls acting under your instructions, but you will not represent Japan diplomatically.[62]

On August 1 the Japanese Chargé d'Affaires turned over the Japanese Legation at Peking to Mr. Denby and proceeded to leave the country.   Five days later, Mr. Denby received a notification from the Chinese Government which was to inaugurate the famous "case of the Japanese spies," the most significant incident in the extension of American protection in the Sino-Japanese conflict.   The notification in question stated that the Tsung-li Yamen had information that Japanese spies had been sent into the interior of China in disguise and that they would be dealt with severely if they were caught.   In reply Mr. Denby counseled moderation and humanity.[63]   Shortly thereafter it appeared that the Prefect of Shanghai observed two Japanese in Chinese clothing in the French concession and induced the French Consul to arrest them.

The latter delivered them over to the consul-general of the United States, who refused to give them up without definite instructions from the United States Legation.   The Chinese Government demanded their delivery.   Mr. Denby suspended action and requested instructions. He did this, as he stated, for two reasons.   One was that the exclusive jurisdiction of the Chinese authorities over subjects of a power at war

---

[61] *Foreign Relations,* 1894, p. 95.

[62] *Loc. cit.;* these documents are also reproduced in Moore, *op. cit.,* vol. IV, pp. 601–610, where the incident is treated at considerable length.

[63] *Foreign Relations,* 1894, pp. 100–101.

with China, resident in the foreign settlements at Shanghai, was sufficiently in doubt to justify the foreign authorities in demanding proof of
guilt and stipulating for a fair trial before giving up such subjects when
accused.   The custom in time of peace as to foreigners residing in
Shanghai, who were subjects of a foreign power having no treaty with
China and hence not enjoying the privileges of extraterritoriality, was to
be tried when arrested for crime by the "mixed court," namely, a
Chinese magistrate sitting with a foreign "assessor."   The foreigners at
Shanghai wished to establish the principle that this procedure should be
followed in time of war against subjects of a belligerent power.   They
were strongly averse to establishing the precedent that China should
have exclusive jurisdiction over such persons.   During the Franco-
Chinese war, Russia, said Mr. Denby, used her good offices for the protection of the French in China, and French subjects arrested at Shanghai were actually brought before the Russian consul for hearing, and
China had made no effort to interfere with them.   The second reason
for suspending action was stated to be that of humanity.   It was suggested that the consuls of the United States should act as arbitrators in
the matter.[64]

With this reasoning the Department of State was not in
agreement; telegraphic instructions were immediately sent
to Mr. Denby at Peking that the two suspects were to be surrendered unconditionally to the Chinese authorities.[65]   On
the same day (August 29) detailed instructions were sent to
Mr. Denby and Mr. Dun in order to clarify the nature of the
protective functions with which they were charged.   The
instruction to Mr. Denby read as follows:

The action of the Government of Japan, in committing the interests
of its subjects in China to the care of the diplomatic representative of
the United States during the existence of hostilities between China and
Japan, renders it expedient that you should be instructed as to the
nature of your duties in the delicate situation in which you are thus
placed.

The Japanese Government, when it solicited the interposition of our
diplomatic representative in China in behalf of Japanese subjects during
hostilities, was informed that such interposition would be permitted

---

[64] Moore, op. cit., vol. IV, pp. 606–607, citing Foreign Relations,
1894, pp. 103–109.

[65] Foreign Relations, 1894, p. 106.

with the consent of the Chinese Government.   Such consent has been given.   Moreover, the diplomatic representative of the United States at Tokyo has, at the request of the Chinese Government and with the consent of the Government of Japan, been charged with the care of the interests of Chinese subjects in the latter country pending hostilities.

The function with which you are thus charged, with the consent of the Government to which you are accredited, is one that calls for the exercise of personal judgment and discretion.   It is an unofficial, not an official, function.   A minister of the United States cannot act officially as the diplomatic representative of another power, such an official relation being prohibited by the Constitution of the United States. But, apart from this fact, the circumstances under which the function in question is to be discharged imply personal and unofficial action.   The state of war into which China and Japan have entered is inconsistent with the continuance of diplomatic intercourse between them.   Your position is that of the representative of a neutral power, whose attitude toward the parties to the conflict is that of impartial amity.   Your interposition in behalf of the subjects of one of them is not to be considered as an act of partisanship, but as a friendly office performed in accordance with the wishes of both parties.   This principle you are constantly to bear in mind, in order that, while doing what you can consistently with international law for the protection of the interests of Japanese subjects in China, you may not compromise our position as a neutral.

By consenting to lend its good offices in behalf of Japanese subjects in China, this Government can not assume to assimilate such subjects to citizens of the United States, and to invest them with an extraterritoriality which they do not enjoy as subjects of the Emperor of Japan. It can not assume to hold them amenable to the laws of the United States nor to the jurisdiction of our minister or consuls; nor can it permit our legation or our consulates to be made an asylum for offenders against the laws from the pursuit of the legitimate agents of justice.   In a word, Japanese subjects in China continue to be the subjects of their own sovereign, and answerable to the local law to the same extent as heretofore.   The employment of good offices in their behalf by another power can not alter their situation in this regard.

On several proper occasions the Government of the United States has permitted its diplomatic and consular representatives to exercise their good offices in behalf of the citizens or subjects of a third power, as in Mexico in 1867 and in the Franco-German war in 1870.   For many years good offices have been exercised by our diplomatic and consular representatives in behalf of citizens of Switzerland in China, as well as in other countries, where the Swiss Republic is without such representatives.   In this relation it is proper to refer to an instruction of this Department to its diplomatic representative in China, of July 25, 1872, in which the protection to be extended by our minister and consuls to Swiss citizens in that country is defined as follows:

"The protection referred to must necessarily be confined to the personal and unofficial good offices of such functionaries.   Although when exercised to this extent merely, this can properly be done only with the consent of the Chinese Government, that consent must not be allowed to imply an obligation on the part of a diplomatic or consular officer of the United States in that country to assume criminal or civil jurisdiction over Swiss citizens, or to make himself or his government accountable for their acts."

But, while you are to act unofficially, you will carefully examine any complaints that may be laid before you in behalf of Japanese subjects, and make such representations to the Chinese Government as the circumstances may be found to warrant; and in all ways you will do what you can, consistently with the principles heretofore stated, for the protection of Japanese subjects in China, and their interests.[66]

With this point of view the Japanese Government itself was in entire agreement and the case was officially closed with the beheading of the two alleged spies by the Chinese authorities at Nanking on October 8.[67]   In other respects the protection which the United States gave reciprocally to Chinese and Japanese during the war of 1894–1895 appears to have been entirely routine except for the fact that the Japanese Government after the conclusion of hostilities offered valuable gifts to the American diplomatic and consular officers who had protected Japanese interests in China.

Inasmuch as the friendly offices so exerted by the agents of the United States in that quarter were in pursuance of formal instructions, and were impartially given, as well to Chinese in Japan as to Japanese in China, at the request of each government and as a usual act of international

[66] *Ibid.,* pp. 106–108.

[67] It appears from Mr. Denby's despatches that the only charge against these men was that they had rendered themselves suspicious by wearing Chinese clothing, although this was by no means uncommon among Japanese in China.   *Ibid.,* pp. 110–116.

consideration, motives of delicacy prompted avoidance of all appearance of personal service on the part of officers who only discharged a simple duty imposed by their own government. The Japanese minister at Washington was therefore requested to make known to the Japanese Government the sentiments of this Government in the matter, expressing due appreciation of its amicable desires with equal regret at being unable to permit acceptance of the proffered gifts.[68]

---

[68] Report of Secretary of State (Olney) to President Cleveland, *Foreign Relations,* 1896, vol. I, p. xxvii. Section 126, title 22, of the United States Code (June 17, 1874) provides that no diplomatic or consular officer shall "ask or accept, for himself or any other person, any present, emolument, pecuniary favor, office, or title of any kind from any such [foreign] government." (Hackworth, *op. cit.,* vol. IV, p. 476.)

CHAPTER III

LATER DEVELOPMENTS, 1899–1945

1. THE BOER WAR, 1899–1900

BY telegram dated October 13, 1899 the American Consul at Pretoria notified the Secretary of State that, pending confirmation from the Department, he had accepted charge of British interests in the emergency on the request of the British Government, transmitted through the British agent in that city.[1] Consul Macrum's action was approved by the Department and the Acting Secretary of State assured the British Ambassador at Washington that the United States Government would be pleased to permit its Consul at Pretoria "to afford to British interests in that quarter the friendly and neutral protective offices usual in such contingencies".[2] The Government of the South African Republic, however, refused to recognize the American Consul as an intermediary between the belligerent governments, although it did not object to his exercising good offices in giving advice and assistance to British subjects.[3] Early in November Mr. Macrum, in response to instructions from the Department, endeavored to transmit money to a certain British officer prisoner and to report on the health of another. His efforts were rebuffed by the Boer authorities who stated that "these requests should come through the proper military channels".[4]

[1] The Consul at Pretoria (Macrum) to the Secretary of State (Hay), unnumbered telegram, Oct. 13, 1899, MS., Pretoria, Despatches, vol. 1.

[2] *Foreign Relations,* 1899, p. 350.

[3] Consul Macrum to Assistant Secretary of State Hill, no. 78, Oct. 27, 1899, MS., Pretoria, Despatches, vol. 1.

[4] *Id.* to *id.,* no. 82, Nov. 9, 1899.

In response to this communication the British Government wished it pointed out to the Transvaal Government that it was departing from the usual practice in not allowing the friendly offices of the United States Consul to be used on behalf of these prisoners:

Lord Salisbury calls attention to the fact that during the Crimean war monies for British prisoners in Russia and for Russian prisoners in England were distributed through the Danish representatives in St. Petersburg and London. Further that during the Franco-Prussian War monies were handed to the French prisoners in Germany through the British Representative in Germany and French Prisoners were allowed to send their letters to France from Germany through the British Foreign Office.

Lord Salisbury desires me to add that it is understood that reciprocal privileges would of course be granted to Boer prisoners in our hands.[5]

When W. Stanley Hollis, as Mr. Macrum's successor, attempted to arrive at a solution of this problem with the Boer authorities, he encountered strong opposition. F. W. Reitz, the State Secretary of the South African Government, said with emphasis to Mr. Hollis, "We got rid of the British agent on the 11th of October last, and God willing, we will never have another one here."[6] After a lengthy discussion they reached an agreement, which Mr. Hollis confirmed in writing on January 31 to Mr. Reitz:

. . . As I understand it, the views of your Government in this matter are as follows:

1. The Government of the South African Republic objects to recognizing the United States (or any other) consular officer as the official representative of the British Government during the present war.

2. The Government of the South African Republic objects to the transmission by the United States Consul of—

(a) Official communications from the British Government and addressed to the Government of the South African Republic.

---

[5] The British Ambassador (Lord Pauncefote) to the Secretary of State (Hay), Nov. 22, 1899, MS., Notes from Great Britain, vol. 132.

[6] *Foreign Relations,* 1900, p. 621.

(*b*) Official communications from the British Government and addressed to British prisoners here.

(*c*) Moneys or funds sent by the British Government to British prisoners here.

On the other hand, I understand that the Government of the South African Republic will have no objection to the performance by the United States consul at this capital of the following services on behalf of the British prisoners of war and their friends:

1. The forwarding of letters and papers sent by friends or relatives of the prisoners.

2. The distribution of funds (under the supervision of the war office of the South African Republic) sent to the British prisoners by their friends or relatives.

Provided that these services are reciprocal and that the Government of the South African Republic will have the right to request the similar services of the United States consular officers in the British Possessions and on behalf of the Boer and Afrikander prisoners of war that are now in the hands of the British authorities.

I further understand that the Government of the South African Republic reserves to itself the right to revoke any or all of the privileges to receive letters, money, and parcels now enjoyed by the British prisoners of war in this Republic, and that the fact that Boer or Afrikander prisoners of war in the hands of the British authorities are not receiving kind and humane treatment, or are denied privileges similar to the privileges now allowed to British prisoners of war in the South African Republic, will, if proven to your satisfaction, be deemed sufficient cause and reason for such action on the part of your honorable Government. . . .[7]

These terms of reference for the protective functions of the American Consul were noticeably restrictive and may have been the result in part of the failure of Mr. Hollis (who was outspokenly pro-Boer) [8] to press for a broader and more official recognition of his position respecting British interests in the South African Republic.   Shortly thereafter Mr. Hollis was transferred to Lourenço Marques and his place at Pretoria was taken by Adelbert Hay, the son of the Secretary

---

[7] *Ibid.,* p. 622.

[8] Consul Hollis to Assistant Secretary of State Hill, no. 97, Dec. 20, 1899, MS., Pretoria, Despatches, vol. 1; also no. 99, Dec. 26, *loc. cit.*

of State.   Consul Hay reported as follows on the situation at
the time of his arrival at Pretoria:

Before my arrival, the local papers published articles, saying that I
was coming with a strong English sentiment and that I had received
my instructions from London.   So I came looked upon as an enemy and
with suspicion, but I am glad to say that I have been able to change
that opinion and now, convinced of my neutrality, every official with
whom I have any dealings, shows me every courtesy and assistance. . . .

My position here in connection with British affairs is a hard one to
define as I can find no specific instructions from the Department of
State on the subject or from the Government of the South African
Republic.

The only thing I have to refer to is a statement of the position of this
consulate drawn up by my predecessor and assented to by the Government here as being in every way favourable to it.   However, I am using
my own discretion in regard to many things and hope I may do what is
right.

[*Postscript*]   I have learned later that the agreement, drawn up by
Mr. Hollis and assented to by the State Secretary is dated January 31,
and no understanding existed till then.   I mention this as I think the
statement *re* our status should not have been expounded by a United
States Consul whose object seemed to be to avoid any service or friend-
liness to the British Government.[9]

This criticism may not have been entirely justified for on
January 5 Mr. Hollis had reported that, although the South
African Government had "taken particular pains to impress"
him with the fact that he was recognized only as the representative of the United States, he had, nevertheless, been
able "to do many little things for the British prisoners here,
and for their friends".   He endeavored to furnish every
British prisoner in Pretoria "with a pipe and a handfull of
tobacco", while his Consulate was "being turned into a post
office of prisoners' letters".[10]

It does not appear from the record that Consul Hay was
able to do much more than his predecessor in protecting

---

[9] Consul Hay to Assistant Secretary Hill, no. 4, Feb. 10, 1900, *loc.
cit.*

[10] Mr. Hollis to Mr. Hill, no. 105, Jan. 5, 1900, *loc. cit.*

British interests. Small sums of money, newspapers, and parcels of tobacco sent by friends were regularly transmitted to British prisoners of war.[11] Much time and effort was consumed in acting on inquiries coming from the British Embassy at Washington via the Department, respecting the welfare and whereabouts of British subjects, including prisoners of war, in the South African Republic.[12] The personal effects of some deceased British prisoners were sent to their next of kin by the American Consul, who also transmitted certain sums of money intended for Boer widows and children.[13]

It does not appear that the American Consul ever visited any prisoner-of-war camps or had much occasion to employ his good offices on behalf of British civilians in the South African Republic. A proposal made by the Netherland Minister at London that the British Government should communicate to him the names of Boers killed, wounded, or taken prisoner by the British forces was agreed to by the British Government on the condition that the Boer authorities would transmit a corresponding list of British prisoners and casualties to the American Consul at Pretoria.[14] There is no evidence that action was ever taken on this matter up to

---

[11] *Foreign Relations,* 1900, pp. 622–623.

[12] Secretary Hay to Lord Pauncefote, notes or memoranda dated Feb. 6, 10, 17, 28, Mar. 3, Apr. 14, 23, 26, May 3, 12, 25, 1900, MS., Great Britain, vol. 25. Most of the persons subject to inquiry were found to be in good health. One report (May 25, 1900) had a certain Mr. Malachlan shot by the Boers on Dec. 25 without any reasonable cause. Consul Hay investigated and reported that Mr. Malachlan was in the best of health but on Dec. 25, last, "was a little excited on account of a Christmas dinner".

[13] Consul Hay to Assistant Secretary Hill, no. 22, June 21, 1900, MS., Pretoria, Despatches, vol. 1; MS., Instructions to Consuls, no. 37, vol. 172, p. 52.

[14] The Secretary of State (Hay) to the Consul at Pretoria, telegram, Dec. 11, 1899, MS., Instructions to Consuls, vol. 170, p. 200.

the time of the occupation of Pretoria by British troops in June 1900.[15]

2. BRITISH IN BOLIVIA, 1899–1903

In the winter of 1899 a revolution broke out in Bolivia, in the course of which the British Minister and Consuls withdrew from the country.   In April George H. Bridgman, American Minister at La Paz, was sent the following telegram by Secretary of State John Hay: "On request British Government you will protect British subjects and interests if necessary.   Notify Bolivian authorities." [16]   The Bolivian authorities being agreeable, Mr. Bridgman took over the British Legation and proceeded to use his good offices in behalf of several British subjects in difficulty with the Bolivian authorities.   During the following spring and summer, however, the revolutionary forces successfully took over the Government of Bolivia but failed to gain British recognition. Accordingly the new Bolivian Government indicated that British recognition might be required before it could permit Mr. Bridgman to continue the use of his good offices in behalf of British interests.[17]   In response to instructions from the Secretary of State based on a request of the British Government, Mr. Bridgman wrote to the Bolivian Minister of Foreign Affairs in November and attempted to regularize the matter by announcing that he and his secretary, Mr. Zalles, had been instructed to assume temporary charge, respectively, of British diplomatic and consular interests in Bolivia. To this the Bolivian Minister of Foreign Affairs replied as follows:

Sir: It is pleasing for me to answer the esteemed note of your excellency dated the 4th instant, No. 11, in which you have the kindness to

---

[15] Consul Hay to Assistant Secretary Hill, no. 23, June 28, 1900, MS., Pretoria, Despatches, vol. 1.

[16] The Secretary of State (Hay) to the Minister to Bolivia (Bridgman), Apr. 16, 1899, MS., Bolivia, Instructions, vol. 2, p. 118.

[17] *Id.* to *id., ibid.,* no. 100, Nov. 20, 1899, p. 132.

inform me that Messrs. George H. Bridgman and Gerardo Zalles had been urged by the British Government, according to dispatch transmitted to the State Department in Washington, to assume the representation of British interests in Bolivia, the first as chargé d'affaires and the second as consul.

It will be very satisfactory to me to receive the usual documents which will accredit your excellency and Mr. Zalles in this new character, and that will procure me the pleasure to cultivate with your excellency *double diplomatic relations.*[18]

In forwarding a copy of this reply to the Department Mr. Bridgman added the following observations:

There could have been no mistake in that the Bolivian Government regarded it as a regular appointment to ministership and consulship, for after quoting the sentence in dispatch and cablegram from Washington, I was careful to explain that, with my secretary, Mr. Zalles [also American consul], we were asked to temporarily assume the duties of chargé d'affaires, I as diplomatic interests might require and Mr. Zalles as consular interests might require, over the subjects and interests of Great Britain until English consular officers were appointed.   As shown in inclosed reply, they seem to make no distinction between temporary arrangement and regular appointment.

. . . They do not state the kind of document they name as "usual", and I do not know what they want, unless it may be a request similar to the one received, signed in the foreign office of the British Government. . . .[19]

In response to this despatch Secretary Hay sent to Mr. Bridgman the following instruction designed to clarify this confused situation:

. . . In reply I have to say that it is somewhat unfortunate that in your request to the Bolivian Government you announced your temporary assumption of the duties of British chargé, and also Mr. Zalles's temporary assumption of British consular representation.   So presented, the Bolivian Government may not unnaturally have attached a formality to your official position which would not have been the case had you followed the general rule of stating that you had been asked to continue your good offices in behalf of British subjects and interests

---

[18] *Foreign Relations,* 1899, p. 109.   Italics by the present writer.
[19] *Ibid.,* p. 108.

pending the designation of British officers.   The object was, not to invite your recognition in the character of British chargé d'affaires ad interim, but to ask that in the absence of any British representative you, as the United States minister, might be permitted to speak, unofficially and by way of good offices, in favor of any British interests which might appear to deserve that kind of mediation on your part.   The latter is the usual way of proceeding when unrepresented foreign interests are provisionally intrusted to a representative of the United States in a foreign country.   The officer whose good offices are thus permitted is in no sense an officer of the unrepresented Government—He does not report to it, nor take its orders.   His communication with it is indirectly effected through his own Government.   Upon your making this clear to the Bolivian Government it is thought there can be no difficulty in the way of your exerting your good offices in the manner asked by the British Government and contemplated by the instructions sent to you.[20]

It appears that Mr. Bridgman eventually managed to clarify the matter to everyone's satisfaction [21] and that he was permitted by the Bolivian authorities to continue to exercise his good offices in behalf of British interests until he was relieved of the charge by the arrival of a British Minister to Bolivia in April, 1903.[22]   During these years the efforts of Mr. Bridgman and Mr. Zalles were successful in obtaining fair trials for several British subjects who had been imprisoned for some length of time on questionable charges and in protecting the archives of the British Legation, part of which had been removed to a convent during the revolution.[23]

---

[20] *Ibid.,* pp. 109–110.

[21] Secretary Hay to Minister Bridgman, no. 114, Mar. 19, 1900, MS., Bolivia, Instructions, vol. 2, p. 142; Secretary Hay to the British Ambassador (Lord Pauncefote), no. 1679, Jan. 26, 1900, MS., Notes to Great Britain, vol. 25, p. 78.

[22] In response to the Bolivian request for the "usual" documentation, Lord Salisbury with some hesitation had addressed a note to the Bolivian Foreign Minister via Mr. Bridgman, but the latter did not find it necessary to present this document. (Lord Pauncefote to Secretary Hay, Feb. 12, 1900, MS., Notes from Great Britain, vol. 132.)

[23] MS., Bolivia, Instructions, vol. 2, pp. 120, 140, 151, 155, 168, 188.

3. THE RUSSO-JAPANESE WAR, 1904–1906

On February 7, 1904, the Japanese Minister at Washington received the following telegram from Baron Komura, the Japanese Minister for Foreign Affairs:

See the Secretary of State as soon as possible and ask him whether the United States Government, if Russia consents, will permit its embassy in St. Petersburg and its consulates in various places in Russia to assume charge and protection of the Japanese subjects and interest in Russia.

You will add that the Imperial Government retain lively appreciation of friendly offices extended to them by the United States during the China-Japanese war, and they venture to hope that nothing will prevent the United States from acting for them in a similar capacity in the present instance.[24]

The American and Russian Governments consented to this request, and while the American Ambassador took charge of the Japanese Legation at St. Petersburg, the American Consul at Niuchwang and the Commercial Agent at Vladivostok immediately busied themselves with making arrangements for the repatriation of Japanese civilians from their respective districts.[25]   Thanks to the speedy completion of these arrangements this repatriation movement was quickly and successfully effected.   Two other large groups of Japanese, however, encountered considerable difficulty and occasioned strenuous efforts on the part of American diplomatic and consular officers in Russia.   One group numbering some 600 Japanese subjects, including several consular officials, was detained at Korsakov on Sakhalin Island and was reported as suffering from lack of food.   Through the good offices of the United States arrangements were finally completed in May 1904 for their repatriation on a British vessel which the Japanese Government had chartered for

---

[24] *Foreign Relations,* 1900, p. 430.

[25] *Ibid.,* p. 431.   France undertook the protection of Russian interests in Japan, *ibid.,* p. 716.

the purpose.[26]   The other group of Japanese consisted of those from the interior of Russia, including Siberia, who found it impossible to make their way eastward and who for the most part were rapidly reduced to a state of destitution through loss of employment.   On the request of the Japanese Government the American representatives in Russia made arrangements for the transportation of these Japanese westward through Russia and in October 1904 some 800 Japanese belonging to this category arrived at the Japanese Legation at Berlin, which had instructions and funds for their repatriation to Japan.[27]

The custody of Japanese diplomatic and consular premises during the war was apparently discharged without untoward incident except for the fact that the American Commercial Agent at Vladivostok permitted the Russian admiral of the port, who was also the president of the local Red Cross association, to use the Japanese consular buildings for housing Red Cross nurses and patients, after removal and storage of the Japanese furniture.   Although the American Commercial Agent explained that he had taken this action "on request" and in order to protect and improve the property, the Secretary of State expressed his regrets that such use of these buildings had been permitted without having previously obtained the consent of the Japanese Government.   Fortunately, the Japanese Government expressed itself as having "no objection to the premises being used for the purpose indicated".[28]

The most significant aspect of the protection of Japanese interests during this war was the work of the American representatives in behalf of Japanese prisoners of war.   Shortly after the beginning of hostilities the French Minister at Tokyo in charge of Russian interests addressed a note to the Japa-

---

[26] *Ibid.*, p. 722.
[27] *Ibid.*, p. 435.
[28] *Loc. cit.*

nese Government, requesting that he be sent regularly a list of the Russian prisoners taken by the Japanese, such lists to indicate the name, rank, age, military unit, and all cases of death among prisoners of war.   On a basis of reciprocity the Japanese authorities approved this proposal, and throughout the war the American Minister at St. Petersburg received and transmitted to the Japanese Legation at Berlin such lists of prisoners of war as were sent to him by the Russian authorities.[29]

In this connection it should be pointed out that article XIV of the annex to The Hague convention of 1899 respecting the laws and customs of war on land had provided for the establishment of prisoner-of-war information bureaus by belligerents for the purpose of maintaining records and answering inquiries concerning prisoners.[30] This convention, however, had not gone so far as to provide for the official interchange of such information during hostilities and in this respect the practice during the Russo-Japanese War marked an important advance over previous procedure.[31]

Even more significant were the visits to prisoner-of-war camps which the representatives of the protecting powers in both Russia and Japan were permitted to. make during the

---

[29] *Ibid.*, p. 716.   The Japanese proposed that these lists be delivered by each side every ten days, but the Russians agreed only to transmit such lists "as often as practicable", *ibid.*, p. 719.

[30] Treaty Series 403; William M. Malloy, *Treaties, Conventions, International Acts, Protocols and Agreements between the United States and other Powers* (Government Printing Office, Washington, 1910), vol. II, p. 2050.

[31] Sayuké Takahashi, *International Law Applied to the Russo-Japanese War* (The Banks Law Publishing Company, New York, 1908), pp. 115–118.   During the Spanish-American War lists of Spanish prisoners were occasionally transmitted to the French Ambassador in charge of Spanish interests at Washington but it does not appear that any information bureau was established or that lists of prisoners and casualties were regularly exchanged (*Foreign Relations*, 1898, pp. 797–798).

course of this conflict. The Hague convention of 1899 had referred to the activities of "Relief Societies for prisoners of war" and had provided that "Delegates of these Societies may be admitted to the places of internment for the distribution of relief   .   .   ." [32] Nowhere in these conventions of 1899, however, was there any mention of an official protecting power or of its rights and privileges in connection with prisoners of war. It is, therefore, noteworthy that the representatives of the protecting powers in Japan and Russia were allowed to inspect prisoner-of-war camps not once, but on several occasions, and that on one such inspection the American Vice Consul making the visit was permitted to sample the food given to the Japanese prisoners for their midday meal.[33]

After the conclusion of hostilities the American Ambassador at St. Petersburg was instructed, if the Russian Government acceded, to continue his "friendly offices in behalf of Japanese Government and subjects pending the reestablishment of the Japanese legation" and to instruct the consuls in Russia accordingly.[34] During October, November, and December the American representatives in Russia completed the arrangements for the repatriation of approximately two thousand Japanese prisoners of war from European Russia.[35]

---

[32] Malloy, *op. cit.*, Art. XV, p. 2051.

[33] *Foreign Relations,* 1905, p. 601. Takahashi, *op. cit.,* pp. 95–102, has published the text of a memorandum addressed to Vice Consul Smith by the Japanese prisoners in the camp at Medved in Novgorod, and one of Mr. Smith's reports of his visit to this camp where most of the Japanese prisoners of war were held in Russia. Takahashi states that the sanction of the Tsar had to be obtained for these visits by Mr. Smith since an imperial ordinance prohibited all visits to prisoners of war in Russia during the course of hostilities.

[34] *Foreign Relations,* 1905, p. 830.

[35] *Ibid.,* pp. 608–610.

4. FRENCH INTERESTS IN VENEZUELA, 1906–1920

In January 1906 diplomatic relations between France and Venezuela were broken as a result of long-standing difficulties respecting unsettled claims of French citizens against the Venezuelan Government. The French Government recalled its Chargé d'Affaires from Caracas, handed passports to the Venezuelan representative at Paris, and requested the United States Government to assume the care of the archives of the French Legation at Caracas and the protection of French citizens in Venezuela.[36] In this manner there began one of the most protracted and administratively complex incidents in the history of American protection of foreign interests.

Complications arose at the very outset when the Venezuelan Government countered the move of the French Government by revoking the exequaturs of French Consuls in Venezuela and by requesting the United States Government to have its representatives take charge of the archives of the Venezuelan Consulates in France. It appears that the French Government, which had only contemplated a break in diplomatic, rather than consular, relations, was somewhat taken aback by this action, which by terminating the issuance of consular invoices practically suspended the trade with Venezuela which had been largely carried by the ships of the French Transatlantic Company.[37] The upshot of the matter was that American Consuls were instructed to take charge of Venezuelan consular archives in France, without performing any consular functions; while the French Consuls, deprived of exequaturs, were left in Venezuela to care for French consular archives under the over-all protection of the American Minister at Caracas. American Consuls in Venezuela were not permitted to exercise consular functions for French nationals but were to extend their informal good offices on be-

---

[36] *Foreign Relations*, 1906, part 2, p. 1432.

[37] *Ibid.*, pp. 1433–1434.

half of such nationals and their property if the situation should so require.[38]

While this anomalous situation was evolving from the exchange of telegrams between Caracas, Washington, and Paris, a local difficulty of considerable significance had developed in connection with the departure from Venezuela of the French Chargé d'Affaires, M. Taigny. On January 10 the American Minister, W. W. Russell, had notified the Venezuelan Minister of Foreign Affairs of the severance of relations by France and of his assumption of French interests. On the following day this note was acknowledged and Minister Russell had an interview with the Venezuelan Minister of Foreign Affairs, to whom he pointed out that M. Taigny would probably be detained for a few days, pending the arrival of a French man-of-war at La Guaira. On the thirteenth Taigny went to La Guaira to meet the incoming French steamer *Martinique,* which was scheduled to arrive the following morning. When the vessel arrived, he went aboard, forcing his way past the customs authorities who had requested to see his papers. With M. Taigny still aboard, the vessel was ordered by the Venezuelan authorities to put off from the dock and no one was allowed to come ashore. On being notified of this state of affairs, Mr. Russell called on the Minister of Foreign Affairs but was informed that M. Taigny had violated the laws of the Republic and that nothing could be done. Mr. Russell then dispatched M. Taigny's baggage to the *Martinique,* which sailed on the following day.[39] The incident provoked a strong protest from the Dean of the Diplomatic Corps at Caracas, to which the Venezuelan Minister of Foreign Affairs replied by stating that "Mr. Taigny, on the date on which he forcibly went aboard the French steamer anchored in the port of La Guaira, had no diplomatic character after Minister Russell,

[38] *Ibid.,* pp. 1435–1438.
[39] *Ibid.,* p. 1451.

in charge of the negotiations between Venezuela and France, passed to this ministry his official note of the 10th instant, and of which note the national executive was immediately informed, and to which note said American Minister Russell received an official answer on the 11th instant. . . ." [40] When the Diplomatic Corps refused to accept this contention, the Venezuelan Foreign Minister reiterated his position in the following words:

> Indeed, after the handing in of the note by Mr. Russell in the name of the French Government and the answer by the Venezuelan Government, what character can be given to M. Taigny from the moment when the French Government categorically and finally declared that relations were broken off and that M. Taigny was withdrawn from the representation which he had? For the Government of Venezuela, and for those who represent the diplomatic corps, surely M. Taigny from this moment was nothing more than a French citizen in Venezuela. . . . [41]

It is interesting to note that in these statements there was the strong implication that not merely the rupture of relations but also the recognition of Mr. Russell as being "in charge of the negotiations between Venezuela and France" had served to deprive M. Taigny of his diplomatic character and the traditional immunity attaching thereto. The United States Government, however, agreed with the foreign representatives at Caracas that "under international law diplomatic immunities and the right to be protected attach to a diplomatic agent even though his powers to represent and negotiate for his government may have been suspended or terminated by recall or otherwise, so long as he may be within the jurisdiction of the state to which he has been accredited, a reasonable time for his withdrawal therefrom being accorded." [42]

---

[40] *Ibid.*, p. 1451.
[41] *Ibid.*, p. 1455.
[42] *Ibid.*, p. 1456.

During the years 1906 and 1907 the activities of the American diplomatic and consular representatives in Venezuela on behalf of French interests were confined to custody of property, to informal assistance to French nationals, and to the transmission of official papers and information respecting actions taken by the Venezuelan authorities on the pending claims of French citizens and companies. To Minister Russell's confidential suggestion that he be permitted to take a more active part in effecting a settlement of these claims, Mr. Adee, on behalf of Secretary Root, replied that in view of the previous failure of our good offices in this matter it would be well not to renew the effort.[43] As a matter of fact the relations between the United States and Venezuela were becoming ever more strained as a result of a number of unsettled claims by American citizens against the Venezuelan Government. After protracted negotiations the United States Government finally broke diplomatic relations with Venezuela on June 20, 1908 and placed "its interests, property, and archives in Venezuela in the hands of the representative of Brazil".[44] Consular relations, however, were not disturbed and the American Consuls in Venezuela, unlike their French colleagues, were not divested of their exequaturs. The clerk of the American Legation at Caracas remained at his post as "in charge of the archives" under the direction of the Brazilian Chargé.[45]

The French Government thanked the United States Government for its services in protecting French interests in

---

[43] The Minister to Venezuela (Russell) to the Secretary of State (Root), June 24, 1906; Assistant Secretary Adee to Mr. Russell, July 3, 1906; Mr. Russell to Mr. Adee, July 23, 1906, MS., Venezuela, Despatches, vol. 60.

[44] For the history of these negotiations see *Foreign Relations,* 1908, pp. 774–822.

[45] Chargé Sleeper to the Brazilian Chargé, June 20, 1908, *ibid.,* p. 824.

Venezuela and stated that the Brazilian Minister to Venezuela would be asked to take charge of French interests in Caracas at the same time that he assumed charge of American interests.[46] This plan, however, produced some unforeseen complications.   The Venezuelan Government accepted the Brazilian representative at Caracas as being in charge of United States interests but refused to permit him simultaneously to protect French interests, on the grounds that the assumption of those interests might cause friction in the good relations between Venezuela and Brazil.[47] This unexpected turn of events left the American Consuls still in charge of French interests, not by intent but simply by lack of anyone to whom they might properly turn over those interests.

This peculiar situation was brought to the attention of the Department of State by a despatch of September 16 from the American Consul at Maracaibo, who reported on the violation by Venezuelan authorities of the United States consular seal which he had placed on the office of the French Cable Company.   The Department transmitted this information to M. Jusserand, the French Ambassador at Washington, and sent back to Consul Plumacher at Maracaibo Ambassador Jusserand's reply which thanked him for the assistance he had so kindly rendered even after French interests were no longer in his official care.[48] This communication produced a puzzled inquiry from Consul Plumacher, couched in his usual forthright and inimitable style:

I beg your pardon to say that I do not understand the meaning of your Instructions or better said the meaning of Mr. Jusserand the French Ambassador.

---

[46] The French Ambassador (Jusserand) to the Secretary of State (Root), June 24, 1908, MS., numerical file, vol. 223, case 2143/11.

[47] John Brewer, "in charge of the archives", to the Secretary of State (unnumbered), Aug. 20, 1908, MS., numerical file, vol. 924, case 15363/1.

[48] The Consul at Maracaibo (Plumacher) to the Assistant Secretary of State (Bacon), no. 2042, Sept. 16, 1908, *ibid.*/3–8–9.

The news that American Officials are no more in charge of the interests of French Subjects is absolutely new to me. . . . Since November from the time that Mr. Jusserand considers that I am not Officialy acting, I have helped two French destitute Subjects to a home passage and always helping the sufering French who call at the American Consulate. So far as my personal acts are concerned I do it with pleasure . . . but here is another point. I am in charge of the property of the French Cable and if I am relieved of the Interests of France I must be duly notified and the person named to whom I have to turn over the French Cable property. I do not want this for personal satisfaction, but to safe the responsability of the United States Consulate which I have the honor to represent. Somebody must take over the French property and relive our responsibility.[49]

The Department regarded this despatch with mingled humor and embarrassment. The Chief of the Consular Bureau noted that "Mr. Plumacher is at sea and has succeeded in getting me there also." On his suggestion the whole question was carefully reviewed in lengthy memoranda, as a result of which the following carefully drafted note was sent to Ambassador Jusserand:

Your note of June 24 last, wherein you expressed the thanks of your Government for the services of American diplomatic and consular officers in Venezuela in the protection of French interests there, and stated that the Brazilian Minister to Venezuela would be asked to take charge of French interests *in Caracas* at the same time he assumed charge of American interests, was duly communicated to the American Consul at Maracaibo.

I beg now to advise you of the receipt of a despatch No. 2074, of the 26th ultimo, from the Consul, from which it appears that he has not understood the arrangement announced in your note as including the management of consular interests, inasmuch as he reports that he has continued to assist French citizens [who] apply to his Consulate for aid. He further reports that he has in charge certain property of the French Cable Company and requests that, if he is no longer charged with the protection of French interests, he be advised as to whom he shall turn over such property.

---

[49] Consul Plumacher to Assistant Secretary Bacon, no. 2074, Jan. 26, 1909, *ibid.*/19.

I shall, therefore, be pleased to learn from you the wishes of your Government in the premises.[50]

In reply Ambassador Jusserand gracefully stated that there was no reason to alter what had been going on "to our great satisfaction and gratitude, as you are about to resume normal diplomatic relations with Venezuela and have consented to take care there of the whole of our interests, as before." [51] On March 10 the Department sent a copy of this communication to Mr. Plumacher with the following word of instruction:

Mr. Russell is returning to Caracas and the Department has authorized him to take charge of French diplomatic interests as heretofore, in the absence of a French representative. You may likewise temporarily continue to look after French interests at Maracaibo.[52]

This instruction should have clarified the situation; but a curious turn of events caused it to make confusion worse confounded.

On January 2, 1909 the Venezuelan Government finally recognized the Brazilian Chargé d'Affaires at Caracas as being in charge of French diplomatic interests. On February 6 Senhor Lorena notified the American Consuls (whom he regarded as still in charge of French interests) that regular consular relations had just been re-established between Venezuela and France and that the American Consuls were to turn over French interests to the newly appointed French Consuls. [53] This instruction was duly carried out, but the Department did not receive word of this event until after the instruction of March 10 had been sent to the Consul at Maracaibo. Accordingly, when Mr. Plumacher received this

---

[50] The Secretary of State (Bacon) to the French Ambassador (Jusserand), Feb. 24, 1909, *ibid.*/19.

[51] M. Jusserand to Mr. Bacon, Feb. 27, 1909, *ibid.*/20.

[52] Mr. Wilbur J. Carr, Chief Clerk, to Mr. Plumacher, no. 453, Mar. 10, 1909, *ibid.*/19–20.

[53] The Minister to Venezuela (Russell) to the Secretary of State (Knox), no. 346, Mar. 22, 1909, *ibid.*/22.

instruction on April 10, he promptly informed the French
Consul (to whom he had relinquished French interests on
February 19) that the Department of State wished him to
"continue to look after French interests at Maracaibo".
M. d'Empaire replied that by order of the Brazilian Minister
in February and by virtue of the resumption of consular relations between France and Venezuela he had officially taken
over the French Consulate, which he saw no reason to relinquish once again to Mr. Plumacher![54] It was not until
the end of May that the Department realized what had happened and instructed the Consul at Maracaibo that he was
not expected to relieve M. d'Empaire of the functions which
the latter had properly assumed in February.[55]

In the interim the United States Government had sent
William I. Buchanan to Caracas as a High Commissioner to
negotiate a protocol with the Venezuelan Government for
the settlement of the claims question and the resumption of
diplomatic relations.   The Brazilian Minister at Washington
suggested that Senhor Lorena might turn over French interests to Mr. Buchanan, but Secretary Root stated that this
was "impracticable inasmuch as Mr. Buchanan is not an
ordinary diplomatic agent and will leave Caracas immediately upon establishing a basis for the resumption of diplomatic intercourse."[56] Diplomatic relations were resumed
on March 14, 1909 with the arrival of Minister Russell in
Caracas and on the following day he relieved the Brazilian
Minister of the diplomatic protection of French interests.[57]

---

[54] Mr. Plumacher to Assistant Secretary Wilson, no. 2097, Apr. 10,
1909, *ibid.*/23–24. *Id.* to *id.*, no. 2101, Apr. 16, 1909, *ibid.*/25.

[55] Mr. Carr to Mr. Plumacher, no. 457, May 26, 1909, *ibid.*/25.

[56] Secretary Root to Ambassador Nabuco, Jan. 15, 1909, *ibid.*/13.
Hackworth, *op. cit.*, vol. IV, p. 492, cites the wording "resident diplo-
matic agent" employed in the telegram of the same date to Mr.
Buchanan.

[57] Minister Russell to Secretary Knox, no. 346, Mar. 22, 1909,
ibid./22.

The French Consuls, of course, remained at their posts and continued to serve under Mr. Russell's supervision until May 1913, when diplomatic relations were finally resumed between France and Venezuela.[58]

The incident, however, was not entirely closed, nor was it to terminate without posing one final problem.   In November 1911 the American Consul at Maracaibo had reassumed charge of French interests, and, for one reason or another, he was not relieved of this duty until July 1920.[59]   At that time the newly appointed French Consular Agent requested that there be turned over to him all the official correspondence of the Consulate referring to the protection of French interests.   Although the American Consul was inclined to accede to this request, he was instructed by the Department to inform the French Consular Agent that "inasmuch as this correspondence is official correspondence of your office and a part of the records of the office and is correspondence conducted by the Consulate at Maracaibo as American Consulate in charge of French interests, and not as French Consulate, and also as it has been bound in with the other correspondence of the Consulate, you regret it is not practicable to comply with his request".   The Consul was authorized, however, to furnish the French Consular Agent with such information from this previous correspondence as might be necessary for handling matters which might arise.[60]

5. WORLD WAR I, 1914–1918

Upon the outbreak of World War I the major task of protecting belligerent interests fell upon the United States, whose representatives during the period of American neu-

---

[58] Ambassador Jusserand to Secretary Bryan, May 6, 1913, MS., file 731.51/57.

[59] Vice Consul Hickey to Secretary Hughes, no. 185, July 20, 1921, MS., file 704.5131/8.

[60] Mr. Carr to Consul Dwyer, Sept. 20, 1920, *ibid./5.*

trality protected the interests of Britain, Italy, and Japan in Germany, Austria-Hungary, and Turkey, and the interests of Germany and Austria-Hungary in France, Russia, Japan, and most parts of the British Empire.[61] The United States also protected Turkish interests in Japan, France, Mexico, and the British Empire, and Serbian interests in Germany, Turkey, and portions of Austria-Hungary. American representatives also handled Belgian interests at several posts as well as Rumanian interests after that country became a belligerent. In addition to these belligerent interests the United States also protected a number of Allied or neutral interests at a number of posts where the regular diplomatic or consular representation of those countries was suspended or interrupted as a result of the war.[62] The magnitude of these protective activities necessitated a special appropriation by Congress of the sum of one million dollars,[63] while the importance of the task induced Secretary of State Bryan to send the following circular instruction dated August 17, 1914 to all diplomatic and consular officers of the United States:

GENTLEMEN: You are instructed, in assuming charge of the subjects or citizens and the interests of a foreign power at war with the country to which you are accredited, to bear in mind the general usages of nations in relation to the functions exercised by you upon such occasions.

In the first place it is important to recall that the care and protection of foreign interests in both peace and war is based upon the consent of both foreign governments concerned. The consent, having been freely given, may as freely be withdrawn by either, and as a consequence you must exercise the extra duties imposed upon you with candid impartiality.

---

[61] Hyde, op. cit., vol. II, 2d rev. ed., p. 1299, makes a statement erroneously implying that the United States protected only "the interests of nationals of belligerents at war with Germany and her allies".

[62] A tabulation of the foreign interests under American protection during the first World War may be found in appendix I.

[63] Foreign Relations, 1914, Supplement, pp. 742–743.

In the second place, the arrangement contemplates the exercise of no official function on your part, but only the use of unofficial good offices. You are not officers of the unrepresented government. A diplomatic or consular representative of the United States can not act officially as a diplomatic or consular representative of another power, such an official relation being prohibited by the Constitution of the United States. But apart from the fact of legal disability the relations of the foreign governments concerned necessarily imply personal and unofficial action. The state of war existing between the country to which you are accredited and the country for which you are acting, is inconsistent with the continuance of diplomatic intercourse between them. Any suggestion on the part of either country for such intercourse should be referred to the Department for its consideration. It is expected that overtures looking to the resumption of diplomatic intercourse will, if made through the medium of the United States, be addressed to this Government for transmission to the belligerent concerned.

Your position, therefore, is that of the representative of a neutral power whose attitude toward the parties to the conflict is one of impartial amity. In your interposition in behalf of the subjects or citizens of one of the belligerents you should use every care so that it will be regarded, not as an act of partisanship, but as a friendly office performed in accordance with the wishes of both parties. You should especially avoid any action which might compromise the United States as a neutral or affect the amicable relations between it and the country to which you are accredited. While you are thus exercising these unofficial functions with impartiality and discretion, you will, nevertheless, examine all complaints, which may be laid in behalf of foreign subjects or citizens under your protection, and give to them such assistance and make such representations to the authorities of the country to which you are accredited as may seem to be appropriate in accordance with these special instructions and the standing instructions of the Department.

In conclusion the Department anticipates that in some cases questions may arise regarding your authority over the buildings and other property of the foreign mission or consulate in your charge. You are advised, therefore, that your function in this respect is merely that of a custodian of the property and archives of the unrepresented government. Any interference on the part of private persons or officials with such property should be the subject of an unofficial representation or protest to the authorities of the government which is, by the rules of international law, charged with the security of diplomatic and consular premises and archives of foreign governments. If in connection with these duties you are requested or it appears desirable as a means of protection to raise the flag of the United States over the building of a foreign mission or consulate, you will bear in mind that this should not be done except with the consent of the authorities of the government to which you are accredited, and in strict compliance with the laws of the land.

As it may be desirable to hold a foreign government, of whose interests you may be in charge, responsible for the reimbursement of expenditures, which you may make as a result of such service, you will keep accurate account of all additional expense incurred in behalf of such government, its subjects or citizens, and their interests, rendering the same to this Department, when required, with such vouchers therefor as you may be able to obtain.[64]

These were probably the most thorough and judicious instructions which had ever been issued to American representatives in charge of foreign interests, but their interpretation in the midst of the passions and problems resulting from the outbreak of war proved to be no easy matter.   A number of American officers found that it was extremely difficult to remain at all times within the bounds of "impartial amity" and to discharge adequately their protective responsibilities solely by means of "unofficial" representations.   A few instances will suffice to illustrate the extraordinary difficulties which beset the path of "candid impartiality" in the early weeks of war.

Two days after the American Chargé d'Affaires at St. Petersburg had taken charge of German interests in Russia, a large crowd attacked and completely wrecked the interior of the German Embassy building in that city.[65] The German custodian was murdered and it was not until after the building was thoroughly ransacked that the Minister of the Interior appeared on the scene with sufficient police to dis-

---

[64] *Ibid.,* pp. 740–741.

[65] The preceding day the American Chargé had decided that in view of the "perfectly calm situation" he would not raise the American flag over the German Embassy!   (*Ibid.,* pp. 37–38.)

perse the mob. Stunned by this outrage, the American Chargé registered an official protest with the Russian Foreign Office, accused the Russian authorities of "criminal negligence", and intimated that the United States Government might request a "formal apology and complete satisfaction and reparation for loss of life and property".[66]

Only three days later, however, a number of Russian soldiers, including officers, entered the Austrian Embassy without the consent of the American Chargé and started to remove the automobiles which belonged to members of the Austrian staff. In response to Chargé Wilson's urgent protest by telephone to the Foreign Office, the Russian soldiers were ordered to withdraw without taking the Austrian cars.[67] Additional difficulty was caused by the imprisonment of Austrian and German Consuls in Russia, concerning which Secretary Bryan informed Chargé Wilson that since the latter had protested this action "both orally and in writing" he should do "nothing more at the present time".[68] Obviously, the Department felt that any further protests would have jeopardized American-Russian relations.

Ambassador Gerard at Berlin found himself confronted with great difficulty in obtaining the release of British subjects interned by the Germans, his problem being heightened by the fact that the British Government was freely permitting Germans to leave England. Finding that his unofficial protests and friendly appeals were of no avail, he took it upon himself to send the following telegram in cipher to Ambassador Page at London: "Please inform British Government that I advise them to allow no Germans to leave England or any British Dominions until I obtain leave British subjects to leave Germany." [69] Although Secretary Bryan

---

[66] *Ibid.*, pp. 733–734.

[67] *Ibid.*, p. 737.

[68] *Ibid.*, p. 738.

[69] *Ibid.*, p. 739.

informed Mr. Gerard that such a communication "should not be made through the good offices of the United States", Ambassador Gerard maintained that his unauthorized and unorthodox action had produced a salutary reaction in Berlin.[70]

Ambassador Morgenthau at Constantinople likewise encountered difficulties in deciding how far he might properly go in protesting arbitrary and illegal action. Early in December Turkish officials in Aleppo broke the American consular seal on the door of the room containing British and French consular archives and removed the archives themselves, despite the protests of the American Consul. Mr. Morgenthau promptly telegraphed Secretary Bryan: "As day after day Turkish officials are becoming bolder, do you approve that I demand immediate return of archives, punishment of guilty officials, apologies from the Sublime Porte and assurances that such violations will not be repeated?" To this question the Secretary replied:

> You should request immediate return of archives and explanation from the Sublime Porte and assurances that such violations of the seal of the United States will not be repeated.
>
> In presenting this urgent request use discretion, remembering that we use only moral persuasion in our efforts to give protection to other nationals and are not under obligation to use force. Our ability to serve other nations depends upon our maintenance of cordial relations with the Ottoman Government.[71]

Personal feelings and local antipathies could not but influence the interpretation of Secretary Bryan's "candid impartiality" in certain quarters. On August 4 the German Minister left Brussels after requesting the American Minister, Brand Whitlock, "to take possession of his keys and seal and hold them provisionally until his Government could formally arrange for protection of German interests in Belgium".

---

[70] *Ibid.*, p. 740.

[71] *Ibid.*, p. 748.

Mr. Whitlock agreed somewhat reluctantly to keep the keys
and seal, but he would assume no responsibility for the
archives of the German Legation or the protection of German
interests or property, pending instructions. By telegraph Mr.
Whitlock then requested the Department not to accept the
protection of German interests in Belgium and he explained
that he would have more than he could do in protecting British, French, and Russian interests, not to speak of the interests of the American colony and American refugees. "In
addition," he added, "intense hostility in Belgium to Germans
would largely nullify my efforts on behalf of our own and
other interests." [72] The Department's reply reflected the
broader concepts of duty, as well as policy, in such a situation:

Your August 4. We replied to German Government that we would
take over their diplomatic and consular offices in Russia and elsewhere,
upon request, with the understanding that such action would not interfere with compliance with similar requests from other governments. If
Germany, under these circumstances, asks some other country to act
for her, you will be relieved to that extent, but we can not refuse to act
if she asks it. We appreciate the heavy burden it imposes upon our
officials to look after the interests of all countries that have asked and
may ask, but we will supply the needed help and make it as easy as
possible. In this critical hour it becomes necessary for our Government
to render every assistance that a neutral can render, not only as an
international duty, but that we may be in better position to exert our
influence for peace.[73]

After these difficulties and others of a similar nature resulting from the initial impact of war had gradually been
overcome, the major problem which developed was the
extent of the protecting power's responsibility in connection
with prisoners of war and civilian internees. In a previous
section we have noted that despite the absence of any mention
of a protecting power in the annex to the Hague convention
of 1899 respecting the laws and customs of war on land, the

[72] *Ibid.*, p. 735.
[73] *Ibid.*, p. 736.

protecting powers during the Russo-Japanese War had achieved a certain measure of official recognition in connection with their exertions on behalf of prisoners of war.[74] Since, however, the Hague convention of 1907 was as silent as that of 1899 on this subject, the outbreak of World War I found the situation in this regard extremely confused. On the one hand there was a wide-spread feeling that the protecting power could not and should not remain entirely indifferent to the treatment of prisoners of war who had served in the military forces of the country whose interests were entrusted to its care. On the other hand there was a recognition of the fact that in entering this field of activity the protecting power would be operating almost without precedents, completely without legal foundation, and in constant danger of jeopardizing its own neutrality.

The attitude of the United States Government toward this problem was at first one of reserve and caution, but American representatives in the field could not ignore the issue. On September 10, Chargé Wilson reported from Petrograd that the condition of Austrians and Germans held as prisoners of war and sent to the interior was very bad and that his daily protests at the Russian Foreign Office had produced nothing but empty promises. Secretary Bryan's reply was brief and pointed: "As no instructions seem to have been sent to you, please explain as to protests and discontinue same until otherwise instructed."[75] The problem, however, could not be avoided. The American Ambassadors at London and Berlin were encountering daily difficulties in their respective protection of German and British interests because of the mounting suspicions in each country regarding the treatment of prisoners of war and civilian internees by the enemy. This situation had become so acute by the end of October that Chandler P. Anderson, the

---

[74] *Ante*, p. 78.
[75] *Foreign Relations,* 1914, Supplement, pp. 750–751.

special legal adviser to the American Embassy in London, suggested the "advisability of his going to Berlin with a view to reporting to Berlin the true condition of German prisoners in England and to visit detention camps in Germany in order to report to the British authorities the condition of British prisoners in Germany."[76] The fact that the United States was simultaneously in charge of both British and German interests in the territory of the other seemed to present a unique opportunity for this type of reciprocal reporting on both sides of the North Sea. The Department of State passed the suggestion on to Ambassador Gerard at Berlin, who was requested to discuss the matter informally with the German authorities and to cable his views on the subject. Mr. Gerard replied that the German Government was perfectly willing to have Mr. Anderson inspect camps in Germany but it desired that someone from the Berlin Embassy should inspect camps where Germans were held in England, Russia, and France. Gerard's own views were expressed in the following telegram of November 3 to the Secretary:

Suggest that there should be an international agreement if possible as to just what each nation should give its prisoners of war, nature of food and clothing; for instance, British claim they give overcoats, suits, underclothes, socks, shoes, etc., and three blankets to all prisoners, civil and military, while here I have had to buy clothes etc., for English prisoners and they have only two blankets, and our Ambassador, Paris, telegraphs Germans in French camps badly in need of clothes. Many Russians here, I am told by Spanish Ambassador, have no blankets. Authorities here have refused to allow me to give seven marks a week to civil prisoners to allow them to get extra food.[77]

The Department's position was that it would be glad to submit any proposals that the German Government might care to make to other belligerents, but that on its own initiative the United States Government could do nothing in the matter. The situation, however, was rapidly becoming crit-

[76] *Ibid.*, p. 751.
[77] *Ibid.*, p. 752.

ical, particularly as a result of Mr. Anderson's trip to Berlin, concerning which the American Ambassador at London reported on November 16 as follows:

. . . Anderson, just returned from Berlin, reports that German Government wishes me and in fact expects me personally to visit the prisons and detention camps in England and report upon them, and expend from the German Government for clothing and other comforts for these war prisoners and interned German subjects. Anderson visited several internee camps and carried report to Berlin. This only partially satisfied German Government, which insists on my personal examination and report.

I am, of course, ready to undertake such work if you think it wise to authorize me to do so, and if British Government consent. I shall not approach British Government till I receive your instructions. Your general instructions for the conduct of other embassies do not cover this point. British Government will assent, I am sure, in case German Government agree to reciprocal actions by Gerard.

British Government a little while ago gave me $15,000 to send to Gerard to aid British prisoners in Germany. Now German Government has put in my hands $15,000 for reciprocal use.

I suggest for your consideration the possibility of instructing me to undertake this work as an act of grace not as a duty, not incurring responsibility for the condition of prisoners nor any other responsibility whatever, except an accurate accounting of expenditures. There are now about 20,000 Germans interned and prisoners in Great Britain. . . .[78]

The reply of Acting Secretary Lansing to Ambassador Page indicated in no uncertain terms the Department's feeling that these developments were taking a dangerous turn and should be brought immediately to a halt:

In view of the reports which have already been made by the several American representatives it would seem inadvisable to go further into the matter at this time. . . .

It appears to the Department that such investigations and reports are futile and might afford opportunity to one belligerent or another to charge the American Government with partiality or prejudice in favor of some one belligerent. The Department, therefore, deems it in-

---

[78] *Ibid.,* p. 753.

advisable to make at present a fresh general investigation or report as to conditions in the prisons and detention camps in England.   Department is to-day sending similar instructions to Berlin and Paris.

You may, of course, expend moneys from funds furnished by the German and Austrian Governments for clothing and other comforts for the war prisoners and the detained subjects of those countries and at all times lend your personal assistance and the assistance of the entire Embassy staff in any way and manner that may tend to the amelioration of the discomforts of those interned.[79]

The Department had chosen a particularly unfortunate time for curtailing the reciprocal inspection of prisoner-of-war camps tentatively begun by American representatives in England and Germany.   As Ambassador Gerard hastened to point out on December 19, Mr. Anderson's visit of inspection in Germany had been permitted by the German authorities on the clear understanding that one of his own staff was to go to England to inspect the camps where Germans were held. Accordingly, the German Government felt, to put it mildly, that the issuance of the "stop-order" at this particular time was decidedly unfair.   In conclusion Mr. Gerard added the following plea:

I must also respectfully urge that if we are to take charge of British interests here, it is part of such duty to see that the prisoners, civil and war, are properly cared for.   The neutrality of the United States is at present so questioned here and the reports of the bad conditions in the camps in England so widespread, that I hope you will ask the British Government to allow me to name some one to visit the camps in England.   Probably when the order was issued you did not know that some one named by me had not made the return inspection in England.   I assure you that this matter is of the utmost importance.[80]

Despite its fear of political complications the United States Government could no longer refrain from assuming the initiative in this pressing matter.   Taking as its starting point the comprehensive and constructive memorandum on the problem prepared by Mr. Anderson of the Embassy at

---

[79] *Ibid.*, p. 754.
[80] *Ibid.*, pp. 754-755.

London,[81] the Department indicated to the British and German Governments that it would be willing to undertake a general program of inspection of prisoner-of-war camps in both countries on the basis of the three following stipulations:

1. Each of the belligerent governments should furnish immediately, for the information of the other, a complete statement of its policy with regard to the treatment of prisoners, with full details showing the supplies furnished and the conditions of their life during internment, supplemented by copies of orders and instructions issued from time to time to the commandants of the prisoners' camps;

2. The belligerents should permit the representatives of the United States in each country to have access to the prisoners and permit the prisoners to furnish written statements about their treatment and conditions of life, and their requirements, which they wish to have communicated to their own government;

3. In undertaking this work the Government of the United States will assume no responsibilities of any kind beyond the mere transmission of the statements and the distribution of the supplies furnished as above indicated, in accordance with such restrictions and regulations as are imposed by the governments concerned.[82]

The British Government accepted this proposal with the single modification that the direct correspondence of prisoners with their own government would have to remain subject to the control of the British authorities.[83] The German Government agreed to the proposal in principle and made a counterproposal (which the British accepted) containing the important provision that the inspecting officials should "be free to converse with the prisoners, in the presence but beyond hearing distance of the commander of the camp or such officer as may be detailed by him, and to hear their wishes and complaints." [84] The plan subsequently found general acceptance by other belligerents, with the result that a large number of American missions and consulates had to

---

[81] *Foreign Relations,* 1915, Supplement, pp. 997–1002.
[82] *Ibid.,* pp. 1004–1005.
[83] *Ibid.,* p. 1009; also cited in Hackworth, *op. cit.,* vol. VI, p. 283.
[84] *Ibid.,* p. 1011.

undertake, in addition to the heavy burden of foreign-interest work already assumed, the arduous and delicate task of inspecting and reporting on camps where prisoners of war and civilian internees were held.[85] This work, carried out on a scale never before attempted, gained world-wide recognition and paved the way which led to the prisoners of war convention signed by the plenipotentiaries of the United States and forty-six other countries at Geneva on July 27, 1929.

It should be emphasized, however, that the inspecting of prisoner-of-war camps, the protecting of official properties, and the facilitating of repatriations were but the more spectacular of the manifold duties undertaken by American representatives in the protection of foreign interests during the first World War. From Vladivostok and Kobe to Stuttgart and Winnipeg American consuls worked unstintingly on the minor but numerous problems which arise in even the most "routine" protection of belligerent interests. An idea of the nature and extent of these activities may be obtained from the following list of typical duties performed by the American Consulate at Alexandria, Egypt, in connection with the protection of German interests:

Assuming custodianship of property, real estate and personal, including residence property, premises and furnishings, furnishings in rented premises, business properties and stocks of merchandise.

Superintending the taking of house-furnishing inventories when the property was either requisitioned under martial law or surrendered to the Public Custodian. Arranging for the removal and storage of furniture, etc., under vacating notices of landlords of absent Germans.

Issuing passports to expelled German subjects.

Arranging for passages and purchasing transportation for expelled, indigent German subjects.

---

[85] For an interesting account of the details of this work in Germany, see James W. Gerard, *My Four Years in Germany* (George H. Doran Company, New York, 1917), chap. X.

Interceding with local authorities in behalf of expelled Germans for extension of time of departure on account of illness and other reasons producing inability to depart.

The periodical and occasional forwarding of funds to Germans of local residence interned at Malta.

Paying and alloting monthly and incidental relief money granted by the local Government to dependent families of interned, expelled and absent German subjects.

Receiving and forwarding protests from and interceding for masters and crews of interned German merchant ships before their adjudication as lawful prize.

Assuming probate jurisdiction over local estates of dead German subjects. . . .

A vast correspondence covering every phase of German interests in Egypt.

Frequent and regular visits to civil and military internment camps and acting as intermediary between prisoners' committees and governing authorities.

[Daily conferences] with German subjects, local civil and military authorities.[86]

To complete the picture it should be borne in mind that these activities, and others of a similar nature, were carried out by many American Consulates not merely on behalf of one set of interests but on behalf of the interests of a half-dozen different nations simultaneously. At Trieste, for example, the American Consulate was in charge of the interests of eight foreign countries for most of the period from August 1914 to April 1917 and in this connection it handled 9,870 pieces of correspondence in addition to the 13,142 units of correspondence handled in the regular protection and servicing of American interests.[87]

Inevitably this amount of daily activity in behalf of "enemy aliens" in all parts of the globe could not but affect

[86] Consul Arthur Garrels to the Secretary of State, Sept. 15, 1919, MS., file 704.00/424.

[87] Consul Ralph C. Busser to the Secretary of State, no. 151, Trieste, Mar. 17, 1920, *ibid.*/494.

the foreign relations of the United States. In most countries the American representatives were extraordinarily successful in maintaining a neutral attitude despite their daily defense of enemy interests being highly unpopular in the eyes of the local authorities with whom they had to deal. But the accumulation of these constant irritations over a period of several years tended to produce a difficult situation. As Ambassador Penfield said with reference to his position at Vienna, "the almost daily communication of some desire of one or other of the enemy governments has slowly but surely caused the authorities throughout the Monarchy to come to regard us as 'three-fourths enemy' ". To make matters worse, the various protected powers were frequently dissatisfied with the services of the American representatives, who, they felt, were not always enthusiastic enough in pressing their particular interests. While Ambassador Penfield felt this situation very keenly, his penetrating commentary on the subject reflected a general condition which prevailed to a considerable degree in most belligerent capitals:

The various governments concerned, and that of Austria-Hungary as well, seem to have persuaded themselves into believing that American officials, instead of acting merely as channels of communication between themselves and the governments with which they are at war have obligated themselves to employ "the full weight of their influence" towards the accomplishment of their desires. That the interests of the intermediary might possibly be prejudiced in the operation, not to speak of his duty as a neutral, does not seem to have entered the minds of these governments.

The fallacies of "representation" and "protection" seem to have taken root in every chancellery with a resulting irritation at the absence of enthusiastic partizanship of the agents of the "protecting" power. If in times of peace the resolution of ordinary questions required months when urged by the accredited representatives of the now enemy power, greater expedition can hardly be expected when the desires of that government are communicated by a neutral intermediary, itself having interests of vital importance to urge on the attention of the government addressed.

That the potency of the representatives of the United States in accomplishing ends purely American has been to a large degree impaired through the generous exercise of good offices in behalf of belligerents, is hardly to be questioned. Our Government assumed the burden gladly, and for my part I have experienced the liveliest satisfaction in whatever benefit I may have succeeded in accomplishing in behalf of the interests committed to this Embassy's charge. The 19,000 communications received and sent by the Embassy in behalf of British, French, Italian and Japanese interests during the first 17 months of the war, as well as the 21,000 communications dealt with during the same period in behalf of Austria-Hungary, in serving as a channel between this Government and the Embassies at London, Paris, Petrograd, and Tokyo, not to speak of an almost countless number of personal interviews, bear testimony of the diligence with which the interests of our fellowmen, regardless of nationality, have been cared for by this Embassy.

At the same time I must not forget that I am the accredited representative of the United States to the Government of Austria-Hungary. The care of my Government's interests and those of its citizens must be my first concern, and any influence derogatory thereto must of necessity cause me the gravest concern.

It is in no spirit of complaint that I bring the foregoing to the Department's attention, but simply that it may be advised of the conditions which exist here, and are to be found elsewhere, I assume.

Practically every note of importance received from the Austro-Hungarian Government relative to its interests in belligerent countries calls upon the Government of the United States to "urge", "insist", or "bring the full weight of its influence" to bear through its accredited representatives on the Government of the enemy power to insure the realization of Austria-Hungary's demands, and does not hesitate to attribute any disappointment to the lack of energy or to actual unfriendliness on the part of the American mission especially concerned.[88]

In view of these difficulties it is not surprising that when the United States entered the war in April 1917 a large number of American representatives were not loath to give up their foreign-interest work to their colleagues from neutral

---

[88] Ambassador Penfield to the Secretary of State, no. 1300, Feb. 14, 1916. (*Foreign Relations,* 1916, Supplement, pp. 816–818).

countries.[89]   Despite the difficulty of the task, however, the United States as a protecting power in World War I undoubtedly succeeded in ameliorating on an unprecedented scale the hardships of war and in expanding and clarifying the nature of the protection of belligerent interests, particularly as regards prisoners of war.

6. NETHERLAND INTERESTS IN IRAN, 1921–1927

Of the many instances of protection of foreign interests by the United States during the period between the two World Wars, the most interesting and significant concerned the protection of Netherland interests in Iran.[90]   The episode began in 1921 when the Netherland Government requested the United States to assume temporarily the protection of Netherland interests in Iran, pending the appointment of a Netherland Minister to Tehran.   The Department of State acceded to this request on the understanding that "this protection will be assumed with the consent of the Persian Government, and will not include the exercise of judicial functions on behalf of Dutch nationals".[91]   It was further understood that such judicial functions as might arise from the extraterritorial rights of the Netherlands in Iran, would be exercised by the Netherland Consul at Tehran.   With the expressed consent of the Iranian Government the protection was duly assumed.

Shortly thereafter the Netherland Consul at Tehran died and the affairs of his Consulate were taken over by the American Consul in that city, with the approval of the

---

[89] See appendix II for list of protecting powers after April 1917.

[90] For list of foreign interests protected by the United States during the period between the two World Wars, see appendix III.

[91] The Acting Secretary of State (Norman H. Davis) to the Netherland Chargé d'Affaires ad interim (Jonkheer W. H. de Beaufort), Jan. 21, 1921, MS., file 704.5691/oug.

American Minister and the Department of State.[92] Netherland consular affairs in southern Iran were in the hands of the British Resident and Consul General at Bushire, who in such matters signed as "Acting Consul for the Netherlands". The protection of Netherlanders under this arrangement appears to have been quite routine until June 1924 when the American Vice Consul at Bushire was informed by the British Resident that he had been ordered to turn over the protection of Netherland interests to the American Vice Consulate.[93] The Vice Consul accepted the charge, and the Department subsequently approved his action although it informed him that "the assumption of the representation of foreign interests should never be undertaken without the Department's specific authorization, except in some case of the most unusual emergency, and then, ordinarily, the advance approval of your supervising American diplomatic officer should be procured, unless existing conditions make communication with that officer impossible." [94]

Shortly thereafter Mr. Fuller raised the interesting question as to whether he was authorized to issue or extend Netherland passports. He pointed out that the Netherland consular regulations provided only for issuance of passports by Dutch Consuls and that the British Resident at Bushire had done so in the capacity of Acting Consul for the Nether-

---

[92] The Minister to Persia (Caldwell) to the Secretary of State (Hughes), telegram no. 11, Mar. 7, 1922, *ibid./2*; the Consul at Tehran (Gotlieb), to the Secretary of State (Hughes), no. 37, Apr. 22, 1922, *ibid./3*.

[93] Vice Consul Fuller to Secretary Hughes, no. 22, June 28, 1924; *id.* to *id.*, no. 28, July 10, 1924, *ibid./13–14*.

[94] Assistant Secretary Wright to Vice Consul Fuller, Aug. 22, 1924, *ibid./13*. The Department subsequently learned that Vice Consul Fuller had requested and obtained the prior approval of the American Minister to Persia. (Mr. Fuller to Mr. Hughes, no. 74, Oct. 24, 1924, *ibid./18*.)

lands. Mr. Fuller felt that in view of the constitutional prohibition on accepting an office from a foreign state,[95] he could not follow the example of his British predecessor. He suggested that he might be permitted to issue such passports in the name of the "American Vice Consul in charge of Netherlands Interests" and to place thereon the seal of the Netherland Consulate.[96] After consulting the Netherland Government, the Department authorized Mr. Fuller to issue passports to subjects of the Netherlands and to sign such papers and other documents in the manner which he had suggested. He was instructed, however, to use only the American consular seal.[97]

In January 1925 a more serious problem arose in connection with the protection of Netherland interests at Tehran. The case in question concerned a judgment rendered by the Foreign Office Tribunal of the Iranian Government against a Netherland subject involved in the failure of a pawnbroker's shop which he had established and operated in a questionable fashion. The American Chargé d'Affaires ad interim at Tehran expressed to the Department his doubts as to how far he should go in "protecting the legitimate interests of the Legation's Dutch protégé and of satisfying at the same time the just claims of Persian subjects against him." [98] This was precisely the sort of difficulty which the Department had hoped to avoid by its original specification that the protection of Netherland subjects in Iran would "not include the exercise of judicial functions on behalf of Dutch Nationals". Unfortunately the Netherland Consul at Tehran, who was

---

[95] See *ante,* p. 19.

[96] Mr. Fuller to Mr. Hughes, no. 66, Oct. 10, 1924, ibid./17.

[97] Assistant Secretary MacMurray to Vice Consul Fuller, Feb. 16, 1925, *ibid./*19.

[98] The Chargé d'Affaires ad interim in Persia (Murray) to the Secretary of State (Hughes), no. 823, Jan. 3, 1925, *ibid./*20. An abbreviated version of this case may be found in Hackworth, *op. cit.,* vol. IV, p. 491.

supposed to exercise such judicial functions, had died in 1922, and his post had not yet been filled by an appointee of the Netherland Government.   In reply the Department informed Mr. Murray that it did not "perceive any basis on which either you or the Vice Consul in Charge at Teheran could properly take action with a view to compelling [the Netherland subject] to satisfy the claims which may be asserted against him." [99]

Meanwhile the Iranian Government had officially requested the American Legation to collect the amount of the judgment against the Netherland national in question and to forward it to the executive section of the Foreign Office Tribunal for delivery to the plaintiff.   This procedure was strictly in accord with the prevailing practice under the Capitulations which the United States, as well as the Netherlands, enjoyed in Iran.[1]   Since the defendant was without funds to pay the judgment, the American Legation at Tehran, with the Chargé's approval, proposed to proceed to liquidate his available assets to satisfy his legal obligations in accordance with "the customary American consular practice" under the Capitulations.   To this proposal the Department replied by urgent telegram as follows:

Representation of Dutch interests is by way of good offices, which do not entail enforcement of claims for or against Dutch subjects.   Instructions mailed.   If consular court has already taken cognizance of case Department suggests it be returned through the Legation to the Ministry of Foreign Affairs with the necessary explanations to be supplemented upon receipt of written instructions.[2]

This instruction completely paralyzed the progress of the case.   While the American Legation and Consulate at Teh-

[99] Under Secretary Grew to Chargé Murray, no. 383, Mar. 31, 1925, MS., file 704.5691/20.

[1] The United States did not relinquish its extraterritorial rights in Iran until 1928.   See *Foreign Relations,* 1928, vol. III, pp. 682–749.

[2] The Secretary of State (Kellogg) to the Legation in Persia, Apr. 3, 1925, MS., file 704.5691/21.

ran were estopped from further action, the Iranian authorities were at a loss as to how to proceed with the case since Iranian law made no provision for bankruptcy proceedings, least of all against Westerners subject to the jurisdiction of their own consular courts under the Capitulations.[3] The impasse was finally broken in July when the Department, in response to a request from the Netherland Government, consented to allow a representative of the American Legation or Consulate at Tehran to attend the proceedings of the Iranian Foreign Office Tribunal in the case of this Netherland subject, but with the clear understanding that this step would not imply any obligation to take further action in the case or to exercise any judicial or quasi-judicial functions respecting other Netherland nationals in Iran.[4]

The difficulties of this case made clear the need for a Netherland representative at Tehran and an Honorary Consul was duly appointed by the Netherland Government shortly thereafter. In January 1926 he took charge of his post and relieved the American Consul at Tehran of his responsibilities vis-à-vis Netherland subjects, although the American Minister theoretically remained in charge of Netherland diplomatic interests until April 1927, when a Netherland Minister finally presented his credentials to the Shah.[5]

---

[3] The Chargé d'Affaires ad interim in Persia (Murray) to the Secretary of State (Kellogg), no. 1017, Apr. 6, 1925, MS., *ibid.*/23.

[4] Under Secretary Grew to Jonkheer van Wyck, Netherland Chargé d'Affaires ad interim, July 14, 1925, *ibid.*/28.

[5] Consul MacVitty to Secretary Kellogg, no. 59, Jan. 19, 1926, *ibid.*/40; Minister Philip to Secretary Kellogg, no. 323, Apr. 22, 1927, *ibid.*/6.   When the American Vice Consulate at Bushire was closed in September 1925, Netherland interests were reassumed by the British Consul General in the absence of any instructions to the contrary. Vice Consul Fuller to Secretary Kellogg, no. 79, Sept. 14, 1925, *ibid.*/32.

7. WORLD WAR II, 1939–1945

Six months before the outbreak of what has come to be called World War II the Department of State envisaged the probability that in the event of hostilities in Europe the United States Government would be called upon to extend its protection to the interests of various belligerents. On March 21, 1939 the Department sent a confidential circular instruction to the American diplomatic officers and certain consular officers in Europe and the Near East, outlining general policies and procedures to be followed in the event of a European war. With reference to the protection of foreign interests this circular contained the following paragraphs:

It is to be expected that the United States will be asked to assume charge of the interests of countries at war. Such request should not be agreed to without the prior approval of the Department. When such approval has been granted a complete inventory of the property, archives, et cetera, taken over must be made and the Department must be informed of the exact date on which your responsibility commences.

Where this Government assumes charge of the interests of foreign governments it is desired that our missions and consulates take over the premises occupied by the governments concerned and wherever practicable continue the employment of clerical and custodial employees. A qualified diplomatic or consular officer of our Government should be placed in charge and have responsibility under the Chief of Mission or principal consular officer for handling questions of representation.

You may take custody of any funds turned over by the office of which you are assuming charge to be expended and accounted for for rent of quarters, salaries of personnel and other purposes directly connected with representation of that country's interests. If additional funds should be required you should telegraph the Department. It is expected that arrangements will be made with the foreign governments concerned to reimburse the United States for all expenditures in their behalf but in the beginning the Department will endeavor to finance such expenditures.

You may expend for the relief of nationals of the country whose interests you assume any funds turned over for that purpose by its departing representative in the manner stated by him in writing so far as that is for legitimate relief and not in violation of local law or regulation.

If in your judgment additional relief funds are required telegraph the Department but assume no obligations until authorized.

Receipts and expenditures of funds turned over by representatives of foreign governments should be entered on the appropriate cash book form in the regular accounts under "Trust Funds".[6]

A comparison of this circular instruction with that issued by Secretary Bryan in 1914 reveals two significant differences.[7] In the first place the instruction of 1939 dealt almost entirely with administrative matters and did not discuss at all the general nature of the protection of foreign interests, which had composed the largest part of the instruction of 1914. This difference reflected the Department's assumption in 1939 that the experience of World War I and of the intervening decades had made the general nature of foreign-interest work so clear as to render unnecessary a further repetition of what had been officially stated on so many previous occasions. Experience was to indicate, however, that further clarification of the general nature of the practice might still be advisable. Accordingly in July of 1940 the Department issued a circular telegram directing the attention of Foreign Service officers to the Bryan instructions of 1914 and concluding with the following paragraph:

It is stressed that the representation of foreign interests involves the exercise of informal good offices and not of an official function. You may not address a formal protest to the Government to which you are accredited in respect of matters affecting foreign interests, or put the weight of your official position behind any request that the represented government may desire to have made to the Government to which you are accredited. In general, in approaching the Government to which you are accredited, you act only as the medium of

---

[6] MS., Instructions in Case of Hostilities, Circular file 300.1 General Program/209 A.

[7] For Secretary Bryan's instruction of 1914, see *ante*, p. 89.

transmission of such communications as it may be appropriate to transmit.[8]

The other important difference between the instruction of 1914 and that of 1939 is to be found in the fact that the latter did not mention the neutrality of the United States which had been so heavily emphasized in the former. Whatever the reasons for this difference may have been, it is significant that in 1939, unlike 1914, no diplomatic or consular officer of the United States was asked to protect the interests of Germany or any of her allies with the single exception of the American Consul at Lagos, Nigeria, who, with the Department's approval, assumed charge of Italian interests within his district.

Upon the outbreak of war the United States assumed the protection of the interests of Great Britain, the British Dominions, and France in Germany, Hungary, Bulgaria, and Rumania. In 1940 this protection was extended to Italy and most of the territory under German occupation, while the interests of Belgium, Yugoslavia, Greece, and the Netherlands were added to the responsibilities of a number of American missions and consulates in Axis countries and territories under their control.[9] In addition to these belligerent interests the United States also protected the neutral interests of Panama, Haiti, and Cuba in certain Axis countries as well as in some Allied and neutral countries where their representatives were withdrawn as a result of the war.

This protection of certain neutral and Allied interests was continued even after the United States entered the war and entrusted. its own interests in enemy territory to the Swiss Government. The Department of State and the American Legation at Bern also became after 1941 the channel of com-

---

[8] Secretary Hull to the Legation in Switzerland, telegram no. 101, July 16, 1940, MS., file 704.00/576 B.

[9] For the complete list of belligerent interests under American protection in May 1941, see appendix IV.

munication between five of the republics of Central America and the Swiss Government, which took charge of their interests in enemy territory. The United States also continued to protect British interests, including those of he Dominions, in certain of the French colonies, while Swiss, Brazilian, Belgian, and Yugoslav interests were in the hands of various American consulates from Tahiti to Tangier. More than a dozen American posts continued to perform consular services for Cuba and Panama,[10] and good offices were still extended to Chinese nationals in six of the American republics.[11] All of which meant that after the Japanese attack on Pearl Harbor the United States was in the unique position of being simultaneously one of the world's most important protecting and protected powers.

This tremendous volume of foreign-interest work necessitated the establishment of a Special Division (later called the Special War Problems Division) in the Department of State, and special "foreign representation" sections in a number of the more important missions and consular offices abroad. In order to reduce the cost and facilitate the transmission of circular instructions respecting the protection of foreign interests in Europe, the American Legation at Bern was designated as the "clearing house" through which such messages would be relayed, while in each country the protective functions were centralized in the diplomatic mission or the principal consular office in the absence of a mission.[12]

In several outstanding respects the protection of foreign interests in World War II differed from that in the first World War. We have already mentioned the fact that in

---

[10] Consular services for Cuba and Panama had been performed by certain American offices since before World War I (MS., General Instructions Consular, no. 442, Jan. 21, 1916, and no. 856, Oct. 18, 1922). For complete list of offices regularly performing such services in 1939 and 1944, see appendices III and VI.

[11] *Ante,* p. 58, and appendix VI.

[12] Acting Secretary Welles to the Legation in Switzerland, telegram no. 37, Apr. 30, 1940, MS., file 704.00/572 A.

the recent conflict the United States protected no interests of Germany or her allies, with the insignificant exception of Italian interests in Nigeria, whereas in World War I the United States had engaged extensively in the protection of the interests of the Central powers.[13]   While this difference applied only to the activities of the United States as a protecting power, there were other differences of broader significance for the practice as a whole.   Between 1914 and 1939, for instance, the media of telecommunication had been vastly improved and greatly expanded throughout the world. This made it possible for the wishes of the protected government to be ascertained within but a few hours and for those wishes to be relayed to the representatives of the protecting power in far less time than had been required during World War I.   These improved facilities, combined with the increased commercial and social interdependence of the modern world, produced a far greater desire for the transmission of personal communications via the facilities of the protecting power than had existed during the earlier conflict.   On the other hand the clash of ideologies, accompanied and enforced by rigid censorship of all types of communication, rendered extremely difficult and delicate the utilization of the improved means of communication and transportation which were available during the recent war.

Even more significant was the enforcement during World War II of controls far more sweeping and stringent than those ever previously imposed on the use of foreign exchange and on every form of "trading with the enemy".   This development, which was practically universal during the second World War, affected the activities of all protecting powers in a multitude of ways, some of which we shall subsequently have occasion to discuss in greater detail.   At this point, however, it may suffice to note as typical the sharp difference between the attitudes of the United States Government in 1917 and in 1942 respecting this subject.   In

---

[13] *Ante,* p. 89.

1917 the Minister of Switzerland in charge of German interests in the United States informed the Department of State that the Swiss Consulate at New York had been given to understand that it should apply for a license under the Trading with the Enemy Act in order to occupy certain premises, the lease for which had been originally issued to the German Government. The Swiss Minister took the position that in as much as the Swiss Government had assumed the protection of German interests in the United States with the express consent of the United States Government, no license should be required for Swiss Consuls to administer the affairs of German subjects in the United States. The Department agreed with the Swiss Minister and informed the War Trade Board that "the Swiss consular officers took charge of the German consulates as representatives of the Swiss Government and that they did not thereby become 'officers', 'officials', or 'agents' of the German Government within the meaning of the Trading with the Enemy Act, and that this act, reasonably construed, ought not to be held to apply to them".[14] In 1942, on the other hand, General Ruling No. 11, issued by the Director of Censorship with the concurrence of the Treasury Department and the Department of State, specifically prohibited unlicensed trade and communication with any enemy national and defined "enemy national" as including:

The Government of any country against which the United States has declared war (Germany, Italy, Japan, Bulgaria, Hungary and Rumania) and any agent, instrumentality, or representative of the foregoing Governments, *or other person acting therefor, wherever situated (including the accredited representatives of other governments to the extent, and only to the extent, that they are actually representing the interests of the Governments of Germany, Italy, and Japan and Bulgaria, Hungary, and Rumania)*.[15]

---

[14] *Foreign Relations*, 1917, Supplement, pp. 615–616.

[15] U. S. Treasury Department, *Documents Pertaining to Foreign Funds Control* (Government Printing Office, Washington, June 15, 1945), pp. 25–26. Italics by the present writer.

The final outstanding difference between the protection of belligerent interests in 1914 and in 1939 concerns the relationship of the protecting power to prisoners of war.   In World War I, as we have previously noted, this relationship was quite undefined until it was clarified to a certain extent through the initiative of the United States Government.[16] The outbreak of war in 1939, on the other hand, found the relationship clearly stated in the Geneva prisoners of war convention which had been signed in 1929 by the representatives of all nations which became belligerents in World War II, with the exception of the Union of Soviet Socialist Republics.   While this convention clarified the position of the protecting power with respect to prisoner-of-war matters, it also laid upon the protecting power far greater responsibilities in this connection than had been assumed even under the special agreements of World War I.

We shall not attempt at this point to survey in any further detail the manifold and complex activities of the United States as a protecting power in World War II.   In subsequent chapters we shall have opportunity to examine a large number of these activities in considering the protection of foreign interests from a functional and analytical point of view.   In that connection comparison will be made with the similar policies and practices of other states which served extensively as protecting powers during the recent conflict.[17]

---

[16] *Ante,* p. 100.

[17] After the United States became a belligerent, American interests in enemy territory were entrusted to the Swiss Government, which also took charge of German, Italian, Bulgarian, and Rumanian interests in the United States.   The Swedish Government protected Hungarian interests in the United States and Japanese interests in Hawaii.   The Spanish Government was in charge of Japanese interests in continental United States until March 1945, after which the Swiss Government assumed this activity.   For more complete lists see appendices V, VII, and VIII.

CHAPTER IV

BASIC PRINCIPLES

F ROM THE preceding chapters it will have been noted
that although the protection of foreign interests has been
essentially an *ad hoc* procedure, certain basic principles have
evolved from the repeated applications of the practice during the past hundred years.   In the present chapter we shall
state and analyze certain of those basic principles which are
most fundamental to the practice as a whole and most widely
observed by all nations engaging in the diplomatic and
consular protection of interests foreign to their own.   While
we shall deal primarily with examples drawn from the American experience, it goes without saying that the multilateral
nature of the practice has been strongly conducive to the
development of a high degree of international unanimity respecting these basic principles upon which the practice has
operated in both war and peace.   Ten basic principles are
clearly discernible in the practice but it should be observed
that each principle is accompanied by a number of variants
and corollaries which, although logically subordinate to the
principle itself, may equal it in practical importance.

1. THE TEMPORARY ABSENCE OF DIPLOMATIC OR CONSULAR REPRESENTATION BY THE POWER DESIRING FOREIGN PROTECTION IS A REQUISITE

The basic condition upon which is predicated the protection by one power of the interests and nationals of another
is the absence of diplomatic or consular representation by
the latter in the state where protection is extended.   We

have noted that as early as the first Capitulation in 1535 the claims advanced by the King of France as protector of various non-French nationals within Turkey were based on the absence of representatives at the Porte of the sovereigns of these unrepresented or unprotected Christians.[1] Thus from the very earliest times there has attached to the practice a feeling of temporary expediency, which has become more pronounced during modern times when the prevailing assumption has been an almost universal national representation among the members of the family of nations.

The temporary absence of representation by the protected power need not, of course, be complete; it may exist in either the diplomatic or consular field and the type of protection requested of the foreign power may vary accordingly. The protection of French interests in Venezuela furnishes an outstanding example of this variation, since American protection was at first diplomatic and consular, then exclusively consular, and finally, after the appointment of French Consuls, merely diplomatic.[2] More recent examples illustrate the same point. Thus in 1941 the United States assumed the diplomatic protection of Haitian interests in Great Britain, France, and Italy, while Haitian consuls continued to function at certain posts in those countries.[3] Similarly in Sweden where the United States protected Costa Rican interests during the recent war, a Swedish businessman at Göteborg continued to act as honorary Consul General of Costa Rica.[4] During the winter of 1943–1944 the United States Vice Consul at Corumbá, Brazil, was in charge of the Peruvian Vice Consulate at that city, although there was no

[1] *Ante.* p. 9.

[2] *Ante,* pp. 80–88.

[3] The Secretary of State (Hull) to the Haitian Chargé d'Affaires ad interim, Mar. 26, 1941, MS., file 704.3800/1.

[4] Secretary Hull to the Legation in Sweden, telegram no. 42, Jan. 24, 1942, MS., file 704.1858/6.

interruption in the regular diplomatic representation of Peru at Rio de Janeiro.[5]

The temporary presence of a special envoy is not considered as altering the absence of diplomatic representation by the protected power. Thus for several months in 1925 there was a special agent of the Netherlands at Tehran with the rank of Envoy Extraordinary and Minister Plenipotentiary, but since he was not a regularly accredited diplomatic representative, his presence did not terminate the diplomatic protection of Netherland interests by the American Minister.[6] Similarly the presence of High Commissioner Buchanan in Venezuela in 1909 did not terminate the diplomatic protection of American interests by the Brazilian representative at Caracas.[7]

Regarded from the converse point of view, these incidents indicate that the diplomatic protection of the interests of one power by another does not in any way preclude direct negotiation between the protected power and the local state even in instances of war or non-recognition. An instance of this sort arose in 1867 when the United States was in charge of Austrian interests in Mexico. Not long after the withdrawal of the Austrian diplomatic and consular representatives from Mexico the Emperor of Austria sent a special mission under the command of Admiral Tegetthoff to negotiate direct with the Mexican authorities for the return of the remains of Archduke Maximilian to Austria. Despite the official Austrian policy of non-recognition of the revolutionary government of Mexico, and the bitter feelings on both sides, Admiral Tegetthoff bore an official letter addressed by Count Beust, Chancellor of the Empire, to Lerdo de Tejada as Minister of Foreign Affairs of Mexico. Al-

---

[5] Acting Secretary Stettinius to the Embassy in Brazil, telegram no. 4099, Nov. 3, 1943, MS., file 704.2332/1.

[6] The Minister to Persia (Murray) to the Secretary of State (Kellogg), no. 1041, May 3, 1925, MS., file 704.5691/26.

[7] *Ante,* p. 87.

though copies of the correspondence between Beust and Lerdo were subsequently sent to Mr. Plumb, the American Chargé d'Affaires in charge of Austrian interests, Mr. Plumb was not invited to participate in the direct conversations which took place between the Austrian Admiral and the Mexican Minister of Foreign Affairs regarding this special and delicate matter.[8]

In times of actual hostilities negotiations between belligerents of a politico-military nature may go through the hands of a protecting power although they have frequently taken place through special emissaries, military commanders, or diplomatic channels in neutral capitals without reference to the protecting power or powers in charge of the interests of those belligerents. In World War II both types of procedure were followed—the initial German offer of surrender was transmitted through Count Folke Bernadotte as special emissary; while the Japanese capitulation came through the Swiss Government in charge of Japanese interests in the United States.[9]

2. EXCEPT IN EXTREME EMERGENCIES PROTECTION IS NOT GRANTED WITHOUT AN OFFICIAL REQUEST FROM THE STATE WHOSE INTERESTS ARE TO BE PROTECTED

It was noted in chapter I that before the middle of the nineteenth century the granting of protection to foreigners was generally regarded as a personal prerogative of the diplomatic or consular officer and might be effected (if he were so minded) merely upon the request of the foreign national seeking his protection. This theory has been outmoded for many years and action of this sort by any diplomatic or consular officer would today be countenanced by his government only in the most extreme emergencies when life or valuable property would be endangered by a moment's hesitation.

[8] *Foreign Relations,* 1867, part II, pp. 478–479.
[9] *New York Times,* May 1, May 6, and August 11, 1945.

With the modern development and expansion of telecommunications such emergencies have become increasingly rare and, while no government would deny in advance the right of its diplomatic or consular officers to extend protection in such circumstances, every government would be inclined to urge extreme caution until an official request for protection was received from the state whose nationals were in distress.[10] In this connection the following exchange of telegrams between the Department of State and the American Minister to Persia in 1914 is very revealing:

AMERICAN LEGATION, TEHERAN, undated
[Received *November* 3, 1914, 1 p.m.]

Russian officers have seized Turkish and Austrian Consuls at Tabriz and sent them to Russia. Germans are threatened and Consul was feloniously assaulted. Paddock [American Consul at Tabriz] has extended temporary refuge and protection to panic-stricken German Consul and subjects. Russians will arrest, expel, and perhaps deport all Germans. Wire instructions.

CALDWELL

DEPARTMENT OF STATE, WASHINGTON
[*November* 5, 1914, 10 p.m.]

Your undated. The Legation should maintain the attitude of strictest neutrality in conformity with the proclamation issued by the President.

You will instruct the Consul at Tabriz that he should use the greatest care and discretion in extending protection to nationals other than American citizens.

Up to the present time the United States Government has not been requested to take charge of German or Austrian interests in Persia.

LANSING [11]

On the other hand the government, rather than the individual officer, may take the initiative in extending protection to foreign nationals in urgent distress even before any request for such protection has been received from their government. Thus on several occasions of public disturbance

---

[10] Pradier-Fodéré, *op. cit.*, vol. III, p. 249, says that a request is required from "la partie intéressée."

[11] *Foreign Relations*, 1914, Supplement, p. 745.

in South or Central American countries, the United States has instructed its Foreign Service officers, and sometimes its military and naval officers, to extend provisional protection to Europeans as well as Americans in the affected areas.[12] In areas where there was no United States representative within reach, British consuls were not infrequently authorized to render assistance to distressed Americans "with or without request from the United States Government".[13]

There is always the danger, however, that such unrequested interposition may produce serious political consequences and might even be interpreted by the government of the protected national as an infringement of its own sovereignty or as a patronizing assumption of its own inability to protect its own nationals. It is in order to avoid any such misunderstandings or complications, that the modern practice of protection generally insists upon a formal request for such protection from the state desiring it. Although in most emergency situations such a precaution might appear to be dictated by an exaggerated regard for sovereign sensibilities, it is none the less true that the practice of protecting foreign interests, if not clearly based on a relationship between sovereign equals, might be construed as, or might even merge into, a "protectorate" situation, particularly in instances where a great power undertakes the protection of the interests of a small neighbor. In response to a misunderstanding on this score which arose in 1943 the United States Government took occasion to make it abundantly clear that in its protection of the interests abroad of certain of the smaller American republics there had never been any impairment of the sovereignty of those republics.[14] The principal safeguard for the sovereignty of the protected power and the

---

[12] Borchard, *op. cit.*, p. 473, and further citations there given.

[13] *Foreign Relations*, 1914, p. 861.

[14] Secretary Hull to the American Legation in Portugal, telegram no. 270, Feb. 20, 1943, MS., file 704.3853/3.

avoidance of political complications by the protecting power is the basic requirement that no protection of foreign interests should be undertaken except on the request of the state desiring the protection.

Strictly speaking, such a request should proceed through the customary diplomatic channels from one foreign office to the other, but in the event of sudden and unexpected emergency it is acceptable if the request be made by the diplomatic or consular official at the place of difficulty. We have seen that this was the more usual form of procedure in the days before the development of the telegraph and radio and it is still considered an acceptable procedure provided that there is good reason to believe that the request represents the official will of the government concerned.[15]

3. THE GOVERNMENT, NOT THE PARTICULAR OFFICIAL, ASSUMES AND GRANTS THE PROTECTION

It is a rule of long standing in the practice of protecting foreign interests that the diplomatic or consular officer in the field who receives a request for such protection must immediately refer it to his own government for its approval. In extreme emergencies he may extend provisional protection on a humanitarian basis, but his action is contingent upon the approval of his government. This requirement appeared in the French consular instructions as early as November 1864 and it has been almost universally accepted ever since.[16] The significance of this rule is that in the modern practice of protection of foreign interests it is the government, and not the individual official, which actually assumes the protection. The individual officer may properly

---

[15] *Foreign Service Regulations,* chap. XII, sec. 4.

[16] Bouffanais, *op. cit.,* p. 41; also *Foreign Service Regulations,* chap. XII, sec. 4; *Règlement consulaire suisse,* Oct. 26, 1923, art. 33; Satow, *op. cit.,* vol. I, p. 194; B. W. von König, *Handbuch des deutschen Konsularwesens,* 8th ed. (Dietrich Reimer, Berlin, 1914), p. 73.

sign himself as "in charge of" certain foreign interests but this is a privilege derived exclusively by delegation of authority from his own government, which is really in charge of the foreign interests in question.

One corollary of this principle is that the protective function is not interrupted by transfer of diplomatic or consular officers or even by change of the mission of the protecting power. As early as the American protection of various European interests in Mexico in 1867 the Secretary of State made it clear that it was the United States Government, and not merely the American Minister to Mexico, which exercised the protective function. Accordingly when Mr. Plumb succeeded Mr. Otterbourg at Mexico City he was informed in response to his inquiry that he should follow the instructions on the subject issued to his predecessor.[17] The Department's circular instruction of April 30, 1940, specifically explained that the function of protection wherever exercised by the United States would be centralized in the appropriate mission or office, not in a particular official.[18] In pursuance of the same principle the American Embassy after removal to Vichy continued the protection of British interests in France which the Embassy had assumed at Paris in June 1940.[19]

Another corollary to the principle is that the government assuming the protection may do so subject to any qualifications which it feels obliged to make. Thus in assuming the protection of Netherland interests in Iran the United States Government specified that it would assume no responsibility for the performance of judicial functions respecting Nether-

---

[17] *Foreign Relations,* 1867, part II, pp. 453, 469, 479.

[18] Acting Secretary Welles to the Legation in Switzerland, telegram no. 37, Apr. 30, 1940, MS., file 704.00/562 A.

[19] The Embassy at Vichy protected British interests only in unoccupied France. The protection of British interests in occupied France was handled by the American Consulate General at Paris, operating under the direction of the American Embassy at Berlin.

land nationals in Iran.[20]   When the Swiss Government undertook the protection of Japanese interests in the United States in June 1945, it agreed so to do only after receiving from the Japanese Government assurances that the Swiss representatives in charge of American interests in Japan and Japanese-occupied territory would be permitted to visit all camps where American nationals were held.[21]   In accordance with the good-neighbor policy and considerations of hemispheric solidarity the United States Government will not undertake the formal "representation in the other American Republics of governments of non-American countries",[22] although it will extend its informal good offices in such circumstances, as it has for many years in behalf of Chinese nationals.

Since protection is a favor granted by the protecting power to the protected state, the protection may be terminated by the former at its own pleasure.   It seldom happens, however, that a protecting power resigns from that position on its own initiative and without the approval or request of the protected state.   One of the few examples of withdrawal of consent by a protecting power occurred in 1945 when the Spanish Government, although not having broken relations with Japan, summarily gave up the protection of Japanese interests, apparently because of the alleged mistreatment of Spaniards in eastern Asia by the Japanese.[23]

4. THE CONSENT OF THE LOCAL POWER IS A REQUIREMENT

Since earliest times, the consent of the local power has been a requirement for the protection of foreign interests

---

[20] *Ante,* p. 104.

[21] Department of State press release 560, July 21, 1945.

[22] The Secretary of State (Hull) to the Yugoslav Minister (Fotitch), Oct. 31, 1941, MS., file 704.60H90 B/1.

[23] *New York Times,* Mar. 25, 1945; *Department of State Bulletin,* Apr. 8, 1945, p. 649.

within the territory of that power in times of peace or war. The necessity for a neutral state protecting the interest of one belligerent within the territory of another belligerent to obtain the latter's consent to such activity is perfectly apparent.

The necessity for obtaining the local state's consent in time of peace is perhaps less obvious but none the less real. While a general "right of legation" obtains between independent states in peaceful relationship with one another,[24] this right, with its attendant obligation, has been invariably regarded as a strictly bilateral matter as between each pair of states in the international family. State "X" has no valid grounds for objection if state "Y" chooses for reasons of economy or convenience to withdraw its representation from state "X" and to request state "Z" to protect its interests within state "X". It has never been maintained, however, that state "X" is under obligation to permit the exercise of this delegated right within its own territory.[25] However, as the protection of foreign interests has developed during the years into an accepted international practice, the tendency has become more and more pronounced to take the consent of the local power almost for granted, particularly in instances where the relations between the local state and the state desiring the protection are on a friendly basis. During World War II this tendency became quite marked even in instances of protection involving belligerent interests. In May of 1940 the American Ambassador to Italy made inquiry of the Department regarding various procedures which he should follow if he were asked to extend protection to certain foreign interests in Italy in the event of Italian entry

---

[24] Hyde, *op. cit.*, vol. I, pp. 212–213; Satow, *op. cit.*, vol. I, p. 190.

[25] J. Tchernoff, *Protection des nationaux résidant à l'étranger* (A. Pedone, Paris, 1899), p. 386; Borchard, *op. cit.*, p. 472; Pradier-Fodéré, *op. cit.*, vol. III, p. 249; Paul Fauchille, *Traité de droit international public*, 8th ed. (Rousseau and Co., Paris, 1921), vol. II, p. 53.

into the European war.   One of his specific questions was the following: "Should the consent of the Italian Government be obtained before taking over foreign interests or is formal notification deemed sufficient?"   In reply Secretary Hull stated: "You should of course promptly notify the government to which you are accredited of your assumption of the representation of any foreign interests.   In the absence of objection on its part, its tacit acquiescence may be regarded as sufficient assent without formal agreement." [26]   In January 1942 the Swedish Minister at Washington notified the Secretary of State that the Swedish Government had acceded to a request of the Japanese Government to assume the protection of Japanese interests in Hawaii.   Although the consent of the United States Government was not specifically requested, the Department formally indicated that the Government consented to this arrangement. [27]   General practice, however, still inclines toward a specific request rather than a simple notification. [28]   When the protection of belligerent interests is at stake, the local power may make its consent contingent upon the assent of the opposing belligerent to the reciprocal protection within its territory of the interests of that local power. [29]

If the local state expresses strong objection (as did Turkey

[26] The Ambassador to Italy (Phillips) to the Secretary of State (Hull), telegram no. 398, May 22, 1940; Secretary Hull to the Embassy in Italy, telegram no. 153, May 29, 1940, MS., file 704.00/566.

[27] The Secretary of State (Hull) to the Swedish Minister (Boström), Jan. 24, 1942, MS., file 705.9458/2.

[28] Serious difficulties may ensue if the notification is not made through proper channels and in a sufficiently formal manner; see *post,* p. 186.

[29] Assistant Secretary Long to Minister Boström, Dec. 18, 1941, MS., respecting the protection by the Swedish Government of Hungarian interests in the United States and the protection by the Swiss Government of American interests in Hungary.

in 1868)[30] the matter should be dropped immediately unless the protecting power wishes to become in effect a party to unwarranted interposition or intervention.   If the local government expresses merely hesitation or reluctance, based perhaps on fear of political complications or lack of certainty respecting the nature and extent of the protection to be exercised, it is entirely proper for the protecting power to set these doubts at rest by such explanations as may be appropriate, without pressing the matter unduly.   Thus in 1867 the United States gave Mexico assurances that the protection which the United States proposed to exercise in Mexico over certain European interests would not be allowed in any way to jeopardize the good relations between the Mexican Republic and the United States.[31]

The consent of the local power may be qualified in any way that it sees fit.   In 1905 the Panamanian Government permitted American diplomatic and consular officers to exercise their good offices in behalf of Chinese subjects in Panama, but in 1907 the Panamanian Government qualified this privilege by requesting that American officers not undertake to administer the estates of Chinese nationals.   The Department did not contest this decision and pointed out to the American Minister that the exercise of such good offices was subject to the consent and approval of the Panamanian Government.[32]

Since the consent of the local power is admittedly necessary for the protection of foreigners within its territory by a third power, it follows that that consent "having been freely given, may as freely be withdrawn" (as Secretary Bryan expressed it).   Such a withdrawal of consent by the local power has rarely occurred in time of peace; in time of war it has happened not infrequently, although it may be protested

---

[30] *Ante,* p. 38; cf. also p. 60.

[31] *Ante,* p. 35.

[32] Hackworth, *op. cit.,* vol. IV, p. 488.

by the protected belligerent. In May 1941 the German Government informed the Government of Switzerland that Swiss protection of Yugoslav interests in Germany had "no object any more", presumably because of German recognition of the so-called "Croatian" state. The Yugoslav Government, however, protested this action as a "flagrant violation of the International Law and the International obligations assumed by Germany".[33] In 1942 the French Government at Vichy requested the United States Government to "consider as having terminated" the protection which for nearly two years the United States had extended to the interests of Belgium, Luxembourg, and Yugoslavia in France.[34] The Governments-in-Exile of Belgium, Luxembourg, and Yugoslavia took the position that such action was "contrary to the laws and usages established by international law".[35]

After the surrender of Germany and the establishment of the Allied Control Council at Berlin in 1945, the United States Government informed the Swiss Government that any further protection by the Swiss of German interests in the United States would be "no longer necessary".[36] On the other hand the Swiss were permitted to protect Italian interests in the United States until the arrival of the new Italian Ambassador at Washington.[37]

The protection of the interests of a belligerent within territory occupied by the enemy of the protected state raises a number of interesting problems. From the American experi-

---

[33] The Assistant Secretary of State (Breckinridge Long) to the Yugoslav Minister (Fotitch), May 19, 1941, MS., file 706.60H54/4; also the Chargé d'Affaires in Switzerland (Morris) to the Secretary of State (Hull), telegram no. 1917, May 15, 1941, MS., file 701.60H62/8.

[34] The Chargé d'Affaires ad interim at Vichy (Tuck) to the Secretary of State (Hull), no. 1080, July 2, 1942, MS., file 704.5551/93.

[35] Mr. Long to Mr. Fotitch, Dec. 4, 1942, MS., file 701.60H51/11.

[36] The Acting Secretary of State (Grew) to the Swiss Minister (Bruggmann), May 8, 1945, MS., file 705.6254/5–845.

[37] Id. to id., Feb. 28, 1945, ibid./2–2745 CS/D.

ence in protecting various Allied interests in Germany during 1940 and 1941 it appears that as a general rule protection may be automatically extended to occupied areas without requesting the special assent of the local, i.e. occupying, power in each instance. Thus the American protection of British interests, including those of Canada, Australia, and New Zealand, in Germany was extended to German-occupied areas on the Continent without question by the German authorities, despite the fact that the original agreement had only referred to the protection of British interests "in Germany".[38]

In Japan, on the other hand, the authorities originally consented to Swiss protection of American interests in Japan *and* Japanese-occupied territory, but subsequently refused to permit the Swiss representatives to visit prisoner-of-war and civilian-internment camps where Americans were held by the Japanese during the period of Japanese occupation in the Philippine Islands, French Indochina, Thailand, Manchuria, Burma, Malaya, and the Netherlands Indies.[39] Since Japan, at the instance of the United States Government, had specifically agreed to abide by the Geneva prisoners of war convention and to apply its provisions "in so far as adaptable" to civilian internees, such action constituted a flagrant violation of the obligations undertaken by the Japanese Government.[40] It is to be noted, however, that the Japanese did not impose these restrictions on the Swiss representatives as officials of the protecting power in charge of American, or other Allied, interests, but upon the Swiss, and other neutral

---

[38] Chargé d'Affaires Kirk to Secretary Hull, telegram no. 1032, Berlin, Sept. 3, 1939, MS., file 704.4162/53.

[39] Secretary Hull to the Legation in Switzerland, telegram no. 307, Dec. 16, 1941, MS., file 703.5494/5; the Chargé d'Affaires ad interim in Switzerland (Huddle) to Secretary Hull, telegram no. 442, Dec. 26, 1941,; Secretary Hull to the Legation in Switzerland, telegram no. 275, Jan. 27, 1944, MS., file 711.94114A/277 B.

[40] Secretary Hull to the Legation in Switzerland, telegram no. 331, Dec. 18, 1941, MS., file 740.00114 European War 1939/2026 b; Mr. Huddle to Mr. Hull, telegram no. 398, Feb. 4, 1942, *ibid./*2108.

representatives, in their own capacity. In so doing, the Japanese were availing themselves of the traditional right of the occupying power to control all foreign relations with occupied territory, including the exercise of neutral consular functions therein.[41]   While this right is well established in international law, it cannot legitimately be used as a pretext for violating article 86 of the Geneva prisoners of war convention, which provides that "Representatives of the protectting Power or its accepted delegates shall be permitted to go to any place, *without exception*, where prisoners of war are interned".[42]

For many years it has been a general assumption that it would not be proper to request or expect that neutral protection should be extended to the occupied portions of the territory of the protected power itself.   Although it does not appear from available sources that this feeling has ever been reduced to a statement of principle, it is clear that the attitude has been wide-spread in practice and has resulted from considerations of national pride on the part of the protected state as well as from a feeling that the occupying power would be justified in not consenting to such protection if it were requested.   As an example of the application of this attitude we may note that during the early phase of the recent war the United States protected Belgian interests in all German-occupied territory except Belgium, and French interests in all areas under the control of the Reich except occupied France.   In so far as the writer is aware, this practice has been universally followed except for three instances which are not precisely analogous but are worthy of note.

The first instance occurred during World War I when the British permitted the Swiss to protect German interests in

[41] Hyde, *op. cit.*, vol. III, pp. 1903–1904.

[42] Convention relating to the treatment of prisoners of war between the United States of America and other powers, signed at Geneva, July 27, 1929, Treaty Series 846 (Government Printing Office, Washington, 1932), p. 57.   The italics are by the present writer.

German East Africa while that territory was under British occupation.[43] The second example concerns the action of Brand Whitlock, the American Minister to Belgium, who remained in Brussels from 1914 to 1917 and in effect acted as a protector of Belgian interests in occupied Belgium. Despite the success of his humanitarian activities, he himself admitted that his situation was "almost untenable".[44] It may possibly have been in memory of Mr. Whitlock's services that the Belgian Government in 1940 asked that the United States Government assume the protection of Belgian interests not merely in Germany or Italy (which would have been the usual phrase) but at the request of the Belgian representative "in any country or part thereof that is or may be occupied by either Germany or Italy". The Department of State, however, acted on the assumption that this request was not intended to include occupied Belgian territory.[45]

The third instance, and the only one in which a protected power specifically requested protection in its own homeland under enemy occupation, occurred in 1940 when the Netherland Government asked that the American Minister at The Hague might be permitted to remain at his post and to protect "formally or informally" Netherland interests in the event of German occupation of The Hague.[46] In response the Department instructed Mr. Gordon at The Hague as follows:

You are authorized, if The Hague is occupied by the German forces, to establish contact with the German Military Governor and to use

---

[43] Escher, *op. cit.*, p. 93.

[44] Allan Nevins (ed.), *The Letters and Journal of Brand Whitlock* (Appleton-Century Company, New York, 1936), p. 140.

[45] Assistant Secretary of State Long to the Belgian Ambassador, June 13, 1940, MS., file 704.5500/8.

[46] The Minister to the Netherlands (Gordon) to the Secretary of State (Hull), telegram no. 192, May 13, 1940, MS., file 356.56/22. Somewhat analogous was Ambassador Bullitt's position in occupied Paris shortly thereafter. See the *New York Times*, June 14, 1940, p. 5.

your good offices in alleviating the situation as far as may be practicable, much as was done by Whitlock in Brussels during 1914–1917. It is obviously impossible to give specific instructions to meet various contingencies and we shall have to rely on your discretion and judgment. Nevertheless you may inform the Netherlands authorities that we have been glad to authorize you to remain in The Hague and to carry on as long as possible as "the diplomatic representative of the United States." [47]

Actually neither Mr. Whitlock nor Mr. Gordon was authorized to act as a protector of Belgian or Netherland interests, respectively, within occupied Belgium or Holland, and the emphasis which the Department placed on Minister Gordon's acting as "the diplomatic representative of the United States" constitutes a further indication of the prevailing practice of not requesting the occupying power to consent to protection of enemy interests within the occupied portions of the territory of the protected state. [48]

An important new element is injected into this problem, however, by article 86 of the Geneva prisoners of war convention, which, as we have seen, permits the representatives of the protecting power to go to any place, "without exception", where prisoners of war are interned. This provision unquestionably gives to the protecting power the right of visiting prisoners of war who may be held in occupied portions of their own territory, even though the protecting power may not be accorded or may not wish to assume any other rights or privileges within such territory. This issue was raised, although in a somewhat beclouded fashion, when the Germans in August 1940 refused to allow representatives of

---

[47] Secretary Hull to the Legation in the Netherlands, telegram no. 87, May 13, 1940, *loc. cit.*

[48] Referring to his own anomalous position, Whitlock wrote: "I am not accredited to Von Bissing or to the German soldiers—thank Heaven! I am accredited to the King of the Belgians. My place is near him, that is, at Havre." (Nevins, *op. cit.*, p. 149.) Professor Nevins, however, refers to Whitlock and his neutral colleagues as the "protecting Ministers" (*ibid.*, p. v).

the American Embassy at Berlin to visit camps in Belgium
and northern France where Allied prisoners of war were held,
on the ground that Belgium and occupied France were "zones
of operation". The Department of State promptly instructed the Embassy at Berlin to inform the German Foreign
Office that—

Department considers second paragraph Article 86 of Geneva Convention confers on you as representative of protecting Power right and
duty to visit prisoners of war wherever held including prison camps in
Belgium and France.   If it is asserted that such camps cannot be visited
because they are within "zones of operation", please refer to Article 7,
first sentence, which provides for removal of prisoners from zone of
combat within shortest possible time.[49]

While this controversy hinged on the "zones of operation"
argument, it also involved the protection of large numbers of
French prisoners within occupied France, although this aspect of the problem was not specifically raised.[50]   Undoubtedly it would have arisen shortly thereafter had not the
Vichy government appointed a special mission to handle all
matters affecting French prisoners of war direct with the
German authorities.[51]

On the basis of these experiences the following conclusions
would appear to be justified respecting this complex problem:

1. The original consent of the local power, unless specifically restricted to the territory of the local power, is generally
interpreted as covering automatically an extension of pro-

[49] The Chargé d'Affaires ad interim in Germany (Kirk) to the Secretary of State (Hull), Aug. 23, 1940; Secretary Hull to the Embassy
in Germany, Sept. 6, 1940, MS., file 740.00114 European War 1939/
204.

[50] The reference to this incident in Hackworth (op. cit., vol. VI, p.
285) implies that the Embassy was acting only on behalf of British
interests, whereas in fact Belgian and French interests, including Belgian and French prisoners of war, were also involved.

[51] Secretary Hull to the Embassy in Germany, telegram no. 2413,
Sept. 6, 1940, MS., file 740.00114 European War 1939/204; id. to id.,
telegram no. 3159, Nov. 29, 1940, ibid./473.

tection to areas subsequently occupied by that power, with the exception of occupied portions of the protected state itself.

2. In situations where the Geneva prisoners of war convention is not applicable, prevailing practice would indicate that the consent of the local power is not meant to apply to the occupied parts of the protected state's territory unless this point is specifically mentioned.

3. In situations where the Geneva prisoners of war convention is applicable, the local power is still not under any obligation to consent to the functioning of a protecting power, but if it does so consent, it cannot refuse to permit that protecting power to exercise all its rights respecting prisoners of war even within the occupied territory of the protected state.

4. Even in a situation where the Geneva prisoners of war convention is observed, the general consent of the local power is not interpreted as conferring upon the protecting power any permission to handle other than prisoner of war matters on behalf of the protected state within occupied portions of that state.

5. A RESORT TO FOREIGN PROTECTION DOES NOT NECESSARILY IMPLY SEVERANCE OF RELATIONS BETWEEN THE PROTECTED POWER AND THE LOCAL STATE

Although almost every instance of severance of relations between states in recent times has been accompanied by a resort to foreign protection, it is not valid to assume that every resort to foreign protection implies a severance of relations between the protected power and the local state. From the examples surveyed in preceding chapters we have seen that foreign protection, both diplomatic and consular, has frequently been requested as a temporary expedient for reasons of economy or convenience when no rupture of relations was contemplated by either the local or the protected power. In the case of the protection of Swiss citizens by American representatives in certain countries the protection extended by the United States actually established as be-

tween Switzerland and the other state a temporary diplomatic or consular relationship where none had previously
existed.[52]   On countless occasions consuls of various nationalities have assumed charge for short intervals of one of
their colleagues' establishments precisely in order to maintain
a consular relationship which would otherwise have lapsed
for some time because of illness, transportation difficulties,
delays in appointment, or economic reasons of various sorts.

Even in the protection of belligerent interests the essence
of the practice is not to intensify but rather to counteract
and ameliorate certain mutually undesirable consequences
of the severance of direct relations between the belligerent
powers.   By providing a channel of communication between
warring states, the protecting power offers facilities for ex-
changing "proposals tending to moderate the transports of
hostile rage", as Vattel expressed it in a slightly different
connection.[53]

Despite these facts, the obvious association of rupture of
relations with a resort to foreign protection has occasionally
raised some doubts regarding this matter.   In 1943, for example, when the United States Government at the request of
the Haitian Government took charge of Haitian interests in
Portugal, the Portuguese Foreign Office raised the question as
to whether this act might indicate or lead to a rupture of
Haitian relations with Portugal.   The United States Government promptly set these fears at rest by pointing out that
no rupture of relations had occurred or had been implied in
many previous instances in which the United States Govern-

---

[52] *Ante,* p. 44.

[53] Emmerich de Vattel, *The Law of Nations,* English ed. (Johnson
and Company, Philadelphia, 1857), pp. 456–457.   Vattel was speaking of the obligation of a belligerent state to admit a special envoy of
the enemy and to provide him with a safe-conduct which might be
requested "through the intervention of some common friend".   The
"common friend" has become the protecting power in modern terminology and practice.

ment had protected the interests of Haiti and certain other American republics in various European countries.[54]

6. OFFICERS IN CHARGE OF FOREIGN INTERESTS DO NOT BECOME OFFICIALS OF THE PROTECTED POWER

No principle governing the protection of foreign interests has been the subject of more lingering confusion and more repeated attempts at clarification than the one above stated. Although the principle, with its several important corollaries, is now universally accepted, it is understandable that it should have been the cause of perennial misunderstandings. Obviously the officer in charge of foreign interests occupies a peculiar position vis-à-vis his own government and that of the protected state. It cannot be denied that he is involved in a dual relationship which is not easy to explain and which is not elsewhere encountered in the conduct of international relations. Further confusion has arisen because of the historical relationship between the modern practice of the protection of foreign interests and the earlier custom of actually employing foreigners as diplomatic and consular officials.

In so far as the United States is concerned, article I, section 9, of the Constitution, as interpreted by the opinion of the Attorney General in 1871, makes it illegal for an officer of the United States Government to accept a commission from a foreign government without the consent of Congress.[55] As far as the writer is aware, that consent has never been given with respect to any American citizen holding a commission as diplomatic or consular officer of the United States. Somewhat similar regulations prevent the diplomatic and

---

[54] The Minister to Portugal (Fish) to the Secretary of State (Hull), no. 785, Jan. 23, 1943; Secretary Hull to the Legation in Portugal, telegram no. 270, Feb. 20, 1943, MS., file 704.3853/3.

[55] *Ante,* p. 20; *Opinions of the Attorneys General,* vol. XIII, pp. 537–538.

consular officers of most other powers from accepting commissions from foreign governments without the approval of
high authority, which appears to be almost never granted.[56]

The officer in charge of foreign interests, then, remains
exclusively the official of his own government, from which
he receives his commission and his instructions.   If he is a
consular officer he does not require another exequatur from
the local government when he extends his protection to foreign interests.   He never displays the flag or coat of arms of
the protected power nor does he employ its seal or the seal of
any of its diplomatic or consular offices in connection with
the protection of its interests.[57]   He does not sign as an official of the protected power, but customarily signs his regular signature and title, adding the phrase "in charge of
_____ interests".[58]   In so far, however, as the diplomatic or
consular officer acts on behalf of the protected power (on
the instruction of his own government) he serves as an agent
of the protected state.   The nature of this peculiar relationship was confused for many years by the fact that the term
"diplomatic or consular agent" was so generally used as
synonymous with "diplomatic or consular officer", a circumstance which produced serious misunderstanding in 1871
when a number of American diplomatic and consular officers thought that they were to become officers of the Swiss
Government when they were instructed to act as its "agents"

---

[56] *Ante,* p. 19.

[57] *Foreign Service Regulations,* chap. XII, sec. 5; Bouffanais, *op. cit.,*
p. 42; Hackworth, *op. cit.,* vol. IV, p. 492; *ante,* p. 106.

[58] *Foreign Service Regulations,* chap. XII, sec. 4, n. 4; Hackworth,
op. cit., vol. IV, p. 486.   British officials on occasion have signed as an
"acting" officer of the protected power (cf. *ante,* p. 105) but this practice does not appear to indicate any official relationship between the
officer and the government of the protected state.   The usual identify-
ing phrases are "in charge of", "chargé de", "encargado de", "betreut
mit", etc.

in protecting certain Swiss citizens.[59]   The nature of this "agency" relationship was never definitively settled until 1931 when a decision was rendered by an arbitral tribunal on the long-pending "Chevreau claims".   These claims originated in the arrest by British forces in Persia in 1918 of M. Julien Chevreau, a French national.   Among other issues, there was involved the determination of responsibility of a British Consul in Persia for certain books and documents entrusted to his care while he was in charge of French interests.   The arbitrator decided that "the British Government cannot be held responsible for the negligence of its consul in his capacity as *gérant* (manager) of the consulate of another Power".[60]   It appears that the relationship of the officer in charge of foreign interests to the protected state is comparable to that of a trustee who undertakes to do his best, but assumes no liability for the consequences.[61]

The unhappily worded instruction of June 16, 1871, which caused so much initial confusion in the protection of Swiss citizens, was quite correct, therefore, in stating that the protected power was responsible for the acts of the foreign official in charge of its interests.[62]   Unfortunately, the instruction also observed that the official in question was responsible to the protected power "for his discharge of those duties".   This statement has been repeated by American writers a number of times since that date and it even appeared in the American

---

[59] See *ante*, p. 46.   The term was so frequently employed in this sense that their misunderstanding is not surprising.   For repeated instances of the usage see Satow, *op. cit.*, vol. II, chap. XI; Moore, *op. cit.*, vol. IV, chap. XV; and Amos S. Hershey, *Diplomatic Agents and Immunities* (Government Printing Office, Washington, 1919).   Bouffanais, *op. cit.*, p. 51, refers also to the confusing use of "gestion", "mandat", and "délégation" in French instructions respecting the protection of foreign interests by French consuls.

[60] Manley O. Hudson, "The Chevreau Claims", *American Journal of International Law*, vol. XXVI, pp. 804–807.

[61] Cf. Bouffanais, *op. cit.*, p. 52.

[62] *Ante*, p. 45.

Foreign Service Regulations as late as the edition of 1941.[63]
As a matter of fact, actual practice has never held the officer
to be responsible to the government of the protected power,
and it would be difficult to imagine a situation in which a
government would permit any of its officials to be treated
as officially responsible to a foreign power.[64] This point was
later clarified in the *Foreign Service Regulations* as follows:

> As the services of an American diplomatic or consular officer are
> made available to a foreign government as a matter of courtesy when
> the United States Government undertakes the protection of the inter-
> ests of the foreign government, it is expected that the foreign govern-
> ment will not hold either the officer or the United States Government
> responsible for services performed in its behalf. The officer remains
> fully responsible for all actions to the United States Government, whose
> officer he is.[65]

7. NATIONALS OF THE PROTECTED POWER DO NOT BECOME ASSIMILATED TO NATIONALS OF THE PROTECTING POWER

We have observed that officers of the protecting power
do not become officials of the protected state. Similarly,
foreign nationals under protection do not become assimilated
to the status of nationals of the protecting power. While this
principle is now widely accepted in practice and appears to
be eminently reasonable, it is significant that a contrary view
was maintained by some governments well into the present
century.

In the earliest days of foreign protection under the Capitulations in countries of the Near and Middle East the protected foreigner was almost entirely removed from local
jurisdiction and, as regards his relations with the local state,

---

[63] *Foreign Service Regulations* (1941), chap. XII, sec. 3, n. 2. This
section may be found in Hackworth, *op. cit.*, vol. IV, pp. 485–486. Cf.
Borchard, *op. cit.*, p. 472; Stuart, *op. cit.*, p. 268; also *ante*, p. 56.

[64] R. Monnet, *Manuel diplomatique et consulaire* (Berger-Levrault,
Paris, 1910), p. 333.

[65] *Foreign Service Regulations,* chap. XII, sec. 5, n. 3.

was actually assimilated to the status of a national of the power whose protection he enjoyed.[66]   This concept of assimilation was to carry over into the modern practice of protecting foreign interests, and during the nineteenth century Germany and Switzerland became its principal, although not its sole, adherents.   We have already noted that in 1871 the Swiss Government, desirous of obtaining the maximum possible protection for Swiss citizens abroad, took the extreme position that—

"A Swiss, by placing himself under the protection of the United States, becomes assimilated . . . while he is under that protection, to a citizen of the United States; his character as a Swiss is for the time being not to be considered, and, so far as the foreign state is concerned, he is covered by the United States flag." [67]

Although the United States, never an enthusiastic supporter of the protégé system even under the Capitulations, refused to accept this Swiss thesis, a number of European powers tended to act in accord with this theory in protecting foreign nationals.   Germany, in particular, went furthest in meeting Swiss desires by extending German protection to such Swiss citizens as might request it, just as though they were German subjects.   They became in effect members of the German colony wherever they were located and received the benefits of any special treaty relations between Germany and the local state.   The Swiss Government recognized the application of German law to their personal affairs even when the procedure differed from Swiss law.   For instance, the Swiss Government accepted as valid marriages performed for such Swiss citizens by German consuls, although Swiss consuls were not authorized to perform such ceremonies.[68]   In a similar way German protection was also extended to

---

[66] *Ante*, p. 11.

[67] *Ante*, p. 52.

[68] Escher, *op. cit.*, pp. 66–67.

Austrians and Luxembourgers during the latter part of the nineteenth century, while Switzerland subsequently undertook to protect the nationals abroad of Liechtenstein in accordance with this "assimilation" theory.[69]

Great Britain is said to have followed the same theory to a rather more limited degree at various times in the nineteenth century.[70] It appears that French practice tended to distinguish between protection of a temporary nature and protection on a continuing basis when the protected power did not maintain any consulate in the area. In the latter case the protected foreigners were to be considered as "protégés français" and French laws and fees were to be applied to them.[71]

The United States has never followed this theory of assimilation and has always maintained that such assistance as might be rendered to foreigners by American diplomatic and consular officers must be of an unofficial nature and that such foreigners have no claim to the official support of the American Government or to the enjoyment of any special rights or privileges obtained by treaty between the United States and the local power. In contradistinction to the theory expressed by Switzerland in 1887, such foreigners as may be under American protection do not lose any "characteristics of their nationality" nor do they acquire any rights of American citizenship by virtue of being temporarily under American protection.[72] The outstanding application of this principle occurred during the Sino-Japanese War of 1894–1895, when the United States, although in charge of Japanese interests, refused to allow a Japanese subject to enjoy the extraterri-

---

[69] B. W. König, *Die deutschen Konsuln* (C. Schünemann, Berlin, 1876), pp. 5–6; Escher, *op. cit.*, pp. 46–47; Herbert Kraus, *Der Auswärtige Dienst des deutschen Reiches* (Stilke, Berlin, 1932), pp. 425, 454.

[70] Escher, *op. cit.*, pp. 47–48.

[71] R. Monnet, *op. cit.*, p. 332.

[72] *Ante*, p. 52.

torial rights obtained by the United States from China.[73] While this decision attracted some adverse criticism from Europeans, who were apprehensive of its effect on their special status in the East, it was generally conceded to be sound in principle.[74]

Since that time the theory of "assimilation" has proved definitely impracticable in the protection of belligerent interests under conditions of modern war.   During the brief war between Turkey and Greece in 1897 the Ambassadors of France, Great Britain, and Russia asserted their protection over Greek nationals, both Catholic and Orthodox, in Turkey and attempted under the Capitulations to shield these Greek protégés from Turkish jurisdiction.   This move was denounced by the Turkish authorities as being "practically equivalent to a declaration of war".[75]   Such protection, designed to bestow neutral characteristics upon enemy aliens, would never have been attempted except under the peculiar regime of the Capitulations, and it has in fact never been asserted by any neutral power protecting belligerent interests in Europe or America.

Even with respect to foreign protection in time of peace the idea of assimilation is no longer supported in either theory or practice.   Foreign protection has been increasingly recognized as a temporary delegation of the protective rights and duties of the power unable at the moment to exercise them through its own instrumentalities.[76]   It follows that the protecting power cannot exercise any rights of protection not possessed by the protected power within the territory of

---

[73] *Ante,* p. 65.

[74] Tchernoff, *op. cit.,* p. 387; Ch. Rousseau, "Les Consuls en temps de guerre", *Revue générale de droit international public,* 1933, vol. 40, p. 513.

[75] "Chronique des faits internationaux", *Revue générale de droit international public,* 1897, vol. 4, p. 530.

[76] Cf. Tchernoff, *op. cit.,* p. 383–384; Borchard, *op. cit.,* p. 471; Escher, *op. cit.,* p. 18.

the local state.[77]   As indicated in the protection by the
United States of Netherland interests in Iran, the protecting
power is under no obligation to exercise all such rights delegated to it by the protected state; the protecting power
merely undertakes, within the limits established by the relations between the local state and the protected power, to do
what it can on behalf of the interests of the latter within the
territory of the former.[78]   As between themselves, the protected power and the protecting power may agree upon the
extent to which the laws or regulations of the latter may be
applied to the nationals of the former, but this in no way
"assimilates" the protected nationals to the protecting power
in the eyes of the local state in which they reside.   The protecting power may properly invoke in behalf of protected
nationals any pertinent treaties between the local state and
the protected power, but it cannot invoke its own treaties
with the local state for the benefit of foreign nationals under
its protection, unless, as in the case of the defunct Capitulations, special provisions cover this contingency.[79]

8. THE PRESENCE OF A PROTECTING POWER DOES NOT ALTER
    THE RESPONSIBILITY OF THE LOCAL STATE FOR ALIENS
    WITHIN ITS JURISDICTION

The use of the terms "protecting power" and "local state"
may appear to imply that the former bears the primary responsibility for actively protecting within the territory of the
latter the nationals of the protected state.   As a matter of
fact no legal responsibility whatever attaches to the protect-

---

[77] Ernst Schneeberger, *Staatsangehörigkeit und diplomatischer
Schutz,* dissertation (University of Bern, 1943), p. 2.

[78] *Ante,* p. 104.

[79] "In the exercise of your good offices you may invoke any provision
of any treaty between Italy and the represented Governments which
specifically provides for the treatment to be accorded enemy interests
during belligerency. . . ." (Secretary Hull to the Embassy in
Italy, telegram no. 153, May 29, 1940, MS., file 704.00/566.)

ing power. The responsibility rests primarily on the local state itself and secondarily on the protected power.

It is an accepted tenet of international law that every state admitted into the family of nations must possess certain essential characteristics, among which is the ability "to assure foreigners within it of a minimum of rights".[80] In the words of Elihu Root, "The rule of obligation is perfectly distinct and settled. Each country is bound to give to the nationals of another country in its territory the benefit of the same laws, the same administration, the same protection, and the same redress for injury which it gives to its own citizens, and neither more nor less; provided the protection which the country gives to its own citizens conforms to the established standards of civilization."[81]

When the protection afforded to the alien falls below this established standard, the state of which that alien is a national has the legal right and the moral duty to take appropriate measures to have this situation corrected.[82] Such measures may lead to forceful intervention and the obtaining of extraterritorial rights and concessions if the local state is habitually unable or unwilling to maintain the accepted international norm in the administration of justice to aliens within its territory. In recent times, however, and as between states maintaining effective administrations, the usual procedure is merely to call the attention of the other govern-

---

[80] Borchard, *op. cit.*, p. 27.

[81] Elihu Root, "The Basis of Protection to Citizens Residing Abroad", the *American Journal of International Law*, 1910, vol. 4, p. 521.

[82] The legal right exists in international law; the moral duty is toward its own nationals. For an interesting discussion see Borchard, *op. cit.*, pp. 29–30. Referring to the protection of British subjects in Mexico, the British Ambassador stated that the British Government were "in honour bound" and felt it "incumbent upon them" to take steps for their protection, in part through the good offices of the United States. (*Foreign Relations*, 1914, pp. 839, 841.)

ment to the particular case in which it appears to have defaulted on its international obligation respecting the treatment of the resident alien. When there occurs a rupture or a temporary lapse in the diplomatic relations through which these representations are customarily made, the aggrieved state forwards its complaint or observation through the facilities of a "protecting power". Similarly the nationals of the protected state employ the facilities of the protecting power in communicating to their own government the information concerning their welfare and treatment which in normal circumstances they would give to a diplomatic or consular representative of their own government.

It is clear, therefore, that the presence of a protecting power in no way alters the primary responsibility of the local state to afford adequate protection to aliens admitted to its territory. This international obligation is not terminated by a state of war, although the accepted standards for the treatment of enemy aliens are necessarily lower than those which would be considered acceptable for friendly aliens in time of peace. While military necessity is of capital importance, it cannot properly be used as a pretext for violating the elemental tenets of justice and humanity which the community of nations endeavors to uphold.

Basically, then, the protecting power is merely the agent of the protected power and is not directly responsible for the protection of the nationals of the latter. It is, therefore, not under any obligation to take the initiative in protecting their interests, in presenting claims or protests to the local state or in putting the weight of its own position behind such claims or protests as it transmits on behalf of the protected power.[83] In two circumstances, however, the protecting power may properly exercise a certain measure of initiative. The inviolability of diplomatic premises is so uni-

[83] *Ante,* pp. 51, 102, 110; *Foreign Service Regulations,* chap. XII, sec. 5, n. 2.

versally accepted that a protecting power would be justified
in protesting on its own behalf any violation of such premises
entrusted to its care.   Similarly, it appears from the experience of World War II that a protecting power may properly
protest on its own initiative any infringement of its rights
under the Geneva prisoners of war convention, if the local
state and the protected power are parties to that convention.[84]

9. IN PROTECTING FOREIGN INTERESTS AN OFFICER IS NOT EXPECTED TO ENGAGE IN ANY ACTIVITIES CONTRARY TO THE INTERESTS OF HIS OWN GOVERNMENT

Since the officer in charge of foreign interests is in no way
an official of the protected power, he is under no obligation to
perform any activities on behalf of that power which would
run counter to the policies or interests of his own government.
This means no unneutral activities in protecting belligerent
interests, no competitive activities in protecting non-belligerent interests, and no unessential activities on behalf of
foreign interests in either peace or war.

The injunction against unneutral activities in connection
with the protection of belligerent interests is so obvious and so
universally accepted as to require but little explanation at
this point.[85]   The only problem which has ever arisen in
this connection concerns the actual definition of what constitutes an unneutral action.   The obvious cases of engaging
in espionage, sending information of military importance to
the enemy, or violating local security regulations need not
detain us.   The difficulty arises in connection with less obvious examples where the officer in charge of belligerent interests might not realize at the moment that his action would
be regarded as unneutral by the local power.   In this connection it is significant to recall that the Department of State
considered as unneutral Ambassador Gerard's proposal in

---

[84] *Ante,* pp. 92, 93; *post,* pp. 181, 184, 186, 221.
[85] For instances of this injunction, see *ante,* pp. 65, 90.

1914 that Germans be detained in Great Britain until British subjects were released by the German authorities.[86]   While Mr. Gerard's intention was actually to facilitate the reaching of an agreement for the reciprocal repatriation of both Germans and British, the Department was entirely correct in feeling that a proposal presented in this unilateral form should not be made by an officer of a neutral protecting power.

On the other hand Minister Whitlock, who was in charge of German interests in Belgium prior to the German occupation in 1914, refused on his own initiative to transmit to the Belgian Government a German peace proposal couched in terms which he considered a "dirty bribe." [87]   Although the Department was spared the embarrassment of passing judgment on this action by virtue of the fact that the proposal was actually transmitted to the Belgian Government through the good offices of the Netherland Government,[88] it can scarcely be denied that a refusal to transmit a proposal from one belligerent to another because of the neutral officer's personal opinion of the proposition might very well be regarded as an unfriendly, if not actually unneutral, action on his part.

During World War II the Department cautioned all Foreign Service officers handling belligerent interests that written material should never be transmitted on behalf of belligerent interests and that even purely personal welfare messages should not be transmitted textually, but should always be paraphrased so as to disrupt any possible code arrangement.[89]   The Department also took extreme care that no accusation of unneutral activity should arise from any assistance rendered by American officers in charge of British

---

[86] *Ante,* p. 93.

[87] Nevins, *op. cit.,* p. 24.

[88] *Foreign Relations,* 1914, Supplement, pp. 51, 53.

[89] Secretary Hull to the Legation in Switzerland, telegram no. 163, Sept. 16, 1940, MS., file 704.00/584A.

interests in unoccupied France to British subjects desirous of leaving French territory.[90]

The *Foreign Service Regulations* of the United States provide that a diplomatic or consular officer shall not "perform any duties in behalf of a foreign power which might be detrimental to American trade or to other American interests".[91] As far as the writer is aware, the principle underlying this instruction has been so well understood and so universally observed by all nations that a test case has never actually arisen. No diplomatic or consular officer has ever been requested by the protected power to further its political or economic interests in competition with those of his own government. On occasion, however, officers in charge of foreign interests have forwarded to the protected power copies of laws, regulations, or statistical publications published by the local state. In general the tendency is for the protected power to restrict its requests to activities strictly essential to the protection of its official property and the welfare and property of its nationals within the local state. Since the services of the officer are provided as a favor to the protected power, there is a natural reluctance to impose upon his time by requesting that he perform unessential services, even though they might not involve competitive interests. He is generally expected to engage only in "current activities" of an essential nature, and he is not expected to undertake lengthy investigations or to compile periodic reports for the protected power.[92]

10. PROTECTION IS ACCORDED TO THE INTERESTS OF A STATE, AS DISTINGUISHED FROM A GOVERNMENT

In diplomatic usage it is customary to refer to those national interests under foreign protection in terms of nation-

---

[90] Acting Secretary Welles to the Embassy in Great Britain, telegram no. 2432, Aug. 16, 1940, MS., file 740.0011 European War 1939/4942.

[91] *Foreign Service Regulations,* chap. XII, sec. 5, n. 4.

[92] Cf. B. W. von König, *Handbuch des deutschen Konsularwesens,* 8th ed. (Berlin, Dietrich Reimer, 1914), p. 73.

ality rather than government. An officer, for example, is said to be in charge of American or British or French interests; he is not generally referred to as being in charge of the interests of the American or the British or the French Government. This distinction is terminology which, although a matter more of custom than calculation, is not without significance; it reflects the fact that protection is accorded to the interests of a state rather than to those of a particular government.[93] This principle accounts for the customary absence of any neutral protecting power in civil wars. It also has an important bearing on the protection of foreign interests when an unrecognized (i.e. non-existent) state, as opposed to an unrecognized government, is involved.

In general it may be observed that the protection of foreign interests is less influenced by the non-recognition of a government than by the non-recognition of a state. No power, for example, would be inclined to permit within its territory the protection of the interests of a state which it did not recognize. Although "Manchukuo" was reported to have declared war on the United States on December 8, 1941,[94] the question of permitting neutral protection of the interests of Manchukuo in the United States was never even broached, since a negative reply from the United States Government would have been a foregone conclusion in view of the firm policy of non-recognition of this Japanese puppet state by the United States.

Since the United States regarded Manchuria simply as territory under Japanese control, efforts were made to arrange for the protection of American interests in Manchuria by representatives of the Swiss Government in charge of American interests in Japan and Japanese-occupied areas. In so

---

[93] Occasionally even in official correspondence reference is made to the protected or represented "government", but the usage is infrequent and is never employed when any distinction is involved between state and government.

[94] *World Almanac,* 1946, p. 41.

doing, the Department made it clear to the Swiss Government that it did not desire in any way to jeopardize the Swiss policy of non-recognition of Manchukuo, and an arrangement was effected whereby American interests were protected by a Swiss citizen in Manchuria who served as Swiss Consular Agent ad interim and Special Delegate of the Swiss Minister at Tokyo.[95] Similarly the United States Government carefully refrained from requesting the Swiss Government to undertake the formal protection of American interests in the so-called "Republic of Slovakia".[96] In September 1939 the Soviet Government refused to consent to the protection by a third power of Polish interests in the Union of Soviet Socialist Republics on the ground that the Soviet Government no longer recognized the existence of a Polish state.[97]

In instances involving only a non-recognized government in an unquestionably recognized state much less hesitation is felt either in requesting or accepting foreign protection. As we have seen, the European powers who refused to recognize the Juarez government in Mexico in 1867 did not hesitate formally to entrust their interests in Mexico to the United States. In 1899 the British Government, although not recognizing the revolutionary government in Bolivia, entrusted its interests to the American Minister and Consul at La Paz. When the Bolivian Government attempted to place upon this action an interpretation implying British recognition, it was made clear that the American Minister and Consul were in no sense acting as British officials and that accordingly no recognition by the British Government was implied.[98]

[95] Acting Secretary Welles to the Legation in Switzerland, telegram no. 589, Mar. 3, 1942, MS., file 703.5493 Manchuria/2.

[96] Secretary Hull to the Legation in Switzerland, telegram no. 460, Feb. 16, 1942, MS., file 703.5462/16.

[97] L. Oppenheim, *International Law*, 6th ed. (Longmans, Green and Company, New York, 1944), vol. II, p. 244.

[98] *Ante*, p. 75.

The United States did not recognize the government of General Huerta in Mexico after the latter set himself up as a dictator in October 1913, but when diplomatic relations were severed shortly thereafter, the United States entrusted its interests in Mexico first to the British and later to the Brazilian Minister at Mexico City, while it permitted Mexican interests to be protected by the Spanish Ambassador at Washington.[99]

The case of the "Vichy Government" in France was peculiarly complex. In November 1942 the United States Government took the position that the Government at Vichy had ceased to exist as the Government of France, as a result of the occupation by German troops of the former "unoccupied zone." The American Government did not question the existence of the French state, although its territory in metropolitan France was obviously under German control. Accordingly the United States requested the Swiss Government to extend its protection to American interests in the formerly unoccupied zone through the facilities of the Swiss Legation at Berlin, which was in charge of American interests in Germany and German-occupied territory. The Vichy Government in turn requested that the Swiss Government undertake the protection of French interests in the United States. This proposal was subjected to very careful study by the Department of State. From the legal point of view there was no objection to Swiss protection of the interests of the French state or nation, as distinguished from the defunct regime at Vichy. In order to bring out this distinction and to keep the arrangement on an informal and strictly humanitarian level, the Department did not employ the words "protection" or "representation" in its reply to the Swiss Minister but merely indicated that the United States Government assented "to the exercise until further notice of the good

---

[99] *Foreign Relations,* 1914, pp. 446, 491, 500, 636–637.

offices of the Swiss Government in behalf of French interests in the United States".[1]

For many years the United States has extended good offices for Chinese nationals in various of the other American republics, regardless of changes in the Chinese Government and in the form of the Chinese state.   Early in 1946 there came to power in Haiti a new Government which was not officially recognized by the United States for almost three months.   During this period, however, the United States continued its protection of Haitian interests in several European countries and the Department merely informed the American Embassy at Port-au-Prince to refrain from formally taking up such matters with the Haitian Foreign Office until such action should become feasible.[2]   Fortunately, no matters of extreme urgency in connection with the protection of Haitian interests abroad arose during this brief period of non-recognition of the Haitian Government.

The surrender of a government does not automatically terminate the protection of the interests of the defeated power, as long as its existence as a state is not questioned by either the protecting power or the local state in which the protection is performed.   Thus the Swiss Government continued to protect Italian and Japanese interests in the United States for some months after the defeat of those powers in World War II.[3]   Even as regards German interests, the Swiss Government did not regard its protection as having automatically ceased with the surrender of the German

---

[1] The Secretary of State (Hull) to the Swiss Minister (Bruggmann), Dec. 2, 1942, MS., file 705.5154/4.   For further explanation of the distinction in American practice between "representation" and "good offices", see *post*, p. 175.

[2] The Secretary of State to the officer in charge of the Mission at Port-au-Prince, no. 551, Feb. 13, 1946, MS., file 340.1015/11–2945.

[3] Respecting Italian interests, see *ante*, p. 128.   Respecting Japanese interests, see Department of State press releases 560, July 21, 1945; 947, Dec. 20, 1945; and 43, Jan. 18, 1946.

Government, although the complete collapse of all indigenous German government and the assumption of governmental authority within the German state by the Allied Control Council at Berlin made the continuation of Swiss protection of German interests abroad obviously impracticable.[4]

From the foregoing examples it becomes apparent that the principle of according protection to the interests of a state rather than a government reflects not so much an abstract distinction as a prevailing realization in official quarters that the protection of foreign interests involves an international relationship based upon the existence of national states and that the long-range humanitarian purpose of the practice is most effectively served by disregarding as fully as possible the short-range political complications between the governments concerned.

---

[4] *Ante,* p. 128.

CHAPTER V

ADMINISTRATIVE PROCEDURES

IN addition to the ten basic principles discussed in the preceding chapter there have evolved in the course of the protection of foreign interests a number of general administrative procedures which are important to an understanding of the subject. These practices, like the basic principles, are not in themselves protective activities; they constitute rather the administrative pattern or framework within which the protective activities take place. These practices are, of course, more susceptible to national variations and interpretations than are the basic principles, yet a considerable degree of international uniformity or similarity has developed even in these administrative matters. It is appropriate, therefore, to consider some of these general administrative procedures before proceeding to a discussion of the specific duties of the diplomatic or consular officer in charge of foreign interests.

1. ASSUMPTION AND TERMINATION OF PROTECTION

In the assumption and termination of the protection of foreign interests certain rather set procedures are commonly followed. Whenever possible the officer assuming the protection consults with the departing foreign official (or officials) respecting the details of the transfer, which are generally numerous and are frequently rendered difficult by conditions attending a rupture of relations or declaration of war. As a general rule, most belligerent governments will permit the representative of the protecting power to have access to officials of the departing mission even when the latter may be in official detention pending their repatriation.

In this way the officer assuming the protection can inform himself quickly with respect to the accounting and filing practices followed by the departing official and can arrange with him for the preparation of a suitable inventory.   Concerning this matter of inventory the *Foreign Service Regulations* of the United States specify as follows:

Diplomatic and consular officers protecting the interests of foreign governments will be held strictly accountable for all property and funds of the protected government which they take over in connection with that protection.   An itemized inventory of property taken into custody shall be prepared in quintuplicate, all copies being signed by the officer assuming protection and by the outgoing official.   Three copies of the inventory shall be forwarded to the Department, one being marked for the protected government; two copies shall be retained in the office files, one of which is to be used when the protection is relinquished.   Additionally, receipts shall be given for property and cash received and receipts shall be obtained when protection is relinquished.[1]

This inventory of property is frequently accompanied by a list of the protected nationals in the area, and when circumstances permit, the transfer or relinquishment of office is recorded in a formal protocol or *procès-verbal,* signed by both officials.[2]   The diplomatic officer assuming the protection then promptly notifies the government of the local state, indicating that the protection has been assumed either subject to or with the consent of that government.   A consular officer assuming the protection will notify only the local authorities, while the diplomatic mission of the protecting power will appropriately notify the foreign office of the local state.

Respecting the relinquishment of protection, the *Foreign Service Regulations* provide as follows:

Officers of the Foreign Service in charge of the interests of a foreign government shall not recommend persons to take over protection, but

---

[1] *Foreign Service Regulations,* chap. XII, sec. 4, n. 3.

[2] *Règlement consulaire suisse,* arts. 93 and 94.   For type of protocol see Department of State press releases 947, Dec. 20, 1945, and 43, Jan. 18, 1946.

at the request of the protected power may be instructed by the Department of State to report on the desirability of persons under consideration for such positions. The report shall be forwarded to the Department for use in its discretion.

Foreign interests files other than the categories of papers described in the following paragraphs of this note as not properly to be included therein, shall, to the extent possible, be relinquished simultaneously with the relinquishment of the function of protection.

Papers of the following categories in the foreign interests files of countries protected by the Government of the United States are considered to form a part of the official archives and may *not* be relinquished:

(*a*) The originals of all communications received from the Foreign Office and office copies of all communications addressed to the Foreign Office (or analogous communications exchanged between the local authorities and offices that are not at capitals).

(*b*) The originals of all communications received from the Department and office copies of all communications addressed to the Department.

(*c*) All documents related to matters of policy in the protection of foreign interests. However, copies (or paraphrases, where necessary) of all such communications of the foregoing categories as relate to foreign interests should be included in the foreign interests files.

In view of the fact that foreign interests accounts form a part of the accountable officers' accounts, the office copies of the accounting forms used in connection with the receipt of funds and expenditures for each government whose interests are protected shall not be included in the foreign interests files. If there are extra copies of such forms, however, they may be turned over with the foreign interests files to the persons to be charged with the protection of the interests concerned for their information and guidance.

There shall not be placed in or attached to foreign interests files any matter intended or suitable for the Government of the United States only.

Property of the protected power shall be relinquished at the time of the relinquishment of the functions of protection. Receipts shall be obtained for all such property.[3]

---

[3] *Foreign Service Regulations,* chap. XII, sec. 7. Most of this section was based on circular telegram no. 275, of Dec. 9, 1941, sent to the Legation in Switzerland for relay to offices and missions in charge of

In October 1941 the Department issued a circular instruction to all offices and missions in charge of foreign interests, suggesting the desirability of preparing memoranda containing all pertinent data respecting the protection of each foreign country's interests. In view of the contingencies of modern warfare and the fact that some officers might find it physically impossible to remain at their post, it was felt that such memoranda would be of great assistance in facilitating the relinquishment of these foreign interests to another government, if that should become necessary. The memoranda in question were to include a complete list of protected properties of all types, budgetary statements, lists of protected nationals indicating those receiving financial relief, and copies of pertinent correspondence respecting the protection of that country's interests.[4]

Confusion is avoided if the officer assuming or relinquishing protection promptly telegraphs this information to his government. The older records in the Department of State indicate that officers rather frequently failed to notify the Department of the exact date on which they terminated their protection of certain foreign interests and that some embarrassment occasionally resulted from this omission.

2. CHANNELS OF COMMUNICATION

Respecting the channels of communication in protecting foreign interests the following provision appears in the *Foreign Service Regulations* of the United States:

An officer in charge of the interests of a foreign government shall not address any communications direct to that government. His communications shall be routed through the Department of State and the American diplomatic mission near the protected government. Similarly, communications from the protected power to an officer in charge

---

foreign interests and communicated to the Swiss Government for its information.

[4] Secretary Hull to the Legation in Switzerland, circular telegram no. 240, Oct. 28, 1941, MS., file 704.00/611A.

of foreign interests shall be routed through the American diplomatic mission and the Department of State. The Department of State may in its discretion permit direct communication in exceptionally urgent cases between the protecting officer and the American mission in the protected country.[5]

As early as 1867 the Department indicated that it did not look with favor upon direct communication between the French Government and the American Minister in charge of French interests in Mexico.[6] The reason for this attitude is perfectly apparent and has become even stronger as it became increasingly clear during the present century that the officer in charge of foreign interests remains exclusively the official of his own government and does not become subject to direct instruction from the government of the protected power. Although this prescribed channel of communication has become customary administrative procedure in the protection of foreign interests, it has not always been strictly observed even by the United States Government. In 1914 when American interests in Mexico were entrusted to the Brazilian Minister at Mexico City, the Department of State corresponded direct with the Brazilian Minister quite frequently, although this was not done until after this procedure had been agreed to by the Brazilian Ambassador at Washington.[7] In view of the urgent matters then being handled, it would have been entirely impractical for communications to have been transmitted from Washington to Mexico via Rio de Janeiro.

When the United States was acting as a protecting power during the first and second World Wars, communications were frequently transmitted by American missions between the protected power in Europe and the local power in Europe without going through the Department in Washington. This

---

[5] *Foreign Service Regulations,* chap. XII, sec. 3, n. 4; cf. Von König, *op. cit.,* p. 72.

[6] *Ante,* p. 36.

[7] *Foreign Relations,* 1914, pp. 642, 645, 648.

channel of communication was limited to strictly routine matters and even then it was permissible only as between the two American missions involved.   Thus the British Government would not correspond direct with the American Ambassador in charge of British interests in, let us say, Germany, but would communicate its desires to the American Ambassador at London who would then relay the message to his colleague at Berlin.   On all matters of real importance, however, the approved channel was from the British Foreign Office to the British Ambassador at Washington to the Department of State to the American Ambassador in Germany.   Under modern conditions of telecommunication surprisingly little time was lost by employing the more lengthy, but more orthodox, channel.   General practice has confirmed the rule that the officer in the field would be well advised to refer to his own government any matter dealing with the delicate subject of protecting foreign interests (particularly belligerent interests), unless the matter in question lies strictly within the limits of approved policy.[8]

3. PLURAL AND PARTIAL PROTECTION

Peculiar administrative complexities occur when the protection extended to certain foreign interests is either plural or partial in character within the same local state.   Although we have previously alluded to these variations, it would be appropriate at this point to consider them in some detail.

The usual pattern is for the protecting power to be in charge of the diplomatic *and* consular interests of the protected power throughout the territory of the local state. Partial protection occurs when the protecting power is in

---

[8] Secretary Hull to the Legation in Switzerland, circular telegram no. 211, Nov. 26, 1940, MS., file 704.00/587A. For examples of the embarrassing complications which may result from a violation of this administrative rule, see *ante,* pp. 93, 95, 120, *post,* p. 174.

charge of either diplomatic *or* consular interests but not both at the same time.   Examples of both complete and partial protection (in two variations) occurred in connection with the protection of French interests in Venezuela in the period from 1906 to 1913.[9]   The consular services which a number of American offices have performed for many years on behalf of Cuba and Panama constitute an outstanding example of partial protection on the consular side.[10]   An example of partial protection of an exclusively diplomatic nature occurred in the protection of Haitian interests in France during a portion of World War II, when Haitian consuls continued at their posts although the Haitian Minister had withdrawn from Paris.[11]   When only consular protection is extended, it is customary for the appropriate notification to the foreign office of the local state to be made by the diplomatic mission of the protecting power at the capital.   Notification may also be made by the mission of the power whose consular interests are entrusted to foreign protection.[12]

In the administration of partial protection the question arises as to the extent to which the consuls of either the protecting or protected power are subject to the instructions of the diplomatic mission of the other power at the capital.   As shown in the Venezuelan incident, older practice tended to regard the consuls as definitely subject to the instructions of the foreign diplomatic mission, but in more recent practice

---

[9] *Ante,* p. 80 ff.

[10] Appendix III.

[11] *Ante,* p. 117.

[12] The Minister at Tangier (Childs) to the Secretary of State (Hull), telegram no. 217, June 14, 1941, MS., file 704.3781/4, respecting notification to the Spanish Government of the performance of consular functions for Cuba by the American Legation at Tangier.   Acting Secretary Berle to the Embassy in Great Britain, telegram no. 5141, Aug. 24, 1943, MS., file 704.3844D/2A, respecting notification to the Foreign Office of assumption of protection of Haitian interests by the American Consul at Kingston, Jamaica.

there has been a noticeable endeavor to avoid confusion by maintaining separate channels of communication and authority respecting diplomatic and consular matters.   In the extension by the United States of consular protection for Cuba and Panama, the tendency in recent years has been for the American Consuls to communicate direct with the United States Government, which obtains the desired information or authorization from the Cuban or Panamanian Government.[13]

Administrative matters become even more complex when the protection is plural rather than partial.   Plural protection occurs when two or more powers undertake the protection of the interests of one state within another.   The most outstanding example of this practice occurred during the Spanish-American War, when the interests of Spain in the United States were protected by both France and Austria-Hungary.   Respecting the administration of this dual protection, the French Ambassador wrote as follows to the Secretary of State:

With a view to simplify in practice the accomplishment of the mission which our respective governments have accepted, the minister of Austria-Hungary and I have made in common accord the following arrangements:

First. The archives of the Spanish legation in Washington will remain stored in the legation of Austria-Hungary.

Second. The care of the consular archives and the protection of Spanish interests will be confided to the consulates-general of Austria-Hungary in New York and Chicago and the consulates of France in New Orleans, San Francisco, and Philadelphia.

Third. In those localities where only one of the two countries has a representative, he will assume the protection of Spanish interests; in those places where the two countries are only represented by consular agents, such protection will be exercised by the French agent.

[13] See, for example, the Secretary of State (Hull) to the Ambassador to Panama (Wilson), no. 2422, Mar. 31, 1943, MS., file 125.2572/452; Assistant Secretary Long to the Cuban Ambassador (Concheso), June 23, 1941, MS., file 704.3781/6.

Fourth. Questions the adjustment of which may necessitate representations to the Department of State will be dealt with either by the minister of Austria-Hungary or by me, accordingly as the Austrian or French consul shall have had the initiative therein.

Fifth. In all other cases I shall charge myself alone with the steps to be taken with respect to the Government of the United States.

I today send instructions in this sense to the French consuls, and I will be grateful to you to be pleased to invite the competent authorities to extend to them, the case arising, all the needful facilities.[14]

Secretary Sherman's reply was quite interesting:

I beg to inform you that the Government of the United States admits your friendly action in assuming charge of the protection of Spanish subjects and interests in the United States, and that the scheme which you and the Austro-Hungarian minister have devised for the practical division of the charge you have simultaneously assumed is provisionally accepted so long as experience shall show its convenience in practice. It is, of course, understood, in conformity with the international usage which obtains in circumstances like the present, that the arrangement contemplates only the friendly offices of yourself or of your esteemed colleague, as well as of the consular representatives of your respective nations, should occasion therefor arise, with regard to Spanish subjects and their interests actually within the jurisdiction of the United States, and embraces no representative office by either of you on behalf of the Government of Spain, between which and the Government of the United States a condition of war unhappily exists.

I shall communicate to the competent authorities copies of the notes thus addressed to me by yourself and the Austro-Hungarian minister, to the end that they may give due heed to such representations as the agents of either country may feel called upon to make in behalf of Spanish subjects and interests in fulfillment of the friendly office of protection thus assumed and admitted. In order, however, that no confusion may exist as to the distribution of protective functions among the respective consulates, I beg that you will favor me with a list of the French consular officers who have been designated to act in the manner stated in your note.[15]

---

[14] The French Ambassador (Cambon) to the Secretary of State (Sherman), Apr. 22, 1898, Moore, *op. cit.,* vol. IV, p. 612; *Foreign Relations,* 1898, pp. 786–787.

[15] Moore, *op. cit.,* vol. IV, pp. 612–613; *Foreign Relations,* 1898, pp. 787–788.

From this reply it is seen that the United States Government did not feel that it was obliged to accept this administrative procedure proposed by the two protecting powers, and it reserved the right to make further suggestions in this regard if experience should indicate that the proposed arrangement was not practical. As a matter of fact, the arrangement, however cumbersome, appears not to have caused any serious difficulties, although it was rendered even more complex by the fact that at the request of the Spanish Government, the Mexican consuls at Laredo, Texas, and Nogales, Arizona, were also permitted to protect Spanish interests, since there were neither French nor Austrian consuls in those areas. This was done with the understanding that such correspondence as these consuls might have with respect to the protection of Spanish interests would be sent to the Mexican Minister at Washington, who would refer the matter to the French Ambassador for action.[16] Mexico, therefore, was not, strictly speaking, a third protecting power, but it was engaging in a partial, consular protection of Spanish interests which were already under plural protection, both diplomatic and consular! Slightly less complex was the situation during the early part of World War I when American consuls handled French interests in those areas of Germany where there were no Spanish consuls, Spain being in charge generally of French interests in Germany.[17]

During World War II the same administrative complications arose on an even larger scale in connection with the protection of various Allied interests in Germany and German-occupied countries. In June 1940 an official of the German Foreign Office pointed out, by way of example, that the American Legation at The Hague had assumed the protection of the interests of South Africa, Belgium, and Egypt, while at Berlin only Belgian interests were in American

---

[16] *Foreign Relations,* 1898, p. 792.
[17] Appendix I.

hands, the interests of South Africa and Egypt being entrusted to the Swedish and Iranian Legations, respectively. It was suggested that for administrative convenience it would be desirable if the interests of any one belligerent were handled by the same protecting power throughout Germany and German-occupied territory.[18] With this suggestion the Department of State was in agreement, and steps were taken to "rationalize" and simplify in so far as possible the protection of all Allied interests by the United States in Germany and German-occupied territory.[19]

The type of plural protection least likely to result in administrative difficulties and confusion is that in which there is a very sharp geographic demarcation of the jurisdictions of the different protecting powers. This was the situation during most of the period of American belligerency in World War II when Japanese interests were protected by Spain in continental United States, by Sweden in the Territory of Hawaii, and by Switzerland in American Samoa.[20] Even under these conditions the practice of plural protection is not to be recommended from an administrative point of view.

For uniformity and simplicity of administration it is obviously desirable for the protected power to entrust its interests in another country to only one protecting power, and in instances involving the protection of belligerent interests there are advantages to all concerned if both belligerents entrust their interests in the other's territory to the same protecting power. M. Fauchille referred to this arrangement as a "particularité curieuse",[21] but his observation reflected an attitude, now all but obsolete, that a protecting power was supposed to be on especially friendly terms with the belliger-

---

[18] The Chargé d'Affaires ad interim in Germany to the Secretary of State (Hull), telegram no. 1621, June 1, 1940, MS., file 704.00/568.

[19] Secretary Hull to the Embassy in Germany, telegram no. 1499, June 6, 1940, *loc. cit.*

[20] Appendix VII.

[21] Fauchille, *op. cit.*, vol. II, p. 52.

ent whose interests it undertook to protect and that the position of the protecting power was rather analogous to that of a "second" in a duel.[22] The experience of World War II indicates that a more uniform administration and a higher standard of treatment of enemy interests by both belligerents result from a reciprocal protection of the interests of those belligerents by the same protecting power throughout the territories under the control of each belligerent.

4. INTERPRETATION OF LAWS AND REGULATIONS

Since it has now become a settled principle that officers in charge of foreign interests do not become officials of the protected power, it naturally follows that they do not automatically acquire any authority to interpret its laws and regulations. It is clear that any such interpretation by individual officers might be extremely dangerous in the protection of belligerent interests and might, in any circumstances, lead to administrative confusion. General practice, therefore, requires that the individual officer refer all such questions to his own government, which, in turn, ascertains the proper interpretation or decision from the government of the protected power and then instructs the official accordingly.[23]

This has been general practice in the protection of belligerent interests for many years. It has not always been the rule, however, as regards the protection of consular interests in time of peace, particularly when these consular services have been extended on a continuing basis for a number of years. As late as 1941 the American *Foreign Service Regulations* required that consular officers in charge of Cuban

---

[22] Typical of this attitude were the older references to the subject which almost invariably alluded to the extension of foreign protection, not by a "neutral" power, but rather by a "friendly" state. Cf. *ante,* pp. 25, 31, 45, 76, 135.

[23] Assistant Secretary Long to the Consul General at Calcutta (Patton), Mar. 31, 1943, MS., file 125.2572/452.

interests at various posts "should inform themselves of the current Cuban practices before issuing or visaing a passport and, when necessary, consult with the Cuban Department of State". Consular officers in charge of Panamanian interests were told that they would "be furnished with pertinent Panamanian regulations".[24] This practice, which represented a sort of "vestigial remain" from the days before the clarification of the relationship between the officer in charge of foreign interests and the government of the protected power, was found to be increasingly confusing and unworkable in recent years. Respecting this subject the *Foreign Service Regulations* now contain the following paragraph:

> The United States Government does not authorize its officers engaged in the protection of foreign governments to perform services requiring the application or interpretation on their part of laws and regulations of the protected countries. Such functions shall be performed only upon the basis of information obtained from the protected power indicating the application of laws and regulations appertaining to each individual case or upon the basis of a general statement from the same source of principles applicable alike to all cases.[25]

Such instructions, decisions, and texts as the officers may need from time to time are sent to them in English by the Department of State, accompanied by such explanation as may be necessary to clarify the desires and administrative policy of the government of the protected power. Similarly in the protection of American interests by the Swiss Government in World War II, every effort was made to avoid placing Swiss officials in the difficult position of having to interpret American laws and regulations. All pertinent information respecting these matters was communicated to the Swiss Government through the American Legation at Bern, which, in informal correspondence with the Division of Foreign Interests of the Swiss Foreign Office, assisted in clarifying and interpreting these laws and regulations whenever their appli-

---

[24] *Foreign Service Regulations* (1941), chap. XII, sec. 3, n. 9 and 10a.
[25] *Ibid.* (1946), chap. XII, sec. 6.

cation raised doubts or questions in the minds of the Swiss officers in charge of American interests.[26]

If an officer in charge of foreign interests were permitted to act directly on the basis of the laws and regulations of the protected power, he might be put in the position of performing services or activities of a sort not authorized, or even expressly forbidden, by his own government. While exceptions may be made occasionally in favor of some special service, as a general rule an officer in charge of foreign interests is not expected to perform any services for the protected power of a type which he is not authorized to perform for his own government. The requirement that he shall receive his interpretations of foreign laws and regulations only from his own government insures that the government of the protecting power will maintain a close control and supervision over his activities in behalf of the protected power.

5. FINANCING OF FOREIGN PROTECTION

The financing of the protection of foreign interests involves two questions: (1) Which government defrays the expenses? (2) How is the payment effected? The answer to the first question is that in modern practice the protected power generally reimburses the protecting power for expenses incurred in the protection of its interests. This has not always, however, been the rule and it is still subject to certain qualifications. In 1870 when Minister Washburne was in charge of German interests at Paris, the German Government placed at his disposal "a credit of 50,000 thalers for the aid of their subjects in Paris".[27] This sum, however, did not entirely cover all the relief which Mr. Washburne advanced to destitute Germans nor did it suffice to defray all

[26] The Chargé d'Affaires ad interim in Switzerland (Huddle) to the Secretary of State (Hull), telegram no. 609, Feb. 16, 1942, sec. 4, MS., file 703.5400/22 C. F.

[27] Washburne, *op. cit.,* p. 70.

the other expenses, such as those for additional clerical help, et cetera, which he incurred in connection with the protection of German interests. He was supported by the Department of State in his feeling that the German Government should not be billed for these expenses, since, as he expressed it, "It would certainly have been unworthy of a great government like ours to permit itself to be paid for hospitalities extended to the subjects of other nations for whom our protection had been sought." [28] It does not appear that any reimbursement was sought from any of the other governments whose interests were protected by Mr. Washburne during the Franco-Prussian War.[29]

By 1914, however, it was no longer considered improper to expect the protected power to defray the extraordinary expenses incurred in its behalf,[30] and by the time of World War II it was generally assumed that the protected power should unquestionably stand these expenses. The only remaining question on this score concerned the determination of what should properly be charged to the protected government. Salaries of officers of the protecting power are never so chargeable, even though the officer's entire time is devoted to foreign-interest work. Salaries of clerks employed by the protecting power are not generally charged unless the clerks in question devote all their time to foreign-interest work and were hired for that purpose.[31] Other types of expenses generally charged to the protected power are the payments made in settling outstanding official and personal obligations of the departing officials of the protected power, the costs of moving

---

[28] Moore, *op. cit.*, vol. IV, p. 601; the parenthetical explanation in Moore's citation implies that the United States Government assumed the entire cost of the relief of Germans in Paris during the siege.

[29] *Ante*, p. 39.

[30] For attitude at outbreak of World War I, see the last paragraph of Secretary Bryan's circular instruction, *ante*, p. 91.

[31] Secretary Hull to the Embassy in France, telegram no. 1362, Nov. 8, 1939, MS., file 362.4115/42.

and storing their household effects, the expenses in connection with maintaining properties on behalf of the protected state, postal and telegraphic charges resulting from foreign-interest work, the expenses of relief and repatriation for nationals of the protected state, traveling expenses in connection with visits to prisoner-of-war camps, together with such other special payments as may be authorized or requested by the protected government.[32]

We come now to the second question concerning the method whereby these payments are effected. In World War I the United States Congress appropriated the sum of $5,000,000 to defray the expenses arising in connection with American protection of foreign interests. Officers in charge of such interests were instructed to keep accurate account of all additional expenses incurred in the course of foreign-interest work and to render same to the Department, together with such vouchers therefor as might be obtained for eventual settlement with the interested governments.[33] This procedure involved a protracted accounting process which it was decided not to duplicate in 1939. Accordingly, in World War II the United States requested from each protected power the deposit of funds in advance, upon which the American officers in charge of that country's interests might draw as needed for defraying the types of expenses authorized by the Department of State and approved by the protected

---

[32] Secretary Hull to the Embassy in Great Britain, telegram no. 1174, Oct. 6, 1939; *mutatis mutandis* to the Embassy in France, telegram no. 1181, Oct. 6, 1939; the Chargé d'Affaires ad interim in Germany (Kirk) to the Secretary of State, telegram no. 764, Mar. 29, 1940; the Chargé d'Affaires ad interim at Bern (Huddle) to the Secretary of State, telegram no. 6325, Sept. 23, 1944, MS., file 704.5462/9–2344 C. F.

[33] *Ante,* p. 91. Bouffanais, *op. cit.,* p. 60, states that French regulations used to require the French officer to obtain his reimbursement direct from the protected government—a provision which he admits was "peu généreuse".

power.   The customary procedure was for American officers assuming certain foreign interests to be authorized to use such funds turned over to them by the departing officials of the protected power (so far as this was permitted by the local state) and then to submit estimates of their expenses for the remainder of the fiscal year.   These estimates would then be totaled and the protected power would be requested by the Department to place this amount in dollars to the credit of the United States Government, which made the equivalent in local currency available to the American officers handling those interests abroad.   Accounts were then rendered on a monthly basis to the interested government.[34]

When the United States became a belligerent in 1941 certain special arrangements were made to provide for the financing of the protection of American interests in enemy territory and the reciprocal protection of certain enemy interests in the United States.   These special arrangements were necessitated by wartime restrictions on use of blocked enemy funds and by the heavy demand for Swiss francs after Switzerland assumed the protection not only of American interests but also the interests of a number of other countries previously entrusted to the United States.[35]   With reference to Hungary, whose interests in the United States were entrusted to the Swedish Government, there was established a bilateral clearing agreement in accordance with which the United States Government placed the sum of $100,000 to the credit of the Swedish Legation at Washington, in return for

---

[34] The Chargé d'Affaires ad interim in Germany (Kirk) to the Secretary of State (Hull), telegram no. 1209, Sept. 12, 1939; Secretary Hull to the Embassy in France, telegram no. 1362, Nov. 8, 1939; the Ambassador to Great Britain (Kennedy) to the Secretary of State (Hull), telegram no. 2277, Nov. 4, 1939; Secretary Hull to the Embassy in Great Britain, telegram no. 670, Apr. 12, 1940; Acting Secretary Welles to the Legation in Switzerland, circular telegram no. 37, Apr. 30, 1940, MS., file 704.00/562A.

[35] Appendix V.

which the countervalue in Hungarian pengos (computed at
the rate of 5.119 to the dollar) was made available by the
Hungarian Government to the Swiss Legation at Budapest
for financing the protection of American interests in Hungary.[36]

With respect to German, Italian, and Bulgarian interests
a different procedure was followed.   The Minister of Switzerland, in charge of the interests of these countries in the
United States, was informed early in February 1942 that
the United States Government had already established a
special Swiss franc account with the Swiss National Bank in
favor of the American Legation at Bern, from which funds
would be supplied to the Swiss Government for defraying the
costs of the protection of American interests in third countries by Swiss representatives.   Accordingly it was proposed
that the United States Government would make dollar credits available to the Swiss Legation for use in protecting the
interests of these three governments in the United States,
provided that these three governments would deposit the
countervalue in Swiss francs with the Swiss National Bank
to the credit of the special Swiss franc account of the American Legation at Bern.[37]   The same proposal, *mutatis mutandis,* was made to the Swedish Legation in charge of
Rumanian interests in the United States and Japanese interests in Hawaii, and to the Spanish Embassy in charge of
Japanese interests in continental United States.[38]   This
proposition became the standing basis for the financing of
the protection of the interests in the United States of all
enemy powers except Hungary.

[36] *Aide-mémoire* from the Department of State to the Swedish Legation, Aug. 25, 1942, MS., file 840.51 Frozen Credits/7126.

[37] The Secretary of State to the Swiss Minister, Feb. 11, 1942, *ibid./*
5254.

[38] The Secretary of State to the Spanish Ambassador, Feb. 11, 1942,
*ibid./*5105; the Secretary of State to the Swedish Minister, Feb. 11,
1942, *ibid./*4977; *id.* to *id.,* Apr. 9, 1942, *ibid./*5799.

In practice the arrangement worked as follows: when the Swiss National Bank received a deposit in Swiss francs from, let us say, the Rumanian Government to be credited to the special Swiss franc account of the American Legation at Bern, the Bank promptly notified the American Legation which telegraphed the exact amount of the deposit to the Department, indicating the equivalent in dollars at the prevailing rate of exchange. The Department of State then issued a check for this dollar equivalent drawn on the Treasurer of the United States to the order of the "Legation of Sweden, Department of Rumanian Interests" and transmitted it to the Minister of Sweden for deposit to the account duly licensed by the Treasury Department for use by the Swedish Legation for the protection of Rumanian interests in the United States.[39]   Similar accounts were maintained by the foreign-interest departments of the other missions at Washington which were in charge of enemy interests, and in order to facilitate the handling of such funds special licenses were issued to these missions by the Treasury Department, permitting them to make the necessary payments, withdrawals and transfers of credit, subject to the provisions of Executive Order No. 8389 of April 10, 1940, and the regulations issued thereunder.[40]

6. THE EMPLOYMENT OF "ENEMY" NATIONALS

In the protection of belligerent interests an interesting administrative problem arises with respect to the employ-

---

[39] The Minister to Switzerland (Harrison) to the Secretary of State (Stettinius), telegram no. 2729, May 16, 1945, MS., file 705.7158/5–1645; the Secretary of State to the Swedish Minister, June 8, 1945, loc. cit.

[40] 3 CFR, Cum. Supp., 645. The text of this Executive order is also found in Documents Pertaining to Foreign Funds Control, issued by the United States Treasury Department, Mar. 30, 1944, pp. 5–9. The texts of the special licenses issued to the missions at Washington of the powers in charge of enemy interests in the United States are not included.

ment by the protecting power of officers and clerks of enemy nationality vis-à-vis the power whose interests they are employed to protect. Consideration of this problem induced Secretary Lansing to send the following telegram to the Ambassador at Madrid when Spain was about to assume the protection of American interests in Germany and Austria-Hungary in 1917:

> Please state to Foreign Office that Department understands that many Spanish consular officers in Germany and Austria-Hungary are German or Austro-Hungarian subjects, or of German or Austro-Hungarian extraction. It is desired by this Government that the interests of this Government shall be entrusted only to those officers who are Spanish subjects by birth.
>
> Please inquire of Foreign Office whether it would appoint, at the expense of this Government, if necessary, consular officers of the latter character to care for American interests in Germany and in case of a break also in Austria-Hungary.[41]

The reply of Ambassador Willard at Madrid was as follows:

> Foreign Office states that it has given attention to Department's wishes and communicated them to Spanish Ambassador, Berlin. The latter states that with this object in view he has centralized, at the Embassy and with the consuls of career, American interests, also with the Vice Consul at Dusseldorff who is a Spanish subject, granting the honorary consuls only limited authority for giving assistance when authorized and transmitting money. Spanish Ambassador also directed the military delegates who visit prison camps and who reside in chief German cities to get into touch with the American consuls and take charge of the archives, leaving protection of Americans in Munich to another Spanish subject who has been appointed consular agent there.
>
> Minister of Foreign Affairs states that from the beginning, considering the difficulties, he has taken all necessary steps to satisfy the Department's wishes and is now completing the necessary Spanish personnel at the Embassy in Berlin, and that he hopes within a short time to obtain results satisfactory to American Government.[42]

---

[41] *Foreign Relations,* 1917, Supplement, p. 610.

[42] *Ibid.,* pp. 611–612.

Surprisingly enough, this antipathy toward the employment of "enemy" nationals by the protecting power was noticeably absent in World War II, although none was apparently employed by any protecting power in the capacity of an officer in handling foreign-interest work. In its protection of Allied interests in Germany and Italy during the early part of the recent conflict, the United States employed many German and Italian nationals in clerical and custodial capacities, without encountering any opposition from the protected powers. Subsequently, in connection with the protection of American interests in Axis countries by the Swiss Government, the United States expressed its own views as follows:

The United States Government would be glad to have its former alien employees, particularly those with long records of faithful service, re-employed by Swiss Government so far as possible. However, it feels that the final responsibility for employment of personnel and determination of salaries in connection with representation of American interests rests with Swiss Government . . . and prefers not (*repeat not*) to pass upon such decisions as Swiss Government may reach. Please so inform Swiss Government.[43]

When a similar question arose in connection with American protection of British interests in Finland, the Department informed the American Legation at Helsinki that it should not have communicated direct with London regarding an increase in salary for a Finnish national employed on British interest work, since matters of employment or changes in compensation of any personnel employed in the protection of foreign interests are generally decided by the protecting power without reference to the government of the protected state.[44]

---

[43] Secretary Hull to the Legation in Switzerland, telegram no. 375, Feb. 7, 1942, MS., file 124.943/492.

[44] Secretary Hull to the Legation in Finland, no. A–11, June 17, 1943, MS. file 124.60D3/334.

7. FORMAL AND INFORMAL PROTECTION

For many years there has been evolving in the practice of protecting foreign interests an administrative distinction between formal and informal protection. The line of distinction has never been very sharply drawn and such distinction as actually existed in practice was frequently obscured by overlapping terminology. We have already noted that in older usage the words "good offices", "representation", and "protection" were used synonymously as generic terms referring to the practice as a whole.[45] In recent years, however, American usage has tended increasingly to employ the words "representation" or "protection" with reference to the practice as generally understood and to use the term "good offices" only in connection with those instances in which it was desired to emphasize the informality of the arrangement. In order to clarify this terminology the most recent edition of the pertinent portions of the *Foreign Service Regulations* employs "protection" as the generic term and distinguishes between informal "good offices" and formal "representation" as types of protection. The pertinent paragraph reads as follows:

Informal Good Offices. Upon occasion foreign governments request the good offices of the United States informally to provide consular and diplomatic services for their nationals in areas where there is no occasion for them to have formal or continuing diplomatic or consular representation. Such good offices are performed as a matter of courtesy at the direction of the Department of State. Recipients of such services shall be informed that because of their extremely informal nature there is no assurance that documents so issued or amended will be given full credence by the local authorities.[46]

In preceding chapters of this study we have described several instances of protection which were obviously more informal in character than the majority. The protection of

[45] *Ante,* pp. 3, 21.

[46] *Foreign Service Regulations,* chap. XII, sec. 3, n. 2; see also appendix VI, sec. C.

Swiss citizens, for example, was always kept on an informal basis, being extended only when, as, and if requested by Swiss citizens in areas where there were no diplomatic or consular representatives of Switzerland.   There was in this protection no idea of "representing" the official interests of the Swiss Government on a continuing basis.[47]   Similarly in protecting Chinese nationals in certain of the other American republics there was no thought of representing the interests of the Chinese Empire, which actually had no treaty relations with these American republics at the time when the United States undertook this informal protection of Chinese subjects.[48]   In both of these instances the protection was intermittent, infrequent, and strictly confined to the personal needs of the individuals concerned.

From later examples it has become apparent that political considerations frequently influenced the distinction between formal and informal protection.   Thus, after breaking relations with the "defunct" Vichy regime in France, the United States hesitated to permit the Swiss Government to represent French interests in the United States, although it consented to the exercise of temporary good offices.[49]   Similarly the United States would not request the Swiss Government to represent American interests in the so-called Slovak Republic, but it was glad to have the Swiss Consul General at Bratislava employ his good offices in behalf of Americans in the area.[50] We have seen that United States policy in recent years has been not to undertake the formal representation of the interests of any non-American power in any of the other American republics, although it permits in such instances the extension of informal good offices.[51]   During the latter part of

---

[47] *Ante,* pp. 46, 49, 53.

[48] *Ante,* p. 59.

[49] *Ante,* p. 151.

[50] *Ante,* p. 150.

[51] *Ante,* p. 124; *Foreign Service Regulations,* chap. XII, sec. 3, n. 3.

1945 and early 1946 the United States was requested by a number of countries to "protect" or "represent" their interests in Germany. In response to such requests the Department of State pointed out that such action might be "out of harmony with existing policy" as applied by the Allied Control Commission at Berlin, which did not accept the "representation in Germany of any governments other than those represented on the Commission itself". The United States Government, however, agreed "to perform temporarily informal good offices on an *ad hoc* basis" in Berlin and the American-occupied zone in Germany on behalf of such countries.[52] Similarly "informal good offices on an *ad hoc* basis" have been undertaken by the United States on behalf of the interests of several countries in occupied Japan.[53]

On other recent occasions the term "good offices" has been used to designate the type of action taken in response to a request from a foreign government for the performance of one particular service when no other protective activities are contemplated. Thus in 1942 the American Consul at Istanbul was authorized upon the request of the Colombian Government to revalidate a passport for a Colombian national, although the United States was not at that time in formal charge of Colombian interests in Turkey. The Consul was instructed to sign the validation with his usual official signature, adding the phrase "acting upon the authority of the United States Government in accordance with a specific request of the Colombian Government dated February 16,

---

[52] The Assistant Secretary of State (Russell) to the Ambassador of the Dominican Republic (Garcia Godoy), Nov. 1, 1945, MS., file 704.3751/9–545; the Secretary of State to the officer in charge of the mission at Habana, no. 587, Mar. 14, 1946, MS., file 704.3262/12–2645.

[53] Acting Secretary Acheson to the Embassy in Cuba, no. A–124, Jan. 25, 1946; Acting Secretary Acheson to the Embassy in Peru, telegram no. 278, Mar. 28, 1946, MS., file 706.2154/3–546.

1942".[54]   In 1943 the Department authorized the American Consul at Cartagena to issue bills of health for Netherland vessels clearing for certain ports, during the temporary closing of the Netherland Consulate in that city.   The Consul was instructed to sign such bills of health "in his capacity as American Consul, and not as American Consul in charge of Netherlands interests".[55]   In 1940 the American Consul at Saigon was authorized temporarily to take charge of the files and seals of the Portuguese consular office in that city, without undertaking in any way to represent Portuguese interests or to perform any consular services for Portuguese nationals.[56]

Since the protection of foreign interests may be, and frequently is, limited or restricted in a number of ways by any one of the three governments concerned, there is no intrinsic difference between informal "good offices" and any other form of protection, nor is it always possible or desirable to distinguish the one from the other unless for reasons of administrative or political expediency one of the three governments has insisted upon emphasizing the informal nature of the arrangement in a particular instance.   When the informality is stressed, however, there are two significant administrative consequences.   The first is that the officer does not sign himself as "in charge of" the interests in question, as he does in the case of the more customary protection of for-

---

[54] Acting Secretary Welles to the Consul at Istanbul, telegram no. 31, Feb. 26, 1942, MS., file 367.2115/2.

[55] Assistant Secretary Long to the Netherland Ambassador (Loudon), Sept. 29, 1943, MS., file 702.5621/4; Secretary Hull to the Consul at Cartagena, no. A–31, Nov. 26, 1943, *loc. cit.*

[56] Secretary Hull to the Consul at Saigon, unnumbered telegram, June 14, 1940, MS., file 704.5351 G/3; the Minister to Portugal (Pell) to the Secretary of State, telegram no. 6, Jan. 8, 1941, *ibid*/6. Incidents of temporary custody of keys and property without exercise of any other protective functions have been of frequent occurrence.

eign interests.[57]   The second is that the local authorities may not give full credence to his acts performed in this very informal capacity, unless their specific assent has been obtained in each instance.[58]   For this reason the more usual and formal type of protection is desirable if the officer may be required to perform many activities requiring official recognition by the local power.   In view of the political or administrative considerations which may have prompted the emphasis upon the informality of the arrangement, the officer exercising only informal good offices generally avoids associating himself in any way with the general interests of the protected power, and he is more than usually circumspect in undertaking on his own initiative any activities in its behalf.   On occasion, however, he may be either instructed or permitted to perform any of those specific duties connected with the protection of foreign interests which we shall consider in the following chapter.[59]

---

[57] *Foreign Service Regulations,* chap. XII, sec. 4, n. 4; Hackworth, *op. cit.,* vol. IV, pp. 486, 492.

[58] *Ante,* p. 175; also Acting Secretary Welles to the Consul at Istanbul, telegram no. 31, Feb. 26, 1942, MS., file 367.2115/2; the Department of State to the Swiss Legation, memorandum, Oct. 28, 1942, MS., file 130.917.

[59] In an instruction dated July 30, 1920, Secretary Colby informed the Chargé d'Affaires ad interim in Japan that "An authorization to exercise unofficial good offices does not include the duty of issuing passports, or documents of nationality, unless such right has been specifically granted by the Government on whose behalf such good offices have been extended." (Hackworth, *op. cit.,* vol. IV, pp. 487–488.)   It is clear from the context of this instruction that the term "good offices" was used in a generic sense and was not intended to designate the particularly informal type of protection to which more recent usage attaches the term.   Respecting the issuance of passports, cf. *post,* p. 229.

CHAPTER VI

SPECIFIC DUTIES

IN THE course of the preceding chapters numerous references have been made to certain specific duties performed by diplomatic and consular officials charged with the protection of foreign interests. Having surveyed the history of the practice, together with the basic principles and the administrative procedures which govern it, we are now in a position to analyze in a systematic manner those specific duties which an officer in charge of foreign interests may be expected to perform. Since the number of these duties is greater, and the attendant difficulties more pronounced, in connection with the protection of belligerent rather than non-belligerent interests, the present discussion will deal primarily with the former. The few consular services, however, which may be more numerous and important in the protection of "peaceful" interests will be appropriately noted in the text. In order that the entire discussion may be as pertinent as possible examples will be drawn almost entirely from the experience of recent years. A certain number of the duties considered in this chapter are exclusively diplomatic; others pertain only to consuls. Many of them may be performed by either diplomatic or consular officers, depending on the circumstances. Accordingly, it has appeared most practicable to present these duties according to the nature of the activity itself, indicating only where necessary the particular type of officer performing the function.

180

1. CUSTODIANSHIP OF PROPERTY

A. *Diplomatic and Consular Premises*

The custodianship of the diplomatic and consular premises of the protected power is one of the oldest and most widely recognized duties of the officer in charge of foreign interests. The inviolability of these premises and their contents, particularly the official archives, in war as in peace has been universally maintained in principle and generally observed in practice for many years.[1] Referring to instances of rupture of relations, Oppenheim says: "If the archives of the legation are not removed, they must be put under seal by the departing envoy and confided to the protection of some other foreign legation."[2] While no principle of international law requires that this must be done, it is the procedure invariably followed in such circumstances with respect to consular as well as diplomatic archives and the premises which house them. If it is believed that the diplomatic or consular officer assuming the protection will need to have access to a portion of these archives in order properly to handle certain types of problems which may arise, the departing official may, of course, leave these portions of his archives unsealed.

Concerning this custodianship the *Foreign Service Regulations* contain the following paragraphs:

Diplomatic and consular officers are custodians of the property of foreign missions or consulates in their charge. They shall, so far as possible, conserve such property. The local authorities shall be promptly notified of the location of all property taken under this Government's protection. There shall be affixed to diplomatic and consular buildings and such possessions of their staffs as may not be taken away a notice under the seal of the mission or consular office stating that the property is under the protection of the United States of America.

If there are no diplomatic or consular buildings in which archives or other property may be stored, a survey shall be made to determine the

---

[1] *Ante,* pp. 14, 40, 77, 91, 93.

[2] Oppenheim, *op. cit.,* 2d ed., vol. I, p. 478. The portion cited has been slightly altered in more recent editions.

possibility of storing such property suitably packed in responsible commercial warehouses or other appropriate repositories. No such property shall be stored within the premises of a United States diplomatic or consular office without the specific permission of the Department of State.[3]

These condensed instructions give but a small idea of the amount and type of work actually involved in the custodianship of diplomatic and consular property. The injunction to "conserve such property", for instance, requires the hiring of reliable janitors, gardeners, and such other tradesmen and artisans as may be necessary to maintain the property in good repair, if that is the desire of the protected power. It may necessitate the renewal of leases, the purchase of fuel, and the payment of public utility bills.[4] In time of war, however, the protecting power does not generally de-

[3] *Foreign Service Regulations,* chap. XII, sec. 4, n. 2. In its annual report for 1942 the Swiss Federal Council made the following statement:

"The mandate to protect foreign interests includes also the safeguarding of archives and the protection and management of Embassy buildings, Legations, Consulates and other property of the Powers represented. Switzerland, as the protecting Power, has seen to it that their immunity was respected. The buildings of the states represented are almost always protected by the placing of special signs. Many of these buildings serve as lodgings or offices for our representatives." (*Rapport du Conseil Fédéral sur sa gestion en 1942.*) Cf. the Minister to Switzerland (Harrison) to the Secretary of State, no. 4947, May 5, 1943, MS., file 854.021/4.

[4] The Acting Secretary of State (Welles) to the Legation in Switzerland, circular telegram no. 37, Apr. 30, 1940; the Secretary of State (Hull) to the Legation in Switzerland, telegram no. 2037, Aug. 25, 1942, MS., file 703.5493 Manchuria/4; Secretary Hull to the officer in charge of the American Mission, Switzerland, no. 1931, Oct. 16, 1943, MS., file 125.2231/85; the Minister to Switzerland (Harrison) to the Secretary of State (Hull), telegram no. 6819, Nov. 1, 1943; *id.* to *id.,* telegram no. 2875, May 6, 1944; Secretary Hull to the Legation in Switzerland, telegram no. 1750, May 20, 1944, MS., file 124.621/551.

sire the paying of insurance premiums on policies covering such property in the enemy country.[5] Customarily portions of such premises are occupied by the foreign-interests section of the mission or office of the protecting power, and the United States authorized Swiss representatives in charge of American interests in the recent war to utilize wherever and whenever necessary any American diplomatic or consular premises in their custody.[6] When the representatives of a protecting power occupy such premises for the conduct of other foreign interests in addition to those of the state owning or leasing such buildings, it is proper for the protecting power to make a reasonable allocation of the maintenance charges between the several protected powers.[7]

The protected power is generally willing for the protecting power's representative to use any furniture, equipment, or office supplies in the premises of which he assumes charge. An interesting incident involving the immunity of such property to local action and the use thereof by the protecting power arose in 1942 when the Swiss Minister at Tokyo discovered that two sizeable shipments of office equipment and supplies, originally consigned to the American Consulate at Mukden and to the American Embassy and Consulate at Tokyo had been held by the Japanese customs authorities since the outbreak of war between the United States and Japan. When the Swiss Minister endeavored to have these official American supplies released to him, the Japanese finally agreed so to do provided that he would sell the office supplies, particularly the cases of paper which was becoming very scarce in Japan. When Minister Gorgé refused, the Japanese threatened to confiscate the entire shipment

---

[5] Secretary Hull to the Legation in Switzerland, telegram no. 2933, Dec. 28, 1942, MS., file 703.5493 Manchuria/5.

[6] *Id.* to *id.*, telegram no. 1707, May 16, 1944, MS., file 125.9551/64 and 65.

[7] Mr. Harrison to Mr. Hull, telegram no. 2923, May 9, 1944, *ibid.*/64.

under their wartime authority.[8] The Swiss Minister protested this proposed action on his own initiative and his action was approved by the Swiss Government and subsequently by the United States Government, which pointed out that it had not confiscated or attempted to force the sale of any office supplies entering the United States for use by the Spanish Embassy in charge of Japanese interests.[9] It appears that as a result of his energetic action Minister Gorgé eventually obtained possession of most of these supplies by purchasing them for the use of the Swiss Legation and placing the value in a blocked account to the credit of the United States Government. The Department of State, however, offered these supplies to the Swiss Government free of charge for use whenever necessary in connection with "the representation of American or Swiss interests".[10] When, because of the bombing of Japan, Minister Gorgé envisaged the necessity of removing the Swiss Legation from Tokyo to the interior, the United States Government assured the Swiss Government that the latter should have no hesitation in using any American diplomatic or consular property in its custody, including office supplies and furnishings, whenever an emergency situation, such as that envisaged by M. Gorgé, would warrant such action in connection with the protection of American interests.[11]

Diplomatic and consular premises are, of course, not immune to local jurisdiction in matters pertaining to public health and safety, and it behooves an officer in charge of a foreign embassy, legation, or consulate to see that no offense is given in these matters, lest the local authorities, either reluctantly or eagerly, seize the opportunity to search the

[8] *Id.* to *id.*, telegram no. 4205, July 16, 1943, MS., file 703.5494/94.

[9] Secretary Hull to the Legation in Switzerland, telegram no. 1772, July 27, 1943, *loc. cit.*

[10] *Id.* to *id.*, telegram no. 2960, Nov. 30, 1943, ibid./115.

[11] *Id.* to *id.*, telegram no. 367, Feb. 4, 1944, MS., file 703.5462/89.

premises.[12]   As a result of several embarrassing incidents of this sort which occurred in the course of American protection of certain foreign interests during the early part of World War II, the Department informed all Foreign Service officers as follows:

When you are called upon, in acting upon any authorization which may have been given you to represent the interests of a foreign government, to undertake the protection of any official premises or property belonging to that government *you should first cause to be removed therefrom all weapons and dangerous material;* and should you take over such premises or property in circumstances precluding the prior removal of any weapons and other dangerous material you should notify the appropriate local authorities and permit them to remove any weapons or dangerous materials which may be found therein, in order that the presence of such articles on premises or among effects otherwise entitled to protection will not serve to compromise you or to weaken your effective protection of the represented interests or expose you to the allegation that you are endangering public safety by keeping under inadequate safeguard dangerous articles, the presence of which is unknown to the authorities.[18]

The provision in the *Foreign Service Regulations* respecting the posting of notices under seal and the notifying of the local authorities is extremely important, particularly in the protection of belligerent interests.[14]   The notices must be conspicuously placed on all entrances to the premises and should contain translations in the local language, or languages, in order that there may be no misunderstanding of the fact that the premises are under neutral protection.   If, despite these formalities, the seals of the protecting power are violated by any local authorities or private persons, the protecting power is entirely justified in protesting on its own

[12] Cf. Moore, *op. cit.,* vol. IV, p. 678.

[18] Secretary Hull to the Legation in Switzerland, circular telegram no. 225, Oct. 16, 1941, MS., file 701.4160H/72.   Italics by the present writer.

[14] *Ante,* p. 181.

initiative against such action.[15]   In cases of belligerent occupation it is important for notification to be given to the occupying authorities as soon as possible in order that no pretext may exist for violating the diplomatic or consular property under neutral protection.   When the Germans entered Lyon in July 1940 they forcibly broke into the British Consulate and removed a number of correspondence files, despite the fact that the building was conspicuously posted with notices bearing the seal of the American Consulate and the signature of the American Consul General, indicating that the building was under the protection of the United States.[16]   When the United States Government protested this violation and demanded that the missing files be returned to its custody, the German authorities attempted to excuse their action on the grounds that they had never received any official notice that the British Consulate at Lyon had been placed under American protection.[17]   In view of the official notices posted on the premises, there could have been no doubt concerning the nature of the property or the fact that it was under the protection of the United States. The incident, however, indicates the need for prompt action in notifying the local military authorities in occupied areas as well as the Foreign Office of their government whenever "enemy" official property is taken under neutral protection.[18]

[15] *Ante,* p. 146.

[16] The Consul General at Lyon (Sholes) to the Secretary of State (Hull), no. 2, July 24, 1940, MS., file 704.4151/98.

[17] Secretary Hull to the Embassy in Germany, telegram no. 2381, Sept. 3, 1940, *loc. cit.;* the Chargé d'Affaires ad interim in Germany to the Secretary of State, no. 3846, Nov. 19, 1940, *ibid./*172.

[18] During World War II despite the protests or objections of the Swiss representatives in charge of American interests, the Italians violated the archives of the American Consulate at Nice, the Germans violated the archives of the American Embassy at Vichy and the American Consulate at Tunis, and the Japanese violated the archives of the American Embassy at Peiping and the consular archives at Canton, Swatow, Shanghai, Hanoi, and Saigon.   The Japanese also requisi-

As a further means of protecting such foreign diplomatic and consular premises, the officer assuming the custody frequently raises over such premises the flag of the protecting power. This is a procedure long sanctioned by usage and it has been both performed by American officers in charge of foreign interests and requested by the United States Government for the protection of American interests entrusted to foreign officials.[19] As late as 1941 the American *Foreign Service Regulations* specifically authorized this use of the American flag, provided that it was done "with the consent of the authorities of the local government".[20] While this provision has been dropped from later editions of these regulations, the procedure may still be permissible, on occasion, although it appears to have been employed less frequently in recent years than was formerly the case.   It is obvious that this use of the protecting power's flag to protect "enemy" interests may subject it to public insult and may thereby

tioned the buildings housing the American consular offices at Shanghai, Hankow, and Tsinanfu.   Thai authorities requisitioned the American Legation building at Bangkok, although they did not violate the archives.   The Minister to Switzerland (Harrison) to the Secretary of State (Hull), telegram no. 5633, Dec. 4, 1942; Mr. Hull to Mr. Harrison, telegram no. 2944, Dec. 29, 1942, MS., file 125.616H6/1; Mr. Harrison to Mr. Hull, telegram no. 5280, Nov. 19, 1942; Mr. Hull to Mr. Harrison, telegram no. 2684, Nov. 30, 1942, file 703.5451/16; the Consul General at Algiers (Wiley) to the Secretary of State, telegram no. 877, May 14, 1943, file 851S.00/249; Mr. Harrison to Mr. Hull, no. 7485, Mar. 6, 1944, file 703.5493/128; *id.* to *id.*, telegram no. 1091, Mar. 18, 1942; Mr. Hull to Mr. Harrison, telegram no. 766, Mar. 23, 1942, file 125.8576/245; Mr. Harrison to Mr. Hull, telegram no. 4039, July 9, 1943; Mr. Hull to Mr. Harrison, no. A–268, July 27, 1943, file 703.5493/94; the Ambassador to France (Leahy) to the Secretary of State, telegram no. 1590, Dec. 22, 1941; Mr. Hull to Mr. Harrison, telegram no. 377, Feb. 7, 1942, file 125.7856/125; Mr. Harrison to Mr. Hull, telegram no. 3161, July 7, 1942; Acting Secretary Welles to Mr. Harrison, telegram no. 1764, July 13, 1942, file 124.921/225.

[19] *Ante,* pp. 40, 91; Hackworth, *op. cit.,* vol. IV, pp. 492–493.

[20] *Foreign Service Regulations* (1941), chap. XII, sec. 3, n. 2.

provoke serious difficulty between the local state and the protecting power.

The United States Government does not generally permit its officers in charge of belligerent interests to accept for storage in foreign diplomatic or consular premises under American seal any property of a non-official character belonging to nationals of the protected power. Even if this were done with the consent of both belligerents, the Department hesitates to authorize such action, since it "might expose the diplomatic property there stored to violation of its immunity".[21] Similarly the United States Government, as indicated in the *Foreign Service Regulations*,[22] does not look with favor upon a request to store even the official archives of the protected mission or consulate in the quarters of the American mission or consular office, lest the immunity of these American establishments be in any way jeopardized by such action. When there are no available premises of the protected power, such archives or other official movable property are to be stored in a reliable public warehouse, after being securely packed and sealed with the official seal of the protecting mission or office.[23] Occasionally, when no suitable public warehouse space is available and when the amount of property involved is small, the Department authorizes the temporary storage in official American premises of the archives of the protected power or the luggage of its departing officials, and on at least one occasion during World War II official American archives were stored in the building of the Swiss Consulate in charge of American interests.[24]

[21] Secretary Hull to the Embassy in Italy, telegram no. 153, May 29, 1940, MS., file 704.00/566; Secretary Hull to the Legation in Switzerland, circular telegram no. 101, July 16, 1940, *ibid.*/576B.

[22] *Ante,* p. 182.

[23] Secretary Hull to the Consul at Fort-de-France, Martinique, unnumbered telegram, Feb. 3, 1941, MS., file 702.4151 C/3.

[24] Acting Secretary Welles to the Legation in Switzerland, telegram no. 2371, Oct. 15, 1942, MS., file 124.921/231; the Secretary of State

Not infrequently the question has arisen as to whether the local state or local organizations should not be permitted to use the vacant diplomatic or consular premises of the protected power, particularly for humanitarian purposes. We have already noted that an instance of this sort arose during the Russo-Japanese War in 1904 when the American Commercial Agent at Vladivostok permitted the local Red Cross Society to use the Japanese consular premises for housing Red Cross nurses and patients. At that time the Department indicated that such action should not have been taken without the prior approval of the Japanese Government, although as it turned out, the latter did not protest.[25] During World War II the Japanese Government through the Swiss Government requested permission to use portions of the American and British Embassy buildings at Tokyo as hospital quarters for prisoners of war. The request made reference to the acute shortage of building materials in Japan which made it impossible to build a new hospital for this purpose. In reply, the American and British Governments indicated that they would not object to such use of their diplomatic premises at Tokyo provided that the Japanese Government was really so lacking in resources of its own that it was physically unable to fulfil its obligations respecting the treatment of the sick and wounded under article 14 of the Geneva prisoners of war convention.[26] Earlier in the recent war the

---

to the officer in charge of the Mission at Helsinki, no. 435, Dec. 1, 1943, MS., file 704.3860D/3; the Secretary of State to the Chargé d'Affaires ad interim in Iraq, no. 573, Sept. 19, 1942, MS., file 701.1238/9.

[25] *Ante,* p. 77.

[26] The Minister to Switzerland (Harrison) to the Secretary of State (Hull), telegram no. 1257, Feb. 24, 1943; the Ambassador to Great Britain (Winant) to the Secretary of State (Hull), no. 8579, Apr. 9, 1943; Acting Secretary Welles to the Legation in Switzerland, telegram no. 532, Mar. 5, 1943, MS., file 740.00114A Pacific War/339.

Japanese had requisitioned the building of the British Legation at Bangkok without asking British permission.   The
British Government registered a formal protest against this
action of the Japanese military authorities, but did not press
the matter further, since it appeared that the Japanese were
using the premises for housing prisoners of war.[27]

B. *Other Official and Semi-Public Property*

International law does not accord in time of war any
immunity from seizure by the local power to the official
property of an enemy state, other than its diplomatic and
consular premises.   Accordingly, an officer in charge of belligerent interests must be guided in such matters by the decision of the local power and must refrain from taking under
his protection any property of this nature before obtaining
the specific approval of the local authorities.   The experience of World War II, however, indicates that a certain degree of immunity is not infrequently conceded to certain types
of property in this general category and that in consequence
the officer of the protecting power may have a number of
duties to perform in connection therewith.

The officer in charge of belligerent interests will generally
have nothing to do with official funds of the protected state,
which are likely to be "frozen" by the local power in accordance with such regulations as those issued in the United
States under Executive Order No. 8389, as amended.[28]   If
any diplomatic or consular funds are turned over to him in
cash by the departing officials of the protected power, he may
generally use such funds for the protection of such interests,
but subject to the approval and requirements of the appro-

---

[27] The Chargé d'Affaires ad interim in Great Britain (Matthews) to
the Secretary of State (Hull), telegram no. 1684, Mar. 9, 1943,
ibid./354.

[28] *Ante,* p. 172.

priate local authorities.[29]   Similarly, the officer in charge of
foreign interests will not usually be consulted or concerned
with official property of an industrial or commercial character which will probably be requisitioned or "vested" by
the appropriate authorities of the local power shortly after
the outbreak of war.   His only duties in this regard are to
report the facts to his own government for the information of
the protected power and to present to the local government
such inquiries as may be made by the protected power relative thereto.[30]

Within the territory of the local state, however, there may
be a considerable amount of property of an official or semi-
public nature which the government of the local state may
voluntarily refrain from requisitioning or vesting and which
may involve custodial activities by the representatives of the
protecting power.   During World War II there were many
examples of such action.   When the United States was in
charge of British interests in Italy, the American Embassy at
Rome extended its protection with the consent of the Italian
Government to the British Pavilion at Venice, the Anglican
Church at Trieste, and the British School at Rome.[31]   The
protection of these institutions was apparently continued by
the Swiss Government, to which the United States relin-

---

[29] The Secretary of State to the Spanish Ambassador, Feb. 11, 1942;
the Secretary of State to the Swiss Minister, Feb. 11, 1942; the Secretary
of State to the Swedish Minister, Feb. 11, 1942, MS., file 840.51 Frozen
Credits/5105, 5254, 5799.

[30] The Department of State to the Swiss Legation, memorandum,
Nov. 20, 1943, MS., file 811.20 Defense Requisitions/269; memorandum from the Special Division to the Office of the Legal Adviser and
other interested divisions, Mar. 31, 1943, MS., file 851.51/2979.

[31] The Embassy in Italy to the Department of State, no. 2142, Feb.
11, 1941, MS., file 704.4165/117; the Chargé d'Affaires ad interim in
Italy (Wadsworth) to the Secretary of State (Hull), no. 2544, Dec. 8,
1941, ibid./196.

quished British interests in Italy when the United States entered the war.[32]   Similarly after the United States became a belligerent the representatives in Washington of the protecting powers were permitted to take custody of various works of art and other exhibit materials belonging to certain enemy governments, which had originally been sent to this country for display at the New York World's Fair.[33] When the German Library of Information at New York was closed, its properties were stored under custody of the Swiss Legation in charge of German interests.   With the permission of the German and Italian Governments the Swiss representatives in charge of American interests extended their protection to the American Church at Berlin and to the American Academy and St. Paul's Church in Rome.[34]   On the other hand the American Pro-Cathedral Church of the Holy Trinity at Paris was requisitioned by the German Army for religious services for the German armed forces.   The property, however, was maintained in good condition by the German authorities.[35]   The American Church at Paris (63 Quai d'Orsay) was permitted to carry on under the supervision of the *Conseil National de l'Église Reformée de France,* although the German military authorities requisitioned for their own use the gymnasium in the basement of the build-

[32] Mr. Wadsworth to Mr. Hull, no. 2588, Feb. 3, 1942, MS., file 706.4154/41.

[33] Assistant Secretary Acheson to the Alien Property Custodian (Crowley), Apr. 21, 1943, MS., file 740.00113 European War 1939/809.

[34] The Secretary of State (Hull) to the Embassy in Germany, telegram no. 394, Feb. 9, 1942; the Minister to Switzerland (Harrison) to the Secretary of State (Hull), telegram no. 1741, Apr. 26, 1942; memorandum from the Special Division to the European Division, July 24, 1943, MS., file 012.1/4034; Secretary Hull to the Legation in Switzerland, telegram no. 342, Feb. 9, 1943, MS., file 365.1163 St. Paul's American Church/3.

[35] The Minister to Switzerland (Harrison) to the Secretary of State (Hull), no. 7276, Feb. 8, 1944, MS., file 351.1163/32.

ing.[36] The Japanese requisitioned the building at Shanghai belonging to the International Committee of the Young Men's Christian Association,[37] and they threatened to force the sale of the American School at Tokyo, although it appears that this property was eventually entrusted to the Mitsui Trust Company and was neither sold nor requisitioned.[38]

When the protecting power is permitted, as an act of grace, to extend its protection to such official or semi-public property as we have considered in this section, the custodial duties of the representative of the protecting power will follow the general pattern for protection of diplomatic and consular premises,[39] subject to appropriate modifications to suit the particular circumstance. With reference to the semi-public property, which is actually privately owned, there arises the additional problem of payment of taxes to the local authorities, for default of which the property might have to be sold at auction even though the local power refrained from seizing the property as a war measure. During World War II this problem was made more acute by the fact that all belligerents had apparently enacted some form of "trading with the enemy act" which prohibited the direct or indirect transmission of funds to enemy territory for the settlement of private obligations or in pursuance of private transactions. As an exception to such regulations the British Government transmitted funds through the American Embassy at Rome in charge of British interests in Italy for payment of taxes and cost of upkeep of the British Pavilion at Venice, the An-

---

[36] *Id.* to *id.*, no. 7277, Feb. 8, 1944, *ibid.*/33.

[37] *Id.* to *id.*, no. 9163, Sept. 6, 1944, MS., file 394.1153/9–644.

[38] Secretary Hull to the Legation in Switzerland, telegram no. 1710, July 22, 1943; Mr. Harrison to Mr. Hull, telegram no. 365, Jan. 17, 1944, MS., file 394.1164.

[39] *Ante,* pp. 181 ff.

glican Church at Trieste, and the British School at Rome.[40] Similarly the United States Government, after careful deliberation, agreed to transfer through official channels sufficient funds to enable the Swiss representatives in charge of American interests in enemy territory to meet the "minimum finaneial needs" of certain types of American privately owned property, provided that (a) the property was devoted to public or semi-public uses; (b) the property was not utilized for profit; and (c) the protecting power was permitted by the enemy government to protect the property "as if it were official property of the United States Government".[41]

C. *Personal Property of Diplomatic and Consular Personnel*

From the experience of recent years it is safe to say that the officer in charge of foreign interests in time of war will be confronted with many problems in connection with the custodianship of the personal property of the departing diplomatic and consular officials of the protected power. While the duties relating to such property are both numerous and troublesome, their execution is generally complicated by the rather indeterminate status of such property after the outbreak of war. To such property owned by a diplomatic representative there traditionally attaches in time of peace a considerable degree of immunity from local jurisdiction, including exemption from search, seizure and some forms of taxation. The degree of immunity, however, may depend upon the nature of the property and the extent to which the property constitutes a part of his official household or is held by the officer (or members of his family and suite) in a purely

---

[40] Secretary Hull to the Embassy in Great Britain, no. A–415, Feb. 9, 1943; the Chargé d'Affaires ad interim in Great Britain (Matthews) to the Secretary of State, no. A–151, Mar. 7, 1943, MS., file 365.116 AM3/32.

[41] Secretary Hull to the Legation in Switzerland, no. A–476, Nov. 17, 1943, MS., file 362.1163/12.

personal capacity, i.e. inheritances, investments, et cetera.[42] During the present century it has become increasingly common for comparable, although not as extensive, immunity to be granted to the private property of consular officials of career, but such action may be dependent upon the terms of bilateral conventions or conditions of reciprocity.[43]   In principle these immunities have been granted in order to facilitate the performance of the diplomatic or consular officer's official duties, and consequently international law has never required that these immunities be observed indefinitely after the officer has departed from the country in which he has left some items of his personal property.   On the other hand, the practice in both World Wars indicates a growing feeling that such immunities as are extended to this category of property in time of peace should also be continued to a certain extent after the outbreak of war, since diplomatic and consular officers, including secretaries and attachés, are obliged to remain at their posts and do not have the opportunity enjoyed by private citizens of liquidating their property in a foreign country with which hostilities may threaten.

In view of these complex and variable considerations the officer assuming charge of belligerent interests upon the outbreak of war will necessarily have to be guided somewhat by circumstances in extending his protection to the various types of property owned by departing diplomatic and consular officials of the protected power.   It is because of these consider-

---

[42] See Moore, *op cit.*, vol. IV, pp. 646–678; Hackworth, *op cit.*, vol. IV, pp. 555–596.

[43] Typical of the changing attitude toward consular officers is the fact that their effects were not exempt from customs duty by the United States Treasury regulations of 1902 but were so exempted by the regulations of 1937, although they were not declared "inviolate" as were the effects of ambassadors, ministers, chargés d'affaires, secretaries, and attachés.   Cf. Moore, *op. cit.*, vol. IV, p. 677, and Hackworth, *op. cit.*, vol. IV, p. 586.

ations that American officers in charge of foreign interests are under standing instructions not to store even the strictly personal effects of the diplomatic or consular officials of the protected power on American official premises, although such property may properly be stored in the official quarters of the protected power.[44]

During World War II it was "the consistent policy of the United States Government to respect private property, real and personal, left in the United States by enemy diplomatic and consular personnel and to request like treatment for property in enemy territory of American diplomatic and consular personnel".[45] The use of the word "personnel" indicated the desire of the Department to see the customary immunities extended to the personal property of clerks as well as officers. While this forthright position taken by the United States Government was not entirely successful in preventing occasional violations by Axis authorities of the personal property of American diplomatic and consular personnel in Axis territory when the United States entered the war, the policy had the general effect of advancing the principle of immunity for such property and, incidentally, of enlarging the sphere of custodial duties respecting such property on the part of the representatives of the protecting powers.

The nature and extent of these duties respecting baggage and personal effects may be seen from the following telegram sent to the Legation at Bern when American official personnel were awaiting repatriation on the official exchange vessels several weeks after the United States entered World War II:

---

[44] *Ante,* p. 188.

[45] Assistant Secretary Shaw to the Minister to Switzerland (Harrison), no. 1794, June 10, 1943, MS., file 123 Cifani, Alfred/35; Acting Secretary Welles to the Legation in Switzerland, telegram no. 520, Mar. 4, 1943, MS., file 123.G65/462; Assistant Secretary Long to Minister Harrison, no. 1735, Apr. 19, 1943, MS., file 123 Keller, Frank A./54.

One. Please ask Swiss Government by telegraph to request its representatives wherever Switzerland represents American interests to endeavor to communicate with American official personnel awaiting repatriation with view to ascertaining and carrying out their wishes concerning disposition of their household and personal effects. State Department personnel entitled to transportation at Government expense is authorized, subject to travel regulations, to proceed with packing, carting, and transportation by freight of effects. They should assist Swiss representatives wherever possible in preparation of vouchers. Charges for packing, carting, and transportation may be paid from United States funds by Swiss representatives.

Two. This Government has expressed its willingness to facilitate the transportation of household effects of official personnel by commercial means after departure of the exchange vessel, since it does not appear that space will be available for shipment on the exchange vessels of household effects other than those already authorized, such as silverware and linen packed in trunks, boxes with handles, or handbaggage.

Three. If safe transportation is not available or if for other reasons shipment is not feasible and if storage space in property owned or leased by United States Government is not available, effects may be stored elsewhere at expense of Government and necessary charges therefor may be paid by Swiss representatives from United States funds. Insurance premiums are not chargeable to Government, but so far as interested persons may wish to place insurance abroad, may be advanced from United States funds by Swiss representatives and later reimbursed to Government by insured. . . .

Four. Charges attributable to weight or volume in excess of maximum allowances prescribed by travel regulations may likewise be paid from United States funds by Swiss representatives, subject to later reimbursement by officer or employee concerned.

Five. Foregoing applies likewise to effects left behind by American official personnel [e.g. in Tokyo, Kobe, Canton, Shanghai, Copenhagen and Berlin] formerly assigned to posts in territories where Switzerland now represents American interests. Department hopes that Swiss representatives, in consultation with American officers awaiting repatriation, will take steps to ascertain the existence of any such effects and to safeguard them (packing them, if necessary, and storing or shipping them as soon as feasible, in accordance with numbered paragraphs two and three, above).

Six. If American official personnel other than State Department's should be uncertain whether their household effects may be packed stored, or transported at Government expense, Swiss representatives are requested to report facts by telegraph for reference to appropriate branch of this Government.

Seven. Please state that Department would appreciate report by telegraph whether Swiss representative at Tokyo has in his custody American officers' effects shipped aboard *Tatuta Maru* but returned to Japan because of that vessel's incomplete journey. . . .[46]

Since the total number of official personnel repatriated from all belligerent countries in the course of World War II amounted to several thousands, and since most of these were under some form of detention while awaiting repatriation, the extent of the work which the representatives of the protecting powers were called upon to perform in this connection may be well imagined.

In addition to his activities in arranging for the dispatching of personal and household effects the officer in charge of foreign interests may also be confronted with the problem of storing or selling those effects which the departing officials do not wish to take with them or cannot so do because of limitation of shipping space or other travel difficulties attendant upon an outbreak of hostilities. During the recent war most belligerent governments permitted the representatives of the protecting powers to sell such effects (mostly automobiles and bulky furniture) on the open market and to deposit the proceeds thereof either to a blocked account in favor of the individual or to the general account maintained for defraying the costs of the protection. In either case the representative of the protecting power must be guided by the appropriate financial regulations respecting the handling of enemy funds, and must notify his own government in order that the government of the protected power may inform the official in question of the disposition of his property and may reimburse him in case the proceeds of the sale were made available for use in the protection of that power's inter-

---

[46] Secretary Hull to the Legation in Switzerland, telegram no. 459, Feb. 16, 1942, MS., file 120.34 Effects/236.

ests.[47]   Since such personal property is often exempt from certain types of local taxation, the officer of the protecting power must examine with care any requests which he may receive for payment of taxes on personal property of this sort.[48]

Finally the representative of the protecting power may be called upon to take under his protection and to administer or otherwise handle in an appropriate manner various types of real estate and intangible property belonging to the departing diplomatic or consular personnel.   With respect to such types of property the protecting officer may properly extend his protection on a provisional basis to prevent theft and looting or molestation by unauthorized persons, but he should promptly notify the Foreign Office of the local power of his action in order that appropriate steps may be taken to clarify his position vis-à-vis such property in the light of the wartime powers of the local state respecting enemy property. The liberal policy pursued by the United States Government during the recent World War permitted the neutral officials in charge of enemy interests in the United States to retain custody of a considerable amount of such property left behind by Axis official personnel repatriated from the United States. With respect to several cases involving real estate the protecting power was allowed to act as administrator, to arrange for the details of management with local realty concerns, and to pay such taxes as might be required to avoid forced sale of the property.   With regard to securities the United States

[47] The Secretary of State to the Swiss Minister, Feb. 28, 1942, MS., file 840.51 Frozen Credits/6090A; the Secretary of State to the Swedish Minister, Mar. 18, 1942, MS., file 701.6411/433A; the Secretary of State to the Spanish Ambassador, Feb. 28, 1942, MS., file 840.51 Frozen Credits/5797A; Secretary Hull to the Legation in Switzerland, no. A–26, Jan. 20, 1944, MS., file 123 C 367/335; id. to id., no. A–124, Apr. 1, 1943, MS., file 125.9252/169.

[48] The Department of State to the Swiss Legation, Apr. 6, 1943, MS., file 702.6211 Taxation/52.

Government permitted the protecting mission to receive the dividends thereon and to deposit them to blocked accounts in favor of the individual owners.[49]   In such cases it was emphasized, however, that this permission did not in any way limit the right of the Alien Property Custodian to vest or otherwise control such property if he should decide that such action would be in the national interest.   Some properties of this nature were vested or were controlled by the Alien Property Custodian under supervisory orders, but efforts were made to avoid the sale of such property and to maintain and administer it in a manner satisfactory to the representative of the protecting power.[50]

The property of other officials or employees not possessing diplomatic or consular status may properly be the subject of inquiry by the protecting power but it is not generally accorded any preferential treatment in comparison with comparable types of property owned by private enemy nationals.[51]

D. *Property of Private Persons*

Although the property of private enemy nationals enjoys under international law no immunity to local jurisdiction, it does not necessarily follow that the duties of the representative of the protecting power in connection with such property will be slight.   While the extent of effective protection which he may be able to exert over such property, particularly in time of war, is customarily less than that which he can extend to the other types of property previously considered in this chapter, the larger volume of private prop-

---

[49] The Secretary of State to the Swiss Chargé d'Affaires ad interim, June 11, 1943, MS., file 740.00113 European War 1939/682.

[50] The Secretary of State to the Swedish Minister, Nov. 20, 1943, MS., *ibid.*/8–1044; the Department of State to the Alien Property Custodian (Crowley), Feb. 10, 1944; the Department of State to the Swiss Legation, memorandum, Mar. 17, 1944, *ibid.*/1304.

[51] The Department of State to the Swiss Legation, memorandum, Nov. 13, 1943, *ibid.*/1090.

erty and the complications attendant upon the handling thereof will generally require a very considerable amount of the officer's attention.

As a general rule it may be observed that while the officer of the protecting power is not expected to take such property into custody or to place it under the seal of his protection, he is expected to do what he properly can to express or informally represent the interests of the foreign owner and to report on the disposition of such property by the authorities of the local state. During both World Wars the extent of the protecting officer's activities with respect to private property was frequently limited by the wartime legislation not only of the local state but of the protected power as well. The influence upon these activities of such legislation as the Trading with the Enemy Act and the First War Powers Act may be gathered from the text of the following telegram of August 1942 to the American Legation at Bern:

One. The United States Government does not (*repeat* not) intend to permit the direct or indirect transfer of funds to enemy territory for the payment of charges arising in connection with private American property, real or personal, in enemy territory, such as taxes, rent, salaries of custodians, insurance premiums, repairs, and cost of packing or storage.

Two. Furthermore, in conformity with its policy respecting the enforcement of the Trading with the Enemy Act, the United States Government will not (*repeat* not) forward or permit to be forwarded, directly or indirectly, from persons in the United States to enemy territory, or from such territory to persons in the United States, private communications concerning private property. However, the United States Government will always welcome reports of a general character upon the treatment of such American property and such brief reports in specific instances as Swiss representatives charged with the representation of the interests of the United States may find it possible to prepare when officially requested to do so. Such requests will be kept to a minimum.

Three. Though Swiss representatives will not be authorized to discharge financial obligations arising in connection with private American property, it is hoped they will not (*repeat* not) overlook any alternative means of protecting such property.

Four. Request Swiss Government so to inform all its representatives charged with representation of interests of United States for guidance in answering inquiries from owners of private American property in enemy territory or their agents and in replying to any demands for payment of charges such as those mentioned above in paragraph one. They should also be informed that in reporting upon the status of an individual's private property, the omission of all verbatim statements of or written communications from custodians, agents, or other nonofficial (*repeat* non-official) persons will facilitate the forwarding of information to interested persons in the United States.

Five. American nationals offered an opportunity to return to the United States but unable to avail themselves of the opportunity because they are physically unable to undertake the voyage of repatriation, and for whom the Swiss representative has recommended and the Department has specifically approved the continuance of financial assistance may pay such of the charges mentioned in paragraph one as are an essential part of the cost of their subsistence, provided that the total monthly payment to an American national is not (*repeat* not) permitted by reason thereof to exceed in any instance the applicable maximum prescribed by the Department's air mail instruction no. 1202 of February 14.[52] However, charges such as salaries of custodians and cost of packing or storage are not (*repeat* not) considered to be a part of the cost of subsistence.

Six. This Government does not (*repeat* not) permit persons in the United States to effect transactions on behalf of enemy nationals in enemy territory by drawing upon funds that such enemy nationals may have in the United States for the payment of charges such as those mentioned in paragraph 1, when such transactions involve any communication with enemy territory. Consequently, in cases of American nationals in the United States possessing funds in enemy territory, the Department is not (*repeat* not) suggesting the possibility of utilizing such funds for the payment of such charges, and this Government would not (*repeat* not) approve communications with enemy territory for such purposes.

Seven. The terms "enemy national" and "enemy territory" as used in this instruction shall be understood to mean enemy national and enemy territory as defined in General Ruling No. 11, issued on March

---

[52] For further details on payment of financial assistance see *post*, pp. 215 ff.

18, 1942, by the Treasury Department pursuant to Executive Order No. 8389, as amended.[53]

In accordance with these instructions, relayed through the Swiss Government, Swiss representatives in charge of American interests submitted many reports, both general and specific, on the treatment of American private property in enemy territory, although the Department limited its own requests to a very few cases.[54] In accordance with the suggestion contained in paragraph three of the above-cited telegram the Swiss officials frequently intervened with the authorities of enemy states in behalf of American private property and succeeded at times in preventing or postponing confiscation or sale thereof, particularly in cases where there were previously appointed local agents or private custodians whose positions the Swiss representatives could support vis-à-vis the local authorities.[55] In general it appears that an officer in charge of foreign interests may properly bring to the attention of the appropriate authorities of the local power any matter affecting the disposition of private property of protected nationals (even enemy nationals), provided that in so doing he makes it clear that he is acting purely on considerations of humanity and equity.

---

[53] Acting Secretary Welles to the Legation in Switzerland, telegram no. 1903, Aug. 3, 1942, MS., file 740.00113 A European War 1939/91; cf. Trading with the Enemy Act, Oct. 6, 1917 (40 Stat. 412) and the First War Powers Act, Dec. 18, 1941 (55 Stat. 839, 50 U.S.C. 616).

[54] An official inquiry was made, for instance, with respect to the Sasebo Prize Court proceedings against certain American ships. (Acting Secretary Welles to the Legation in Switzerland, telegram no. 513, Feb. 21, 1942, MS., file 390.1115/1683.)

[55] e.g. the Minister to Switzerland (Harrison) to the Secretary of State (Hull), no. 5283, June 8, 1943, MS., file 362.115 Alexander Kohut Memorial Foundation; id. to id., no. 4650, Apr. 1, 1943, MS., file 362.1153; id. to id., telegram no. 3833, June 28, 1943, MS., file 740.00113 European War 1939.

The handling of estates left abroad by deceased nationals of the protected power requires a special word of explanation. The duties of diplomatic and consular officers with respect to estates left by their own nationals are both varied and complex,[56] and for this reason it has apparently never been assumed that an officer in charge of foreign interests should be expected to become involved in such matters to any great extent.   During the recent war, however, American, Swiss, and Swedish officers (and perhaps others as well) were authorized to handle to a limited degree the estates of deceased nationals of the protected power.   The nature of these duties assumed by American officers in charge of British interests may be seen from the following circular instruction of October 1941:

One. In connection with the estates of British subjects leaving property within the jurisdiction of American Foreign Service officers charged with the representation of British interests, the British Government has made known certain wishes, hereinafter summarized for the guidance of such officers.

Two. In the absence of special provisions by treaty, the devolution and transfer of real property are governed by the law of the place where the property is situated. When real property is left by the decedent within the jurisdiction of the Foreign Service officer, the officer shall, if feasible, informally observe the proceedings and report to the British Government through the established channels any apparent irregularity or unnecessary delay in settling the estate. The provisions of this paragraph shall not prevent the exercise of good offices when necessary in places where the local law requires the participation of the decedent's consular representative in the observance of certain minor formalities connected with the settlement of the estate.

Three. If the decedent has left locally a legal representative, partner in trade, or trustee by him appointed to take care of his personal property, the officer shall record such circumstance in issuing the report of death of the decedent and shall not (*repeat* not) take the property under his immediate protection.

---

[56] See "An Act to provide for the disposition of the estates of American citizens who die abroad" (22 U. S. C. 75–77) ; Foreign Service Serial no. 130, circular instruction, Mar. 4, 1944.

Four. Otherwise, the officer shall act as provisional conservator of the personal property (if authorized by treaty provisions, local laws or authorities, or established usage so to act). As provisional conservator, the officer shall inform the British Government, through the established channels (by mail or by telegraph, as urgency or other circumstances may require), respecting:

(A) Name and address of decedent,
(B) Evidence of nationality,
(C) Brief description and approximate value of personal estate,
(D) Names and addresses of next of kin.

Five. The officer is not (*repeat* not) empowered to administer or distribute the estate. He may, however, sell perishable articles for cash, following the procedure established for American estates by Section XIII–13, *Foreign Service Regulations,* as amended by Footnote 7 thereto. His function as provisional conservator shall cease when the British Government indicates the specific disposition to be made of the property and its wishes have been given effect. If, however, the local authorities assume jurisdiction over the personal property, the officer shall, if feasible, informally observe the proceedings and report to the British Government through the established channels any apparent irregularity or unnecessary delay in settling the estate. The provisions of this paragraph shall not prevent the exercise of good offices when necessary in places where the local law requires the participation of the decedent's consular representative in the observance of certain minor formalities connected with the settlement of the estate.

Six. Any sums necessarily expended by the officer as provisional conservator of the estate (such as expenditures for telegrams, local transportation, packing, and storage) shall be paid from such cash as may form a part of the estate or, if cash is lacking or insufficient, from funds allotted for the representation of British interests, the vouchers being appropriately marked to enable the British Government to recover from the estate or the heirs if it so desires.

Seven. The officer's services in British estate matters shall be gratis except in so far as it may prove necessary in connection with such estates to perform notarial services. . . .

Eight. If any doubt should arise concerning the propriety of any action contemplated within the authority of this instruction, the Department should be consulted. . . .[57]

---

[57] Secretary Hull to the Legation in Switzerland, circular telegram no. 213, Oct. 3, 1941, MS., file 300.413/10.

After the United States became a belligerent the Swiss Government was requested to authorize its officers in charge of American interests to handle the estates of deceased American nationals along substantially the same lines, while Swiss and Swedish officers in charge of various enemy interests in the United States discharged similar functions in connection with their foreign-interest work, subject, of course, to the requirements of the Alien Property Custodian and other appropriate agencies of the United States Government.[58] The transmission of messages respecting private property, including estates, will be considered in section 3 of this chapter.

2. ASSISTANCE IN REPATRIATION MOVEMENTS

Ever since Minister Washburne's experience at Paris in 1870 it has been expected that the representative of the protecting power would assist in the repatriation of nationals of the protected state.[59] This assistance may take a variety of forms and is frequently of as much value to the local state as it is to the protected power and its nationals. During the second World War such repatriation movements or exchanges of nationals were carried out on a larger scale than ever before and the duties of the protecting missions in belligerent countries were correspondingly greater. The experience of the recent war indicates that the representatives of the protecting powers, in addition to transmitting the many proposals and counterproposals of the belligerent governments respecting such exchanges, may be called upon to perform a variety of duties.

It has already been noted that among these duties may be the task of disposing or assisting in the disposition of personal

---

[58] *Id.* to *id.,* telegram no. 1215, May 21, 1943, MS., file 300.113; the Department of State to the Swiss Legation, memorandum, Nov. 9, 1942, MS., file 740.00113 European War 1939/512; the Department of State to the Swedish Legation, memorandum, Mar. 8, 1943, MS., file 311.643/68.

[59] *Ante* p. 42.

property owned by departing diplomatic and consular personnel. When non-official persons are included in such repatriation movements, similar assistance must be rendered to them, and for both officials and non-officials under detention while awaiting repatriation the representative of the protecting power may have bills to settle, travel necessities to buy, and requests for various privileges to present to the authorities of the local state.[60]

He may also be called upon to assume a large measure of responsibility in compiling the names of non-official persons desiring repatriation and in arranging final passenger lists in accordance with instructions which may either designate certain persons by name or indicate groups or categories of persons to be given preference in repatriation on an equitable and humanitarian basis. When the latter method is followed, as it was in the repatriation of Americans from the Far East, the protecting officials will have their responsibilities correspondingly increased under difficult circumstances requiring the utmost in tact and discretion.[61] Officers of the protecting missions generally accompany the persons being repatriated aboard special vessels or trains and see to it that the terms of the exchange agreement are adhered to by all parties.[62] They may be expected to observe the customs ex-

[60] The Secretary of State to the Secretary of the Treasury, Jan. 29, 1943, MS., file 840.51 Frozen Credits/9126; the Department of State to the Spanish Embassy, memorandum, Apr. 9, 1943, ibid./9860; the Department of State to the Swiss Legation, memorandum, Apr. 25, 1942, MS., file 740.00115 European War 1939/2545; id. to id., Apr. 23, 1942, MS., file 701.6211/1655; id. to id., memorandum, Feb. 3, 1942, ibid./1537A; the Department of State to the Spanish Embassy, Jan. 29, 1942, MS., file 701.9423/41.

[61] Department of State press release 10, Jan. 12, 1944; Secretary Hull to the Legation in Switzerland, telegram no. 1311, June 2, 1943, MS., file 701.0090/1627A; Acting Secretary Welles to the Legation in Switzerland, telegram no. 816, Mar. 28, 1942, MS., file 701.6211/1635.

[62] Secretary Hull to the Legation in Switzerland, telegram no. 995, Apr. 20, 1942, MS., file 340.1115A/2565.

aminations, to verify passenger lists, and even to assist in the collection of currency from repatriates if provision has been made for such funds to be reciprocally credited to their special accounts for protection purposes.[63]

3. TRANSMISSION OF PRIVATE MESSAGES AND DOCUMENTS

In the protection of foreign interests in time of peace the transmission of private messages and documents is a function of routine character and limited scope for the representative of the protecting power. When the normal postal service and telecommunication facilities are available to the national of the protected power, the officer of the protecting power will only rarely have occasion to transmit private messages or documents on his behalf. In time of war, however, the officer in charge of foreign interests may expect to receive constant appeals for the use of his official channels of communication for the transmission of private messages and documents which would otherwise be impossible or slow or uncertain. In such matters the officer will have to be guided by the pertinent regulations of all three states concerned and will have to be constantly mindful of his status as a neutral, while still endeavoring in so far as proper to discharge the humanitarian duties of his difficult position.

The subject is both complex as a whole and variable in individual situations, but an indication of the general practice in the matter during World War II may be gained from the following telegram to the American Legation at Bern, which reveals not only the policy of the United States Government but also the type of activities in this regard which were expected of the Swiss representatives in charge of American interests in enemy territory:

---

[63] The Secretary of State to the Spanish Embassy, memorandum, Aug. 19, 1943, MS., file 390.1115A/1680; Secretary Hull to the Legation in Switzerland, telegram no. 1311, June 2, 1943, MS., file 701.0090/1627A.

One. The United States Government does not (*repeat* not) intend to permit, by open mail, diplomatic channels, or otherwise, directly or indirectly, the transmission from the United States to enemy territory or from enemy territory to the United States of documents intended for private use, such as birth, marriage, or death certificates; divorce decrees; legal notices concerning estates, lawsuits, et cetera; powers of attorney; affidavits; deeds of real property; miscellaneous legal documents concerning property or litigation; commissions to take testimony or other documents pertaining to depositions; subpoenas, citations, complaints, or other forms of legal process; or forms submitted in connection with claims for pensions, disability allowances, insurance benefits, et cetera.

Two. With the exceptions hereinafter stated, the United States Government does not (*repeat* not) intend to permit, by open mail, telephone, telegraph, diplomatic channels, or otherwise, directly or indirectly, the transmission from the United States to enemy territory or from enemy territory to the United States of private messages such as those pertaining to private property, business, estates, or the discharge of financial obligations.

Three. Subject to censorship, brief paraphrased messages of a personal nature, including welfare and whereabouts inquiries, may be transmitted by telegraph or, where possible, by mail to or from enemy territory through the facilities of the International Red Cross, the American Red Cross, and other national Red Cross societies, or those of other organizations or societies licensed by the Director of Censorship.

Four. Only where efforts to communicate through Red Cross facilities are unsuccessful or in other exceptional circumstances will the United States Government permit, subject to censorship, the transmission to or from enemy territory, by official telegrams in plain language, of brief paraphrased messages of a personal nature.

Five. The foregoing statements of policy are not (*repeat* not) to be construed as modifying or limiting the provisions of section IV of the convention relative to the treatment of prisoners of war, signed at Geneva on July 27, 1929.

Six. The term "enemy territory" as used in this instruction shall be understood to mean enemy territory as defined in General Ruling No. 11, issued on March 18, 1942, by the Treasury Department pursuant to Executive Order No. 8389, as amended.

Seven. While the Red Cross facilities mentioned in paragraph three are available to all persons regardless of nationality, the utilization by the United States Government of official channels in those instances mentioned in paragraph four will be restricted to messages transmitted in behalf of nationals of the United States.

Eight. In connection with its responsibility for the protection of nationals of the United States abroad, the Department will on occasion undertake through diplomatic channels official inquiries (as distinguished from the personal messages mentioned in paragraphs three and four) concerning the welfare and whereabouts of nationals of the United States in enemy territory.

Nine. The Department wishes to continue to receive for its records and use in connection with the protection of nationals of the United States in enemy territory all possible information concerning the births, marriages, divorces, and deaths of such nationals. Swiss representatives charged with the representation of the interests of the United States should be asked particularly to continue to forward all such information, supported when possible by transcripts of the official records.

Ten. The Department would also be pleased to receive for its records and use in the protection of private American interests in enemy territory reports concerning the status of private American property, real or personal, including American business and commercial interests; estates of, or bequeathed fully or partially to, nationals of the United States; and semi-public American institutions of an educational, religious, or philanthropic character. The United States Government hopes that the Swiss Government may find it possible to authorize its representatives charged with the representation of the interests of the United States in enemy territory to forward such reports so far as their heavy wartime responsibilities permit.[64]

In order that this policy might be the more consistently applied, the substance of this telegram was embodied in a circular note to "Their Excellencies and Messieurs Chiefs of Mission" at Washington, which concluded with the following paragraph:

Owing to the necessities of the military situation, the United States Government is constrained to request the respective Governments of the Chiefs of Mission hereby addressed to give written assurances that the foregoing conditions governing the transmission from the United States to enemy territory or from enemy territory to the United States of

---

[64] Secretary Hull to the Legation in Switzerland, telegram no. 195, Jan. 23, 1943, MS., file 811.711/3693A.

private messages or of documents intended for private use will be strictly observed.[65]

It will be recalled that during the latter part of World War II the United States was in the anomalous position of being simultaneously a belligerent and a protecting power for certain Allied interests in the territory of other Allied and neutral countries. At the same time the United States Government served as the channel of communication between certain of the other American republics and the Swiss Government, which was in charge of the interests of those republics in enemy territory.[66] In these unusual circumstances the United States applied to its activities as a protecting power or a channel of communication the same policy concerning the transmission of private messages and documents to or from enemy territory as it applied to the protection of American interests by the Swiss Government.[67]

4. PAYMENT OF RELIEF AND PENSIONS

In the protection of either belligerent or non-belligerent interests the representative of the protecting power may be expected to handle matters pertaining to the payment of relief and pensions to protected nationals.[68] Like the transmission of private messages and documents, this function is

---

[65] The Secretary of State to the missions at Washington, circular note, Feb. 12, 1943, *ibid.*/3690A.

[66] *Ante*, p. 111; also appendix VI.

[67] The Secretary of State to the Minister to Switzerland, no. 1730, Apr. 15, 1943; Assistant Secretary Long to the Ambassador to Guatemala (Long), no. 57, June 26, 1943, MS., file 740.00115 European War 1939/6852; cf. the censorship provisions of the First War Powers Act, Dec. 18, 1941 (55 Stat. 840, 50 U. S. C. 618).

[68] Most protected powers will desire the payment of financial relief to certain of their nationals abroad in either war or peace, but some countries do not make such payments in any circumstances. See Secretary Hull to the Legation in Switzerland, telegram no. 214, Dec. 4, 1940, MS., file 704.5565/26.

generally routine in time of peace, but becomes much more difficult and important in time of war.   In the protection of non-belligerent interests the duties of the officer of the protecting power in this matter generally consist of investigating the case and forwarding the necessary papers with his own recommendation to his government for transmittal to the government of the protected power, whose decision in the matter is communicated back to him in due course.   Under conditions resulting from the outbreak of war, however, the demands for financial relief tend to increase, while both the determination of the individual's eligibility for either relief or pension money and the facilities for paying either become rather complicated.

During the early months of World War II American officers in charge of foreign interests handled applications for relief and pension payments largely on an individual basis. As the volume of such work increased, the various protected powers gradually adopted more uniform standards and procedures to be applied to all such cases arising in given areas and tended to entrust such matters more extensively to the officers in charge of their interests.   The following excerpts from a circular telegram of July 1940 illustrate the type of duties which the diplomatic or consular officer of the protecting power may have to perform in such matters:

. . . Officers who are in charge of British interests and have received allotment of British funds may in their discretion grant to all destitute British subjects such relief as may be necessary up to a monthly maximum of ten pounds sterling per person.   They will require each recipient of such relief payments first to sign an undertaking to repay to the British Government the amount received and second to furnish for endorsement on the receipt the names and addresses of relatives or friends in the United Kingdom who might, if necessary, assist with repayment.   Receipts including undertakings should be prepared and submitted to Department with accounts in manner specified in Circular 37, April 30, 6 p. m. to Bern.

In the special case of Germany and German-occupied Poland, there has been authorized because of exchange difficulties a monthly maximum of fifteen rather than ten pounds sterling per person per month.

If an officer in charge of British interests determines that the maximum monthly amount fixed for individual relief payments to distressed British nationals fails to a serious degree to meet the requirements of individual cases or of the majority of cases in a given area, he shall report the facts in detail to the mission, which will take up the matter direct with the Embassy at London if possible, otherwise with the Department. The Department does not desire to be informed of exceptional changes authorized in respect to the maximum of relief payments in individual cases but it should be notified whenever the British Government directly authorizes a new maximum for a given territory. . . .[69]

In November these instructions were amplified as follows:

. . . Represented governments providing funds for relief their distressed nationals have indicated that relief shall be conditioned first upon verification nationality of individual and second upon determination of financial distress. Decision as to financial need is final with examining officer. Relief payments may be denied upon positive showing that applicant does not possess nationality of represented country or upon officer's negative finding in respect to financial need. When in a specific case examining officer from available evidence and mission from its knowledge of precedents determine that doubt exists as to nationality applicant for relief or, for extraneous reasons not involving nationality or need, that represented government might exceptionally wish relief denied, payment of relief may be deferred and decision of represented government should be obtained through established channels of communication. In this connection, requirements of British and Australian governments that recipients relief payments shall where possible provide names of relatives who might, if necessary, repay funds advanced is not intended to be indispensable condition for payment of relief. The Governments named have indicated that applicants unable fulfill such requirement would, however, usually be presumed to be entitled to less pretentious scale of living. Latter portion second sentence circular III of July 23 to Bern should be interpreted in this light.

[69] Acting Secretary Welles to the Legation in Switzerland, circular telegram no. 111, July 23, 1940, MS., file 740.00115 European War 1939/459.

In amplification of paragraph seven circular 163 September 16 to Bern, promissory note voucher must be executed and accompany negotiable paper offered in satisfaction of individual relief payment because, since Department's Officers are not authorized to negotiate paper for nationals of represented governments, the beneficiaries' obligation is not discharged until paper offered as discharge is eventually negotiated by represented government.   If represented government in specific case determines in advance that negotiable paper to be presented is sufficient for its purposes and requests promissory note be waived in that case, request may be complied with but voucher for payment should be endorsed to show note was omitted at request represented government and paper was accepted without responsibility.

All despatches and reports relating to foreign interests work should be submitted in quintuplicate. . . .[70]

A few months later these authorizations were extended by the British Government to include the payment of pensions and salaries owed by the British Government, the payment of burial expenses for British subjects, the increase in normal relief for cases involving surgery, and the making of relief payments to certain limited categories of British persons who were not legally British subjects.   In connection with payments to persons not legally British subjects the Department warned the American officers that the "appropriate local officials" should be informed of each case and that if objection was expressed, "payments to that individual should be suspended and a report embodying all the facts of the case should be forwarded immediately to the Department and to the American Embassy at London for the information of the British Foreign Office".[71]

---

[70] Secretary Hull to the Legation in Switzerland, circular telegram no. 211, Nov. 26, 1940, MS., file 704.00/587A.

[71] *Id.* to *id.,* circular telegram no. 224, Dec. 11, 1940, MS., file 740.00115 European War 1939/606; *id.* to *id.,* circular telegram no. 66, Apr. 9, 1941, MS., file 300.4115/15; Acting Secretary Welles to the Legation in Switzerland, circular telegram no. 146, July 21, 1941, MS., file 365.4115/69.

When the United States became a belligerent in the second World War its basic policy respecting such payments and the procedures whereby they should be effected by Swiss representatives in charge of American interests were set forth in a detailed instruction to the Legation at Bern which was subsequently relayed by the Swiss Government to its appropriate officers. This instruction is of such basic importance to the subject as to warrant the repetition at this point of considerable portions of its text, as amended in 1944:

1. To lighten the burden of work and the expense involved in making individual payments, whether from official relief or pension funds or from private funds, to American nationals in territories where the interests of the United States are represented by Switzerland, the United States Government proposes that Swiss representatives charged with such representation make no distinction between the several kinds of payments in advancing funds to American nationals found to be in need. All such American nationals able to qualify for financial assistance in accordance with the rules hereinafter stated will be entitled to receive from the Swiss representatives monthly payments corresponding to their established needs up to the maxima hereinafter set forth in a tentatively established scale. From time to time, the scale will be revised upward or downward upon the basis of such recommendations as may be made by Swiss representatives charged with the representation of the interests of the United States. It would be of great assistance to the Department if upon recommending increases in the maxima, the Swiss representatives would furnish cost of living statistics (current market prices) showing in each instance the rise in the cost of staples in comparison with a previous period. All recipients, with the exceptions specified below, will be limited to the maximum monthly payments for their place of residence, regardless of their ability to repay to this Government amounts greater than the sums advanced. Furthermore, the financial assistance herein authorized is intended entirely to supplant the transfer of any other funds to the American nationals concerned. It is realized that a limitation upon the amount that American nationals may expend in enemy territory, even from their own resources, will entail some hardship. The conservation of foreign exchange, however, is an essential factor in the present economic policy of the United States and it is expected that Americans everywhere will

willingly share with those in the armed forces the sacrifices that must be made in winning the war.

2. The maxima may be exceeded to meet such extraordinary expenditures as may be essential to the health or safety of American nationals for medical, surgical, or dental care, for hospitalization, for reasonable legal defense against political or criminal charges, or for a decent though modest burial where such is not provided by friends or relatives nor by the local authorities. This paragraph may be interpreted to cover also reasonable rental charges for graves, burial niches, or other repositories of the ashes or remains of American nationals in enemy territory, provided that the payment of such charges is essential to the undisturbed tenure of such places of burial. Payment should be made only after submission of each case for approval by the Department, which will notify the nearest of kin if names and addresses are furnished and will authorize payment if the necessary funds are deposited with the Department. Subject likewise to the approval of the Department in each instance, such charges may be paid to protect the places of burial of stateless persons closely related to American nationals able to establish that they have previously paid such charges.

3. Payments should be made against receipts in quadruplicate embodying promises to repay without interest the sums advanced.   .   .   .

4. Receipts should indicate the evidence of American nationality borne by recipients of payments and the names and addresses of persons, firms, or organizations, if any, to whom the United States Government may look for reimbursement of the sums advanced.   .   .   .

5. The Department will inform interested persons in the United States of its willingness to accept private deposits.   .   .   .

6. Swiss representatives charged with the representation of the interests of the United States may explain to the recipients that the financial assistance herein provided should not be considered as public bounty but as loans from public funds to American nationals finding themselves in an abnormal position by reason of the war. It is accordingly expected, as already indicated, that all sums advanced will eventually be repaid.   .   .   .

7. Territories where the interests of the United States are represented by Switzerland are hereby divided into ten classes and the basic maximum monthly payment for an adult is hereby established tentatively for each class as follows: [Classes I to X, $60 to $130]

8. In a single household with more than one adult member of the family, only one adult may receive the basic maximum monthly pay-

ment. . . . Monthly payments may not be increased to discharge indebtedness.

9. [Classification of territories]

10. Except upon the specific authorization of the American Legation at Bern, payments may be made only to persons who, upon the date of the severance of diplomatic relations (which for the purpose of this instruction is considered to be December 7, 1941), were in possession of valid American passports, valid American certificates of registration, or letters from American diplomatic or consular officers informing them that their applications for registration had been approved by the Department for a period extending beyond December 7, 1941. Seamen's certificates issued by the Insular Collector of Customs and the United States High Commissioner at Manila are also acceptable as establishing Philippine citizenship. Eligibility to financial assistance is dependent upon paragraphs ten and eleven of this instruction and not upon the current validity of the applicant's *schutzpass* or similar documentation.[72] Once established, eligibility to financial assistance continues unless the beneficiary performs a known act of expatriation or some other adverse reason for termination of financial assistance is known to the Swiss representative, the Legation at Bern, or the Department. A refusal of an application for renewal of a *schutzpass* or registration would of course terminate financial assistance. The Department has also decided to terminate financial assistance to those American nationals who when given an opportunity to do so fail to return to the United States, except in those rare cases in which the Swiss representatives inform the Department that in their opinion the individuals offered repatriation are physically unable to undertake the voyage to the United States. . . . The Department does not wish Swiss representatives to render any assistance to persons claiming American nationality to enable them to engage in work in industry which might prove helpful to the war effort of enemy countries and the Department desires to be informed of the names of any Americans who seek such assistance with a statement of the circumstances of each case. . . .

11. Applications for payments desired by persons unable under the terms of the preceding paragraph to establish their claims to American nationality should be referred to the American Legation at Bern, which may, at its discretion, approve or disapprove them. . . .

12. Applications referred to the Legation at Bern should be transmitted by mail if mail communications are reasonably expeditious

---

[72] For explanation of *Schutzpass,* see *post,* p. 231.

Otherwise they may be transmitted by telegraph at the expense of the United States Government, in which event, to effect an economy, several applications should be grouped in one telegram stating only such essential facts as the name and the place and date of birth of each applicant and a brief description of the evidence of nationality in each applicant's possession. . . .

13. Aliens, including alien spouses and alien children of American nationals, cannot qualify for payments from funds of the United States Government except as hereafter indicated . . .

14. It is recognized that the Swiss representatives charged with the representation of the interests of the United States may find it necessary to make payments by mail to American nationals residing in regions remote from the offices of the Swiss representatives. It is suggested that receipts might be obtained by mail and payments effected by money orders. Receipts not signed in the presence of a Swiss representative should if possible be signed in the presence of another American national and should in any event bear the right thumbprint of the person signing the receipt.

15. Since prisoners of war and interned civilians are supported by the detaining Power, it is expected that payments made to them will generally not exceed a sum sufficient to provide spending money for miscellaneous personal needs not supplied by the detaining Power. . . . The Department has also authorized provisionally the granting of financial assistance to interned merchant seamen (including aliens having the status of American seamen) on the same basis as it is granted to prisoners of war.

16. In view of previous inquiries, Swiss representatives may be informed that, for the purposes of this instruction, citizens of the Commonwealth of the Philippines are considered to be American nationals. . . .[73]

From these instructions it is apparent, even without considering the perplexing details of individual cases, that the payment from public funds of financial assistance to destitute individuals is among the most important and technically diffi-

---

[73] For complete text see appendix XI; for the original instruction on this subject see Assistant Secretary Long to the Chargé d'Affaires ad interim in Switzerland (Huddle), no. 1202, Feb. 14, 1942, MS., file 340.1115A/2455A, Diplomatic Serial no. 3451; also Department of State Information Sheet dated Mar. 10, 1942.

cult duties performed by the neutral diplomat or consul in charge of the interests of a major belligerent.

5. PROTECTION OF PRISONERS OF WAR AND CIVILIAN INTERNEES

The prisoners of war convention signed at Geneva on July 27, 1929 by the delegates of the United States and forty-six other countries mentions the protecting power in only twelve of its ninety-seven articles.[74] The Red Cross convention signed on the same day by the same delegates contains no reference whatever to the functions of the protecting power in connection with the special treatment which this convention provides for captured sanitary and religious personnel as distinguished from regular prisoners of war.[75] It would be highly erroneous, however, to assume from these facts that the duties of the representatives of the neutral protecting power are small in either number or importance with respect to regular prisoners of war and to the captured personnel referred to in the Red Cross convention.[76] Two of the references to the protecting power in the prisoners of war convention are extremely broad in scope. Article 42 provides that "[Prisoners of war] shall also have the right to address themselves to representatives of the protecting Powers to indicate to them the points on which they have complaints to formu-

---

[74] Arts. 31, 39, 42, 43, 44, 60, 62, 65, 66, 77, 86, 87. 47 Stat. (pt. 2) 2021.

[75] Convention for the amelioration of the condition of the wounded and the sick of armies in the field (Treaty Series 847; 47 Stat. (pt. 2) 2074).

[76] Although the captured members of sanitary and religious formations are not prisoners of war in the strict sense, they are entitled, while awaiting return to their own forces, to at least the same standard of treatment as that provided for regular prisoners of war. Accordingly, in the present discussion it should be understood that the rights and duties of the protecting power respecting prisoners of war also apply to the captured members of sanitary and religious formations.

late with regard to the conditions of captivity." The second paragraph of article 86 states that the "Representatives of the protecting Power or its accepted delegates shall be permitted to go to any place without exception where prisoners of war are interned", and "shall have access to all places occupied by prisoners and may interview them, as a general rule without witnesses, personally or through interpreters". Obviously the combined effect in practice of these two provisions tends to bring to the attention of the protecting power almost all matters affecting the treatment of captured members of the armed forces of the protected power.

The exact extent of the protecting power's responsibility or obligation under the prisoners of war convention is not easy to define. The only provision of the convention which employs mandatory language with reference to the protecting power is to be found in the first paragraph of article 87, which declares that "In case of disagreement between the belligerents as to the application of the provisions of the present Convention, the protecting Powers *must*, in so far as possible, lend their good offices for the purpose of settling the differences." [77] All other references to the protecting power merely specify either the rights of the prisoners, or the duties of the detaining power, vis-à-vis the representatives of the protecting power. In these references certain duties of the protecting power and its representatives are clearly implied, but they are not stated in a mandatory form. The obligation of the detaining power, for instance, to permit representatives of the protecting power to visit any place where prisoners of war are interned, does not constitute a requirement that the protecting power avail itself of this right, although such action on its part is certainly implied and presumed. Whether the protecting power takes full advantage of the rights and privileges granted to it by the convention is left entirely to its own discretion.

---

[77] Italics by the present writer.

It appears, however, that all the powers which engaged in the protection of belligerent interests during World War II were themselves parties to the prisoners of war and Red Cross conventions and were, therefore, deeply concerned with the observance of these conventions, not only as temporary protecting powers but also as original signatories of the documents in question. As a result of this fact there was a general tendency on the part of all protecting powers during the recent war to assume responsibility under these conventions and to interpret their rights and privileges thereunder as duties which they were obliged to perform in the interest of humanity and to the fullest extent commensurate with their facilities and the maintenance of their own neutrality. In the same manner their activities respecting prisoners of war were extended to civilian internees, whom all the major belligerents in World War II, except the Union of Soviet Socialist Republics, agreed to treat in accordance with the terms of the prisoners of war convention in so far as the provisions of that convention were adaptable to persons in civilian status.[78]

It would far exceed the scope of this study to enter into a detailed discussion of the application of the provisions of the prisoners of war and Red Cross conventions during the recent conflict and the manifold activities undertaken in this connection by representatives of the various protecting powers. A convenient approach to the subject may be made, however, by considering these activities as falling into two general categories, i.e. functions of liaison and functions of control.

The functions of liaison require but little explanation. They consist of such duties as the forwarding of capture lists, death reports, and certain types of personal documents per-

---

[78] Secretary Hull to the Legation in Switzerland, telegram no. 330, Dec. 18, 1941; id. to id., telegram no. 376, Feb. 7, 1942, MS., file 740.00114 European War 1939/2108.

taining to prisoners of war and internees; the transmission of funds, books, and relief parcels; and the verbatim presentation to the detaining power of announcements, inquiries, and protests originating with the protected power.[79]   These duties, although both numerous and important, are relatively routine in the sense that they require the exercise of but little initiative and the assumption of but little responsibility on the part of the protecting power or its representatives.

Far more significant and difficult are the duties which we have termed the functions of control.   These activities consist of inspecting prisoner-of-war and internee camps, interviewing prisoners and internees without witnesses, seeing to it that they receive a fair hearing in case of trial, presenting to the detaining power the complaints of those under detention respecting any aspect of their treatment, and helping to resolve disagreements between the belligerents as to the application of the pertinent conventions or special agreements relating to prisoners of war and civilian internees.[80]   These are the functions which the drafters of the prisoners of war convention undoubtedly had in mind when they specified that the "High Contracting Parties recognize that the regular application of the present Convention will find a guaranty in the possibility of collaboration of the protecting Powers charged with safeguarding the interests of belligerents".[81]   An indication of the extent of these activities and the degree of initiative assumed in such matters by the protecting power may be seen in the following excerpts in translation from the report of the Division of Foreign Interests of the Swiss Federal Council for the year 1942:

Prisoners of War—Intervention in favor of prisoners of war has been one of the principal tasks of the Division.   Delegates from the Special

---

[79] Cf. prisoners of war convention, arts. 21, 23, 24, 36, 37, 39, 66, 76, 77.

[80] Cf. *ibid.*, arts. 42, 44, 62, 86, 87.

[81] Art. 86 in the section entitled "Organization of control".

Divisions of our Legations have periodically visited many camps, workshops and hospitals containing prisoners. Detailed reports have been transmitted to the legations of the interested States.

The Powers signatory to the Geneva Convention have everywhere made an effort to apply it in letter and in spirit to the treatment of prisoners; even states which had not adhered to the Convention consented to apply its regulations. The Representatives of Switzerland for their part took upon themselves the task of seeing that these regulations were observed as strictly as possible. They encountered a generous understanding on the part of the Detaining Powers; the competent Authorities in fact attempted, where it was still necessary, to remedy the subsisting difficulties. It may be observed that, in general, the equipment of the camps, as well as the treatment of the prisoners of war, shows constant improvement.

The intervention of the Division contributed to the operation, in Smyrna, in the month of April, of an exchange permitting the reciprocal repatriation, provided for by the Geneva Convention, of seriously wounded Italians and English, as well as of members of the sanitary personnel. This exchange had been prepared by a mixed medical commission. It is to be hoped that, through the good offices of Switzerland, it will be possible for still other repatriations of prisoners of war and of seriously wounded to be effected. . . .

Protection of Internees—In many places, either for reasons of economy or for reasons of national security, the internment of the nationals of enemy States was resorted to. At this juncture, some Powers declared themselves in agreement to apply by analogy, as far as possible, to civilian internees, among whom there are a large number of enemy sailors, the regulations of the Geneva Convention of July 27, 1929, on the treatment of prisoners of war. But in other cases the persons arrested have been treated as [ordinary] prisoners. Particularly in the countries with a tropical climate, the internments have resulted in a state of things which, with the means at its disposition, the Division has attempted to change. Our Representatives have visited regularly the numerous Internment Camps; detailed reports have been addressed to the interested Powers. Complaints and desires submitted to the competent Authorities, either in the course of direct negotiations between the Representative of the Protecting Power and the Detaining Power or at the desire of the Powers represented, have resulted in perceptible improvements in the treatment of the internees.

The measures to be taken for the protection of alien nationals have become more important in proportion as the prospects of reciprocal repatriation diminished and the distress caused by the restrictions placed on the free disposal of their property and by the obstacles set before their professional activity increased.[82]

All protecting powers during World War II endeavored to inspect prisoner-of-war and internee camps on a periodic basis (generally about every three or four months, travel facilities permitting) and they employed in their interviews with the spokesmen of the prisoners or internees and the authorities of the detaining power a more or less uniform type of questionnaire. The questionnaire employed by the Swiss representatives contained about fifty points upon which precise information was to be obtained.[83]   The form used by the American representatives in charge of various belligerent interests during the early part of the recent war required much the same type of information arranged under twelve major headings as indicated in the following outline: [84]

(1) HOUSING
      a) General description:
           Location; building; grounds; security measures; air raid chambers
      b) Interior arrangements:
           Quarters; bedding; heat; light
      c) Bathing and washing facilities
      d) Toilet facilities
(2) FOOD AND COOKING
(3) MEDICAL ATTENTION AND SICKNESS
(4) CLOTHING
      a) Laundry
(5) MONEY AND PAY
      a) Canteen
(6) RELIGIOUS ACTIVITY

---

[82] *Rapport du Conseil Fédéral sur sa gestion en 1942,* pp. 23–24.

[83] A copy of this questionnaire may be found in the Department under file 740.00114 European War 1939/3399.

[84] From bulletin no. 9, Nov. 4, 1940, of the Embassy in Germany; cf. Secretary Hull to the Embassy in Germany, telegram no. 938, Mar. 31, 1941, MS., file 740.00115 European War 1939/927.

(7) RECREATION AND EXERCISE
        a) Welfare work
        b) Books; cinemas; Sundays
(8) MAIL
(9) WORK
Article 27 *a*) Has work been found for officers and non-commissioned officers who would like to be employed?
Article 27 *b*) Are prisoners receiving accident benefits when injured?
Article 28 *c*) Amount of pay and punctuality of payments
Article 29 *d*) Aptitude of prisoners for work
Article 30 *e*) Hours of work
Article 31 *f*) Are prisoners employed directly in war industries?
Article 32 *g*) Are conditions of labor made more onerous as a form of punishment?
        h) Extent of industrial accidents and safety measures
(10) DISCIPLINE
        a) Differences, if any, between treatment of French, British, and Belgian prisoners
        b) Forms of punishment
        c) Description of punishment cells
        d) Number of infractions
(11) COMPLAINTS
(12) GENERAL IMPRESSIONS

Such reports are forwarded to the government of the protecting power for its confidential information. Early in World War II, however, a number of belligerents felt that it would be helpful on occasion to use the information in such reports to relieve worry on the part of prisoners' families and to reassure the enemy prisoners in their hands respecting reciprocity of treatment. As a protecting power, the United States insisted that the actual text of the reports of its representatives must be treated as strictly confidential, although it consented to the release of information based on these reports, provided that the treatment of the subject was sufficiently temperate in tone to avoid recrimination and retaliation.[85] Camp reports were also interchanged on occasion

---

[85] Secretary Hull to the Embassy in Great Britain, telegram no. 626, Apr. 5, 1940, MS., file 740.00115 European War 1939/303.

between different protecting powers and on a regular basis between the protecting powers and the International Committee of the Red Cross.[86]

It is interesting to note that with respect to this highly important function of inspecting and reporting on prisoner-of-war and internee camps the *Foreign Service Regulations* are entirely silent and the files of the Department reveal but few instructions to the field. This is explainable, however, by the nature of the subject and the desirability of affording to the officer in the field as much opportunity as possible for the exercise of his personal discretion. In theory the officer is expected merely to report the facts as he sees them; in actual practice he is expected to do far more than that if conditions permit. On occasion the long-range effectiveness of his activities of control may be even greater if he is not obliged to report automatically everything which he sees or hears respecting the treatment of prisoners of war or civilian internees.

The right of the protecting power's representative to interview prisoners and internees without witnesses and to report his findings to the opposing belligerent places him in a powerful position. While it is understood that his reports should never suggest retaliatory action, it is perfectly clear that such reports, however factual, may induce retaliation by the protected power. For this reason the officer protecting prisoners of war and civilian internees will not infrequently endeavor on his own initative to have corrected what he may consider substandard conditions before it becomes necessary for him to report them through official channels. In this manner he actually serves as an informal arbiter, helping to standardize the interpretations of the pertinent conventions or agreements and to bring the treatment of prisoners and internees to the level of the highest, rather

---

[86] Secretary Hull to the Embassy in Germany, telegram no. 1209, May 9, 1940, *ibid./79.*

than the lowest, common denominator between the belligerents.   The effectiveness of such activity is greatest in those
instances in which one neutral state serves as the protecting
power for both belligerents, as frequently occurred in both
World Wars.[87]

Apart from the long-range advantages of avoiding retaliation, this interpretive function of the representative of the
protecting power may also be of direct and immediate advantage to the detaining power in the handling of prisoners
of war and civilian internees in its custody.   The neutral
officer in the course of his visits of inspection will have frequent occasion to interpret the pertinent conventions or
agreements to the prisoners and internees under his protection, thereby forestalling unnecessary complaints and im-
proving the morale of individuals whose captivity inevitably
deprives them of the broad perspective in such matters, even
when the conditions of detention are in accord with the prevailing international standards.   The officer in charge of
belligerent interests will be expected not to neglect such
opportunities to indicate his impartiality and thereby
strengthen his position vis-à-vis the local authorities.

It goes without saying that the neutral officer who is
privileged to conduct unwitnessed interviews with persons
under forcible detention must constantly guard against the
slightest suspicion which would undermine his prestige in
the eyes of the local authorities.   During World War II it
became standard practice for the representative of the protecting power to refuse to accept from, or give to, any prisoner or internee any paper or object (however harmless)
which had not been subjected to inspection and censorship
by the authorities in charge of the camp.   It was also found
to be good practice to discuss with the camp commander all
complaints expressed by the persons in his charge.   In this
way misunderstandings may frequently be clarified "on the

---

[87] Cf. *ante,* p. 164, and appendices I, II, VII, VIII, IX, X.

spot" and the camp commander given an opportunity to correct any conditions which may have escaped his attention and for which he might be censured if they became the subject of a formal protest submitted through official channels to his superiors.

From the experience of World War II it is apparent that the functioning of a protecting power has become an essential feature in the observance of any international agreement respecting prisoners of war and civilian internees.   Although wide disparities existed in the treatment accorded to such persons by various belligerents, a number of these differences were actually attributable to the prisoners of war convention itself rather than to any lack of activity on the part of the protecting powers and their representatives.[88]   Unquestionably the general effect of these activities was to strengthen the convention and to ameliorate the treatment of prisoners of war and civilian internees in countless ways not always apparent in the midst of hostilities.

6. PERFORMANCE OF CONSULAR SERVICES

Consular services embrace a wide range of activities of which the most numerous are those involving passports, visas, notarial acts, and shipping.[89]   When the protection of foreign interests involves consular functions, either by themselves or in conjunction with diplomatic protection, the consular offi-

---

[88] For example, the prisoners of war convention provides that the food ration and the sleeping quarters for prisoners of war shall be essentially the same as for the troops in base camps of the detaining power.   The differences in these standards as between, let us say, the United States Army and the Japanese Army created a disparity in treatment which in effect was sanctioned by the convention itself, and was, therefore, not to be rectified by formal protests.

[89] See *Foreign Service Regulations,* chaps. X (Legal Services), XV (Documentation of Merchandise), XVII (Civil Vessels and Aircraft), XVIII (Protection of Seamen), XXI (Nationality, Passports, etc.); also Hyde, *op cit.,* vol. II, pp. 1356–1367.

cers of the protecting power may be called upon to perform a number of these services on behalf of the nationals of the protected power.   Respecting such services the *Foreign Service Regulations* contain the following provisions:

1. *Passports and visa services.*   Passports may be issued in behalf of a represented government only to the extent that official passport blanks provided by that government are available for the purpose.

Passport services shall not be performed except in accordance with such general instructions as the represented government may issue for the guidance of the officer to whom application is made.   If the officer has any reason to doubt the *bona fides* of an applicant for passport services or has reason to believe that the performance of a service would require the application or interpretation of laws and regulations of the represented government, over and above the provisions of directives from the represented power already available to him, he shall refer the application to the represented government through the Department of State.   If application forms of the protected country are not available, the use is authorized of American forms appropriately amended or, when justified by the volume of work, of especially devised forms prepared at the expense of the protected government.   Original signed applications shall be forwarded for transmission through established channels to the Foreign Office of the protected country.   Copies shall be made for the files of the office at which the application is made, for the foreign interests files of that office, and for the American diplomatic mission.

Visa services may be performed for a represented government only to the extent that such services are specifically requested by that government in each individual case.

2. *Notarial services.*   In accordance with the usual policy of the United States Government, notarial services performed by diplomatic or consular officers of the United States in connection with the protection of foreign interests will be considered to be purely United States services, subject to the Tariff of United States Foreign Service Fees, and all such fees collected will be payable into the United States Treasury.   Under Item No. 38 of the Tariff, notarial services analogous to those performed gratis for American nationals . . . may likewise be performed gratis for protected nationals.   Officers shall use American fee stamps for such services and shall enter the services in the regular record of fees, assigning to each service a number from the regular series.   Except where they are clearly inapplicable, the Foreign

Service Regulations concerning notarial services shall be observed. . . . No fee stamps of a foreign government may be used or canceled in connection with the protection of foreign interests.

3. *Services other than notarial performed gratis.* All services other than notarial services performed by diplomatic or consular officers of the United States in connection with the protection of foreign interests shall be performed gratis. Whenever the gratis service involves a document of any character, a notation to the following effect shall be made on the document: "Performed gratis, subject to interested party's settlement with protected government of fee prescribed by its tariff". All such gratis services shall be numbered from a separate series of numbers for each government represented and shall be recorded in a separate Record of Fees headed "Services for the Government of _____" maintained for each Government represented. An extra copy, marked "Copy for the Government of _____" shall be submitted with the regular office accounts in order that it may be forwarded to the protected power.[90]

During the early phase of World War II the Department found it frequently necessary to instruct the American officers in charge of certain foreign interests of the particular desires of each protected power respecting the performance of such services on behalf of its nationals.[91] While it would be inappropriate to consider all the variations in procedures which this entailed, it is helpful to note the following circular instruction which concerned the general procedure to be followed in passport and visa cases:

. . . In performing passport services for nationals of represented governments Department's officers shall make such records and entries of services as are customary and required under consular procedure of respective countries. Wherever such procedure does not involve execution of formal application for service, Department's officers shall nevertheless cause formal application to be executed. If it is not fea-

---

[90] *Foreign Service Regulations,* chap. XII, sec. 6, n. 1, 2, 3.

[91] e.g. Secretary Hull to the Legation in Switzerland, telegram no. 195, Sept. 15, 1941, MS., file 855.0128/56, respecting Belgian interests; Acting Secretary Welles to the Legation in Switzerland, telegram no. 129, Aug. 6, 1940, MS., file 740.00115 European War 1939/487, regarding Australian, Canadian, and South African interests.

sible otherwise to obtain a formal application, a procedure modeled upon that outlined by Section 171 Foreign Service Regulations may be followed. In such case certificate of action taken shall include statement regarding infeasibility of requiring personal appearance of applicant. If application forms of represented country are not available, use is authorized of American forms appropriately amended or, where justified by volume of work, of specially devised forms prepared at expense represented government. Original signed applications should be forwarded to mission for transmission through established channels to foreign offices represented countries. Copies should be made for files of American consular office, files of office of represented country and files of mission.

Mission will maintain centralized file and take any necessary measures to insure uniformity of practice.

Department does not desire that its officers assume any responsibility for administration immigration laws represented governments but in exceptional cases it will consider authorizing issuance visas to individuals designated by represented governments. Accordingly, applicants for visas to enter territory of such governments should be informed in absence specific instructions to contrary effect that authorization to grant such visas is lacking. Any communication from authorities of represented government making request that visa services be performed should be reported to Department promptly and in detail in order that it may determine whether it wishes to authorize compliance. . . .[92]

The volume of passport work was sufficiently large during World War II to justify the use of "specially devised forms" by a number of representatives of the protecting powers. The Swiss Government, confronted with a tremendous volume of such work, actually prepared a special type of Swiss "protective passport" (*Schutzpass*) for use in foreign-interest work.[93]

Shipping services, such as those pertaining to invoices, manifests, crew lists, bills of health, and the protection of seamen in foreign ports, may arise in connection with the protection of non-belligerent interests. In the experience of the United States as a protecting power such services have

---

[92] Secretary Hull to the Legation in Switzerland, circular telegram no. 211, Nov. 26, 1940, MS., file 704.00/587A.

[92] Cf. *ante,* p. 217.

been performed for foreign nationals either as a good office on isolated occasions or on a continuing basis in connection particularly with the long-standing consular protection which the United States has extended in many parts of the world to Cuban and Panamanian interests.[94]

Since the proper performance of consular services frequently involves the detailed interpretation of the laws and regulations of the protected power, the consular officer will be well advised to refer all requests for such services to his own government which will then obtain from the protected power either a decision to apply in the particular case or a general statement of policy and procedure in such matters to cover general categories of cases.[95] It is interesting to note that prior to 1914 American consular officers were permitted to retain those fees for services performed on behalf of the protected government which they were not obliged to remit to that government. In February 1914 the Comptroller of the Treasury rendered a decision in this matter, as a result of which the following paragraph was inserted in the *Foreign Service Regulations:*

. . . When an office of the United States has been authorized to undertake representation of the interests of a foreign government . . . any officer of the United States who discharges consular duties for that foreign government is not a consular officer of the foreign government but is an agent of it only insofar as the discharge of duties and responsibility for his official acts are concerned. The tariff of fees of the foreign government should be followed, if available, but if not, the United States Tariff of Foreign Service Fees is applicable. To the extent to which the laws or instructions of the foreign government permit the consular officer to retain fees collected in its name, these fees are the fees of the consular office and must be paid over and accounted for to the Government of the United States. Fees collected by a diplomatic

---

[94] For an instance of a shipping service performed in connection with "good offices" see *ante,* p. 178; for the extent of consular services on behalf of Cuba and Panama see appendix III.

[95] On the general question of interpreting the laws and regulations of the protected power, see *ante,* p. 165.

or consular officer for these services, which the officer is not authorized to retain, shall be disposed of and accounted for in accordance with the instructions of the Secretary of State.[96]

For many years it has been general practice for the protecting power to authorize its consular officials to collect only such fees as were required by the protected power for consular services other than notarials. During the recent war the large volume of foreign-interest work handled by the United States induced the Department to inform all protected powers that in the emergency American officers would not collect fees for the performance of any consular services on behalf of the protected powers, although fees for certain types of notarial services for protected nationals would still be charged for as an American service, i.e. not a service performed for the protected power.[97] While this waiver of the collection of consular fees was not universal among all protecting powers during World War II, its incorporation in the present edition of the *Foreign Service Regulations* [98] is indicative of a growing feeling that the collection of fees is a matter for settlement between the protected power and its own nationals and constitutes, therefore, an unnecessary burden to impose on the representatives of the protecting power.[99]

---

[96] Hackworth, *op cit.*, vol. IV, pp. 495–496; the quotation is from the *Foreign Service Regulations* of 1939, chap. V, sec. 21.

[97] Secretary Hull to the Legation in Switzerland, circular telegram no. 96, May 14, 1941, MS., file 704.00/602 B; Assistant Secretary Shaw to the Ambassador to Panama (Wilson), no. 704, Apr. 17, 1942, MS., file 619.00228/954.

[98] *Ante,* p. 230.

[99] As a protecting power during World War II Switzerland waived all such fees on its own behalf and collected only those required by the governments of the powers under Swiss protection. The difficulty in making such collections is indicated by the fact that these fees "were estimated according to the rate for fees annexed to the Swiss Consular Regulation of October 26, 1923, and the amounts collected were placed to the credit of the protected Powers". (*Rapport du Conseil Fédéral sur sa gestion en 1942,* p. 22.)

Since consular officers protecting foreign interests are in no sense honorary officials of the protected power,[1] they are not subject to the legislation of the protected power in such matters.[2]

7. MISCELLANEOUS ACTIVITIES

In addition to, or in conjunction with, the duties already considered the officer in charge of foreign interests may be obliged or expected to engage in a number of other activities on behalf of the protected power and its nationals. These activities, although miscellaneous in character, may be quite important and numerous in the aggregate of his duties.   One of the most common of these miscellaneous activities is the transmission of official communications from the protected power to the local power.   We have already mentioned this activity in conjunction with several of the specific duties previously discussed in this chapter, but the activity far exceeds the scope of these particular duties. Especially in the protection of belligerent interests the protecting power and its representatives may be asked to transmit to the opposing belligerent a large number of messages dealing not only with the protection of persons and property in enemy territory but also with many phases of the conduct of hostilities.   From the experience of World War II it would appear that such subjects may include the observance or violation of the rules of land and naval warfare, the notification of hospital ships, the granting of safe-conducts for persons or vessels, the detailed arrangements for mutual exchanges of nationals, and the preliminary terms of surrender.[3]

---

[1] *Ante,* pp. 136 ff.

[2] The Ambassador to Panama (Hines) to the Secretary of State (Byrnes), no. A–1909, Dec. 4, 1945, MS., file 619.00228/12–445; Assistant Secretary Russell to Ambassador Hines, no. 171, May 21, 1946, *ibid.*/4–146.

[3] e.g. Secretary Hull to the Legation in Switzerland, telegram no. 3039, Dec. 7, 1943, MS., file 740.00117 European War 1939/150;

With respect to such subjects as these the protecting power and its representatives will generally transmit the message or protest verbatim and without comment.[4]   Whenever the communication concerns the protection of persons or property in the territory or under the control of the local state, however, the protecting power or its officers in the field may exercise some discretion in the matter. If the message is a protest based upon reports of the representatives of the protecting power concerning such serious matters as violation of the prisoners of war convention or of diplomatic premises under seal, the protecting power may support the protest by one of its own or may informally indicate to the local state that it cannot but feel that the protest was merited by the facts.[5]   If, on the other hand, it is believed that the presentation of the message or protest might be likely to confuse or worsen the situation, the protecting power may properly consult with the protected power and explain its reasons for hesitation in the matter.   Such action would not be undertaken by the protecting power without careful consideration but it would be entirely appropriate if the protecting power were convinced that the message or protest was based on a misunderstanding which it was in a position to clarify.

In order that such misunderstandings may be kept to a minimum it behooves the representatives of the protecting power to keep their own government and the government of the protected power as fully informed as possible on all matters pertaining to the interests of the latter in the territory of the local state.   This entails on the part of the diplomat or consul a considerable amount of political and economic re-

---

Secretary Hull to the Embassy in Panama, no. 2951, Dec. 9, 1943, MS., file 819.0128/61; Secretary Hull to the Legation in Switzerland, telegram no. 3566, Oct. 19, 1944, MS., file 740.00115 Pacific War/8–2444; also *ante,* pp. 119, 197.

[4] Cf. *Foreign Service Regulations,* chap. XII, sec. 5, n. 2.

[5] *Ante,* p. 146 n.

porting with respect to the interests of the protected power in addition to the similar but more extensive reporting which he normally does in connection with the interests of his own government.   Such matters as laws and regulations or official statements and important press notices concerning the treatment of the nationals or property of the protected power should be reported by the officer in charge of foreign interests. In the protection of belligerent interests it is advisable to limit such reports to strictly factual material since the government of a neutral protecting power will hesitate as a rule to transmit to the protected power reports containing conjecture or recrimination emanating from the opposing belligerent.[6]

In discharging various of his specific duties the officer protecting foreign interests may find it necessary to maintain informal liaison with certain international societies and with local agencies, both public and private, within the state to which he is assigned or accredited.   Liaison with the local delegates of such societies as the International Committee of the Red Cross and the War Prisoners' Aid of the Young Men's Christian Association may be quite important in the protection of prisoners of war and civilian internees.[7]   With respect to enemy aliens not under detention liaison with local charitable organizations may be of value in alleviating instances of distress which may come initially to the attention of the representative of the protecting power.   Liaison with War Graves Commissions may also be an activity of the officer in charge of belligerent interests.[8]

An officer in charge of foreign interests is not generally authorized or permitted to present formal claims on be-

---

[6] The Chargé d'Affaires ad interim in Germany (Heath) to the Secretary of State (Hull), telegram no. 1598, May 31, 1940, MS., file 740.0011 European War 1939/3416.

[7] Cf. arts. 78, 79, 87, 88 of the prisoners of war convention.

[8] The Chargé d'Affaires ad interim in Italy (Wadsworth) to the Secretary of State (Hull), no. 2544, Dec. 8, 1941, MS., file 704.00/611.

half of protected nationals against the local state, even when there has been no severance of relations between the protected state and the local power.[9]   On occasion, however, local states have consented to accept such claims for consideration when presented by the representative of the protecting power.[10]   Such presentation of formal claims should never be made by the officer in charge of foreign interests without the express approval of his own government.[11]

Except in connection with consular services an officer in charge of foreign interests does not generally sign official documents on behalf of the protected power.   Occasionally, however, a diplomatic officer may be called upon to sign a document for a foreign state either in conjunction with the formal protection of the interests of that state or as an isolated good office not involving other protective duties.   As an instance of the former it may be noted that the French Ambassador at Washington, who was in charge of Spanish interests during the Spanish-American War, signed as a plenipotentiary of Spain the initial protocol of peace terms and suspension of hostilities.[12]   As an example of the occasional signature of documents as a good office not involving other protective functions, it may be observed that the Russian delegates to the Hague Conference of 1907 signed the conventions on behalf of Montenegro and that in 1946 the American Chargé d'Affaires ad interim at Rome was authorized to sign a protocol respecting the International Institute of Agriculture on behalf of Paraguay and Nicaragua.[13]

---

[9] *Ante,* pp. 51, 62.

[10] Cf. Borchard, *op. cit.,* pp. 471, 473.

[11] *Foreign Service Regulations,* chap. XII, sec. 5, n. 2.

[12] *Foreign Relations,* 1898, pp. 824–826.

[13] See, for example, the conventions respecting land warfare, Treaty Series 540, p. 12, and maritime warfare, Treaty Series 543, pp. 12–13; Secretary Byrnes to the Embassy in Paraguay, telegram no. 47, Mar. 13,

Last but not least, the officer in charge of foreign interests may be expected to engage in a certain amount of general protective activity respecting the nationals of the protected power within the state to which he is assigned or accredited. Such activity involves primarily efforts designed to prevent the protected nationals from being in any way victimized or persecuted or deprived of a fair hearing in court. Although the prisoners of war convention gives to the representative of the protecting power certain definite rights in connection with judicial proceedings against prisoners of war (which may by agreement be extended to civilian internees),[14] the status of the protecting power with respect to legal proceedings of any sort involving other nationals of the protected power in either war or peace has never been defined. Traditionally, however, the protecting power and its representatives have exerted themselves in such matters, although the exact degree of assistance has naturally varied in accordance with the circumstances in each case. In the protection of various European interests in Mexico after the downfall of Maximilian the American Minister successfully urged clemency for certain European notables who had been associated with the ill-fated Emperor of Mexico.[15] In the protection of British interests in Bolivia at the turn of the present century American officers used their influence to expedite fair trials for several British subjects who had been held unduly long by local authorities on questionable charges.[16] In connection with the protection of Netherland interests in Persia from 1921 to 1927 the United States, although it specifically denied any responsibility for the "exercise of judicial functions on behalf of Dutch nationals",

---

1946, MS., file 501.SA/3–946; Secretary Byrnes to the Embassy in Nicaragua, telegram no. 74, Mar. 13, 1946, MS., file 561.A1/3–1146.

[14] Prisoners of war convention, arts. 60–66.

[15] *Ante,* p. 35.

[16] *Ante,* p. 75.

became involved in such a case by the very nature of its position as protecting power, complicated by the capitulatory privileges which Netherland subjects then enjoyed in Persia.[17] During World War II American officers in charge of Canadian interests were instructed to act in accordance with the following statement from the Canadian authorities:

It is assumed that, in determining what action should be taken in the case of arrest or detention of a Canadian national, the United States representative on the spot will take into consideration the attendant circumstances and the nature of the charges. It would be expected, for example, that he would go much further in providing protection to a Canadian national arrested on political charges than to one arrested and charged with an ordinary criminal offence.[18]

There are two definite limitations which determine just how far an officer in charge of foreign interests may proceed in such matters even in the most meritorious cases and under the most favorable circumstances. Since it is not a function of the diplomatic or consular officer to act as a lawyer or attorney for the nationals of his own country, it follows that he should not act in such capacity on behalf of the nationals of a foreign state temporarily under his protection.[19] Secondly, in bringing to the attention of the authorities of the local power any instances of apparent miscarriage of justice or harsh treatment involving a protected national the officer must not go so far as to jeopardize his own prestige in the eyes of the local power or to involve his own government by an official representation. While remaining within these limitations, he may still have opportunity for a wide range of activities in such cases. He may help

[17] *Ante*, p. 106.
[18] Secretary Hull to the Legation in Switzerland, circular telegram no. 203, Sept. 20, 1941, MS., file 351.4215/365.
[19] *Foreign Service Regulations*, chap. X, sec. 3; 22 U.S.C. 106–108; *Règlement consulaire suisse*, arts. 47, 50; *General Instructions to His Majesty's Consular Officers*, chap. V, arts. 31–34; Hyde, *op. cit.*, vol. II, p. 1367.

to obtain for the protected national competent legal assistance, and may give him friendly advice respecting his situation and possible courses of action. He should certainly
report the matter to his own government for the information
of the protected power. If he feels that the case is very
meritorious he may informally intercede with the authorities of the local power in an endeavor to bring about an
examination or reexamination of the matter by responsible
officials.[20] The history of the protection of foreign interests
indicates that while matters of this sort must be handled
with great tact, no protecting power would expect its representatives to allow considerations of discretion or expediency to stultify their efforts to maintain those international
concepts of justice and humanity which constitute at once
the origin and the goal of the practice of protecting foreign
interests.

---

[20] Such intercession may be made through the usual diplomatic or
political channels but not direct to courts.   (See the case of the *Gul
Djemal* in Hackworth, *op. cit.,* vol. IV, p. 498.)   For a typical example
of effective intercession by the representative of a protecting power
during World War II, see Assistant Secretary Long to the Minister to
Switzerland (Harrison), no. 1663, Feb. 3, 1943, MS., file 371.1121
Brown, James/15.

APPENDICES

APPENDIX I

Foreign Interests Protected by the United States in World War I

An official tabulation as of February 14, 1916

(Division of Information, Series M, No. 79, 1916)

Place	Protected power	Date of assumption of charge
AUSTRIA-HUNGARY [1] . .	France	August 5, 1914
	Great Britain . . .	August 13, 1914
	Italy	May 24, 1915
	Japan	August 25, 1914
	San Marino . . .	October 4, 1915
At Budapest [2]	France	August 12, 1914
	Great Britain . . .	August 13, 1914
	(Canada) . . .	August 14, 1914
	Italy	May 24, 1915
	Japan	September 7, 1914
	Russia	August 7, 1914
	Servia	August 7, 1914
At Carlsbad [2]	France	August 14, 1914
	Great Britain . . .	August 6, 1914
	Russia	August 1, 1914
	Servia	September 22, 1914
At Fiume [2]	France	August 5, 1914
	Great Britain . .	August 14, 1914
	Japan	September 3, 1914
	Montenegro . . .	August 11, 1914
	Russia	September 8, 1914
	Servia	August 11, 1914

[1] In charge of diplomatic interests.   [2] In charge of consular interests.

243

Place	Protected power	Date of assumption of charge
AUSTRIA-HUNGARY—Con.		
At Prague [2]	France	August 13, 1914
	Great Britain . . .	August 15, 1914
	Russia	August 6, 1914
At Reichenberg [2] . . .	France	August 17, 1914
	Great Britain . . .	August 14, 1914
	Japan	September 3, 1914
	Russia	August 9, 1914
At Trieste [2]	France	August 13, 1914
	Great Britain . . .	August 14, 1914
	Japan	September 6, 1914
	Russia	August 7, 1914
	Servia	August 7, 1914
At Vienna [2]	Great Britain . . .	October 23, 1914
BELGIUM [1]	Austria-Hungary .	August 10, 1914
	Denmark.	September 26, 1914
	Germany	August 10, 1914
	Great Britain . . .	August 19, 1914
	Japan	September 26, 1914
	Servia	September 26, 1914
At Antwerp [2]	Great Britain . . .	October 7, 1914
	Japan	October 7, 1914
At Ghent [2]	Great Britain . .	October 29, 1914
In the Congo [2]	Germany.	September 14, 1914
BULGARIA [1]	Great Britain . .	October 16, 1915
CHINA [3].	Switzerland . . .	May 18, 1915
At Canton [2]	Switzerland . . .	June 3, 1915

[1] In charge of diplomatic interests.
[2] In charge of consular interests.
[3] Exercising good offices.

Place	Protected power	Date of assumption of charge
CHINA—Continued		
At Harbin [2]	Germany	August 6, 1914
	Turkey	April 9, 1915
At Newchwang [2] . . .	Germany	August 25, 1914
At Swatow [2]	Netherlands . . .	July 12, 1915
COLOMBIA		
At Barranquilla [2] . . .	Venezuela	December 4, 1914
DOMINICAN REPUBLIC		
At Macoris [2]	Great Britain . .	August 10, 1914
FRANCE [1]	Austria-Hungary .	August 11, 1914
	Germany	August 3, 1914
	Guatemala . . .	September 9, 1914
	Nicaragua	August 27, 1914
	Servia	September 3, 1914
	Turkey	November 7, 1914
At Algiers [2]	Turkey	November 9, 1914
At Bordeaux [2]	Turkey	November 15, 1914
At Dunkirk [2]	Roumania	April 20 and January 11, 1915
In Guadeloupe	Germany	November 21, 1914
At Havre [2]	Turkey	November 7, 1914
At Lyon [2]	Turkey	November 15, 1914
In Martinique	Germany	September 10, 1914
At Nantes [2]	Turkey	November 15, 1914
At Nice [2]	Austria-Hungary .	August 6, 1914
	Germany	August 6, 1914
	Turkey	November 15, 1914
At Paris [2]	Turkey	November 15, 1914
At Rouen [2]	Austria-Hungary .	September 1, 1914
	Germany	September 1, 1914
	Turkey	November 15, 1914
At Saigon, Cochin China.[2]	Austria-Hungary .	August 17, 1914
	Germany	August 7, 1914

[1] In charge of diplomatic interests.
[2] In charge of consular interests.

Place	Protected power	Date of assumption of charge
FRANCE—Continued		
At Tahiti [2]	Germany	November 17, 1914
At Tamatave, Madagascar.[2]	Germany	November 17, 1914
At Tunis [2]	Germany	August 31, 1914
GERMANY [1]	France where Spain not in charge.	August 11, 1914
	Great Britain . . .	August 5, 1914
	(Canada) . . .	August 14, 1914
	Japan	August 20, 1914
	San Marino . . .	October 4, 1915
	Servia	August 31, 1914
At Apia, Samoa [2] . . .	France	August 10, 1914
	Great Britain . . .	August 5, 1914
	Germany	October 22, 1914
At Berlin [2]	Great Britain . . .	August 10, 1914
At Hamburg [2]	Panama	September 29, 1914
At Tsingtau, China [2] . .	France	August 11, 1914
	Great Britain . . .	August 5, 1914
	Russia	August 3, 1914
GREAT BRITAIN [1] . . .	Austria-Hungary .	August 14, 1914
	Germany	August 14, 1914
	Turkey	November 5, 1914
In Australia—	Austria-Hungary .	August 9, 1914
	Germany	August 7, 1914
At Melbourne [2] . . .	Turkey	November 15, 1914
At Sydney [2]	Germany.	August 7, 1914
	Turkey	November 15, 1914
In British Africa—		
At Bloemfontein [2] . .	Austria-Hungary .	August 13, 1914
	Turkey	November 9, 1914

[1] In charge of diplomatic interests.
[2] In charge of consular interests.

Place	Protected power	Date of assumption of charge
GREAT BRITAIN—Con.		
In British Africa—Con.		
At Capetown [2]	Austria-Hungary .	August 17, 1914
	Germany.	August 8, 1914
	Turkey	November 15, 1914
At Durban, Natal [2]. .	Austria-Hungary .	August 14, 1914
	Germany.	August 9, 1914
At Johannesburg [2] . .	Austria-Hungary .	August 20, 1914
	Switzerland . . .	October 6, 1914
	Turkey	November 9, 1914
At Port Elizabeth [2] . .	Austria-Hungary .	August 18, 1914
At Zanzibar [2]	Germany.	August 5, 1914
	Italy	August 5, 1914
In Canada—		
At Calgary [2].	Germany.	October 16, 1914
At Campbellton [2] . .	Germany.	November 21, 1914
At Charlottetown [2] . .	Germany.	November 21, 1914
At Cornwall [2]	Germany.	November 21, 1914
At Dawson [2].	Germany.	November 21, 1914
At Fernie [2]	Germany.	November 21, 1914
At Fort Erie [2]	Germany.	November 21, 1914
At Halifax [2]	Germany.	November 21, 1914
At Hamilton, Ontario [2]	Germany.	November 21, 1914
At Kingston, Ontario [2]	Germany.	November 21, 1914
At Moncton [2]	Germany.	November 21, 1914
At Montreal [2]	Germany.	August 7, 1914
At Niagara Falls [2] . .	Germany.	November 21, 1914
At Orillia [2]	Germany.	November 21, 1914
At Ottawa [2]	Germany.	November 21, 1914
At Prescott [2].	Germany.	November 21, 1914
At Quebec [2].	Germany.	November 21, 1914
At Rimouski [2]	Germany.	November 21, 1914
At St. John, N. B.[2] . .	Germany.	November 21, 1914
At St. John's, Quebec [2].	Germany.	November 21, 1914
At St. Stephen [2] . . .	Germany.	November 21, 1914
At Sarnia [2]	Germany.	November 21, 1914

[2] In charge of consular interests.

Place	Protected power	Date of assumption of charge
GREAT BRITAIN—Con.		
In Canada—Continued		
At Sault Ste. Marie [2] .	Germany.	November 21, 1914
At Sherbrooke [2] . . .	Germany.	November 21, 1914
At Sydney, N. S.[2] . .	Germany.	November 21, 1914
At Toronto [2]	Germany.	August 27, 1914
At Vancouver [2] . . .	Austria-Hungary .	August 17, 1914
	Germany.	August 6, 1914
At Victoria [2]	Germany.	November 21, 1914
At Windsor [2]	Germany.	November 21, 1914
At Winnipeg [2]	Germany	November 21, 1914
At Yarmouth [2]	Germany.	November 21, 1914
In the United Kingdom . .	Turkey	November 5, 1914
At Belfast [2]	Turkey	November 14, 1914
At Birmingham [2] . . .	Turkey	November 14, 1914
At Cardiff [2]	Turkey	November 14, 1914
At Glasgow [2]	Turkey	November 14, 1914
At Hull [2]	Turkey	November 15, 1914
At Liverpool [2]	Germany.	August 5, 1914
At London [2].	Turkey	November 14, 1914
At Manchester [2] . . .	Turkey	November 13, 1914
At Newcastle [2]. . . .	Turkey	November 14, 1914
At Plymouth [2]	Turkey	November 14, 1914
At Sheffield [2]	Turkey	November 14, 1914
At Southampton [2] . .	Turkey	November 14, 1914
At Swansea [2]	Turkey	November 8, 1914
In Other British Colonies—		
At Aden, Arabia [2] . .	Germany.	August 13, 1914
At Apia, Samoa [2]. . .	Germany.	October 22, 1914
At Belize, B. H.[2] . . .	Austria-Hungary .	August 25, 1914
	Germany.	November 21, 1914
At Bombay, India [2] .	Austria-Hungary .	August 22, 1914
	Germany.	August 3, 1914
	Switzerland. . . .	August 22, 1914
	Turkey	October 9, 1914

[2] In charge of consular interests.

Place	Protected power	Date of assumption of charge
GREAT BRITAIN—Con. *In Other British Colonies—* Continued		
At Bridgetown, Barbados.[2]	Austria- Hungary .	September 3, 1914
At Calcutta [2]	Austria-Hungary .	August 17, 1914
	Germany.	November 17, 1914
In Ceylon [2]	Austria-Hungary .	August 10, 1914
	Germany.	August 10, 1914
	Turkey	November 13, 1914
At Colombo, Ceylon [2].	Turkey	November 14, 1914
At Georgetown, British Guiana.[2]	Germany.	November 17, 1914
At Gibraltar [2]	Germany.	October 24, 1914
	Turkey	November 15, 1914
At Hamilton, Bermuda.[2]	Germany.	November 17, 1914
At Hongkong [2]. . . .	Austria-Hungary .	August 18, 1914
	Germany.	August 8, 1914
At Karachi [2]	Germany.	November 17, 1914
At Madras, India [2] .	Austria-Hungary .	August 19, 1914
	Germany	August 13, 1914
	Turkey	November 7, 1914
At Malta, Maltese Islands.[2]	Germany	November 17, 1914
	Roumania	September 17, 1914
	Turkey	November 9, 1914
At Nassau, N. P., Bahamas.[2]	Germany	November 21, 1914
	Norway	August 3, 1915
At Penang, Straits Settlements.[2]	Austria-Hungary .	August 17, 1914
	Germany	August 10, 1914
At Port Antonio, Jamaica.[2]	Germany	November 21, 1914
At Rangoon, India [2] .	Germany	August 14, 1914
	Turkey	November 15, 1914
At St. John's, N. F.[2] .	Germany	November 21, 1914

[2] In charge of consular interests.

Place	Protected power	Date of assumption of charge
GREAT BRITAIN—Con.		
In Other British Colonies—		
Continued		
At Sandakan, Br. North Borneo.[2]	Germany	November 17, 1914
At Singapore, Straits Settlements.[2]	Austria-Hungary .	August 17, 1914
	Brazil	December 14, 1914
	Germany	August 8, 1914
	Spain	October 17, 1914
	Switzerland . . .	October 6, 1914
	Turkey	November 15, 1914
At Turks Island, Bahamas.[2]	Germany	December 11, 1914
GREECE		
At Saloniki [2]	Austria-Hungary .	December 31, 1915
	Bulgaria	December 31, 1915
	Germany	December 31, 1915
	Turkey	December 31, 1915
ITALY [1]	Norway	August 4, 1915
JAPAN [1]	Austria-Hungary .	August 18, 1914
	Germany	August 27, 1914
	Turkey	June 29, 1915
At Dairen, Manchuria [2] .	Germany	September 10, 1914
At Hakodate [2]	Norway	October 20, 1915
At Kobe [2]	Germany	August 26, 1914
	Switzerland . . .	September 8, 1914
At Nagasaki [2]	Germany	August 25, 1914
	Switzerland . . .	September 8, 1914
At Seoul, Korea [2] . . .	Germany	August 26, 1914
At Yokohama [2]	Austria-Hungary .	August 29, 1914
	Germany	August 27, 1914
LIBERIA [1]	Turkey	December 4, 1915

[1] In charge of diplomatic interests.
[2] In charge of consular interests.

Place	Protected power	Date of assumption of charge
MEXICO		
At Aguascalientes [2] . .	Turkey	January 9, 1915
At Chihuahua [2]	Turkey	January 9, 1915
At Ciudad Juarez [2] . .	Turkey	January 9, 1915
At Durango [2]	Turkey	January 9, 1915
At Ensenada [2]	Turkey	January 9, 1915
At Frontera [2]	Turkey	January 9, 1915
At Guadalajara [2] . . .	Turkey	January 9, 1915
At Hermosillo [2]	Turkey	January 9, 1915
At Manzanillo [2]	Turkey	January 9, 1915
At Matamoros [2]	Turkey	January 9, 1915
At Mexico City [2] . . .	Turkey	January 9, 1915
At Monterey [2]	Turkey	January 9, 1915
At Nogales [2]	Turkey	January 9, 1915
At Nuevo Laredo [2] . . .	Turkey	January 9, 1915
At Piedras Negras [2] . .	Turkey	January 9, 1915
At Progreso [2]	Turkey	January 9, 1915
At San Luis Potosi [2] . .	Turkey	January 9, 1915
At Tampico [2]	Turkey	January 9, 1915
At Vera Cruz [2]	Turkey	January 9, 1915
MOROCCO [1]	Austria-Hungary .	September 9, 1915
	Germany	August 26, 1914
At Mogador [2]	Sweden	July 22, 1915
PERSIA		
At Tabriz [2]	Germany (temporarily).	September 7, 1914
PORTUGAL		
In Portuguese Angola [2] .	Germany	June 8, 1914
RUSSIA [1]	Austria-Hungary .	August 8, 1914
	Germany	August 5, 1914
At Batum [2]	Norway	November 19, 1914
	Turkey	October 30, 1914
At Petrograd	Austria-Hungary .	August 14, 1914

[1] In charge of diplomatic interests.
[2] In charge of consular interests.

Place	Protected power	Date of assumption of charge
RUSSIA—Continued		
At Riga	France	August 2, 1915
	Great Britain . . .	August 12, 1915
At Rostoff-on-Don . . .	Germany	April 13, 1915
At Vladivostok	Germany	November 17, 1914
At Warsaw	France	October 18, 1915
	Great Britain . . .	October 13, 1914
	Servia	October 17, 1914
SERVIA [1]	Austria-Hungary .	August 19, 1914
	Germany . . .	August 19, 1914
At Nish [2]	Austria-Hungary .	June 4, 1915
TURKEY [1]	Belgium	November 10, 1914
	France, except in Palestine.	October 31, 1914
	Great Britain . . .	November 2, 1914
	Italy	August 20, 1915
	Montenegro . . .	August 20, 1915
	Russia	August 20, 1915
	San Marino . . .	October 4, 1915
	Servia	November 2, 1914
	Switzerland . . .	November 14, 1914
At Aleppo [2]	Belgium	November 9, 1914
	France	November 3, 1914
	Great Britain . . .	November 1, 1914
	Servia	November 3, 1914
At Alexandretta [2] . . .	Belgium	November 9, 1914
	France	November 3, 1914
	Servia	November 3, 1914
At Alexandria [2]	Persia	May 25, 1915
At Bagdad [2]	Austria-Hungary .	June 29, 1915
	Norway	December 4, 1914
	Sweden	December 4, 1914
At Beirut [2]	Denmark	March 19, 1915
	Netherlands . . .	June 14, 1915

[1] In charge of diplomatic interests.
[2] In charge of consular interests.

Place	Protected power	Date of assumption of charge
TURKEY—Continued		
At Damascus [2].	Denmark.	November 27, 1914
	Greece.	November 14, 1914
At Haifa [2].	Netherlands . . .	March 24, 1915
At Jerusalem [2].	Italy.	June 17, 1915
	Russia	June 17, 1915
At Lebanon [2]	Uruguay	April 24, 1915
At Smyrna [2].	Great Britain . . .	November 5, 1914
	Italy.	August 4, 1915
	Russia	August 4, 1915
	Spain	August 30, 1915
At Trebizond [2].	Persia	December 31, 1914
In Tripoli [2]	Greece.	November 14, 1914
EGYPT [1]	Austria-Hungary .	May 25, 1915
	Brazil	September 18, 1914
	Germany.	September 4, 1914
	Salvador	January 27, 1915
	Switzerland. . . .	October 6, 1914

[1] In charge of diplomatic interests.
[2] In charge of consular interests.

APPENDIX II

Protection of Foreign Interests in World War I After the United States Became a Belligerent

(Based on unofficial data in Journal du droit international *(Clunet),
1918, vol. 45, pp. 161–162)*

Interests of	In	Protected by
France	Germany	Spain
	Belgium	Spain
	Bulgaria	Netherlands
	Turkey	Netherlands
	Austria	Switzerland
Great Britain	Germany	Netherlands
	Austria	Spain
	Turkey	Netherlands
Belgium	Bulgaria	Netherlands
	Germany	Spain
	Austria	Spain
	Turkey	Sweden
United States	Germany	Spain
	Austria	Spain
	Belgium	Spain
	Turkey	Sweden
Brazil	Germany	Switzerland
Italy	Germany	Switzerland
	Austria	Switzerland
	Belgium	Spain
	Turkey	Spain
	Bulgaria	Netherlands
Russia	Belgium	Spain
	Austria	Spain
	Germany	Spain
	Bulgaria	Netherlands
	Turkey	Netherlands

Interests of	In	Protected by
Serbia	Germany	Spain
	Austria	Spain
	Bulgaria	Netherlands
	Turkey	Sweden
Rumania	Germany	Spain
	Bulgaria	Spain
	Turkey	Spain
	Austria	Switzerland
Portugal	Germany	Spain
	Austria	Spain
	Bulgaria	Spain
	Belgium	Spain
Montenegro	Rumania	Spain
	Turkey	Spain
Guatemala	Germany	Spain
Japan	Germany	Spain
	Austria	Spain
	Belgium	Spain
	Bulgaria	No protecting power
	Turkey	No protecting power
Cuba	Germany	Spain
China	Germany	Netherlands
Austria	United States	Sweden
	British Empire	Sweden
	France	Switzerland
	Italy	Switzerland and Spain
	Rumania	Switzerland
	Greece	Spain
	Portugal	Spain
	Japan	Spain
	Morocco	Netherlands
	Egypt	Netherlands
	Russia	Denmark

Interests of	In	Protected by
Germany	United States . . .	Switzerland
	Great Britain . . .	Switzerland
	France	Switzerland
	Italy	Switzerland
	Rumania	Switzerland
	Tunis	Switzerland
	Cuba	Spain
	Portugal	Spain
	Guatemala	Spain
	Panama	Spain
	Gibraltar	Spain
	Porto Rico	Spain
	Hawaiian Islands . .	Spain
	China	Netherlands
	Morocco	Netherlands
	Tangier	Netherlands
	Brazil	Netherlands
	Greece	Netherlands
	Indo-China	Netherlands
	Russia	Sweden
	Egypt	Sweden
Bulgaria	Great Britain . . .	Sweden
	France	Spain
	Italy	Spain
	Rumania·	Switzerland
	Russia	No protecting power
Turkey	Great Britain . . .	Sweden
	France	Spain
	Italy	Spain
	Russia	Spain

APPENDIX III

Partial List of Foreign Interests Protected by the United States During the Period Between the World Wars[1]

Interests of	Place	Approximate dates
Argentina	Rangoon	1915–1923
	Saigon	1923–1925
Belgium	Tripoli	1936
Bolivia	Calcutta	1930–1932
Brazil	Singapore	1914–1930
	Colombo	1914–1929
	Peking	1924
	Saigon	1923–1925
	Valencia	1936–1939
Bulgaria	Athens	1920–1922
Chile	Calcutta	1930–1932
China	Colombia	Since about 1929
	Dominican Republic .	Since about 1930
	Ecuador	Since about 1908
	Haiti	Since about 1918
	Honduras	Since about 1924
	Venezuela	Since about 1936
	Chile	1909–1922
	Guatemala	1920–1934

[1] A complete tabulation of all foreign interests protected by the United States during the period between the two World Wars would require many pages. A large number of these instances, however, were of short duration or consisted merely of retaining custody of small amounts of property without the performance of any other protective functions. Many such cases have been eliminated from the above list, which is designed to be illustrative rather than definitive. The data have been derived from an informal tabulation based on official materials in the Department of State, but the dates of assumption and termination are only approximate for a number of listings. As indicated by the large number of consular posts in this list, the great majority of these instances involved consular rather than diplomatic services.

Interests of	Place	Approximate dates
Colombia	Saigon	1922–1925
	Bolivia	1935–1936
	Peru	1933–1935
Costa Rica	Saigon	1923–1925
	Montreal	1930
Cuba	Tirana	
	Algiers	
	Saigon	
	Tehran	
	Baghdad	
	Monrovia	
	Wellington	
	Bangkok	Intermittently or on a
	Cartagena	continuing basis
	Singapore	since about 1899
	Rangoon	
	Alexandria	
	Malta	
	Tangier	
	Georgetown	
	Soerabaya	
	Batavia	
Denmark	Maracaibo	1906–1922
	Bangkok	1927–1929
	Hankow	1927–1928
Dominican Republic .	Rangoon	1916–1925
	Montevideo	1920–1924
France	Port Limon	1918–1921
Germany	Barbados	Taken over at out-
	Belize	break of World War
	Kingston	I; not clearly relin-
	Trinidad	quished until 1924–
		1927
Great Britain	Constanza	1922
	Martinique	1924
	Honduras	1924
	Dominican Republic (Puerto Plata)	1927–1928

Interests of	Place	Approximate dates
Hungary	Dominican Republic.	1925
	Haiti	1925
	Hong Kong	1924–1935
	Costa Rica	1924–1936
	Guatemala	1926
	Honduras	1925
Iran	Karachi	1928–1929
Italy	Honduras	1924–1925
	Nairobi	1920–1925
Mexico	Caracas	1923–1933
Netherlands	Vera Cruz	1924–1925
	Iran	1921–1927
	Canton	1927
Norway	Maracaibo	1906–1924
	Barranquilla	1918–1924
	Tampico	1926
Panama	Algiers	
	Colombo	
	Belize	
	Shanghai	
	Tientsin	
	Chefoo	
	Alexandria	As of 1941; intermit-
	Port Said	tently or on a con-
	Bombay	tinuing basis at most
	Calcutta	of these posts since
	Karachi	before World War I
	Tehran	
	Dairen	
	Belfast	
	Jerusalem	
	Penang	
	Istanbul	
	Johannesburg	
Spain	Amoy	1926–1927
Sweden	Hong Kong	1922–1924
	Batavia	1927
	Peiping	1937

Interests of	Place	Approximate dates
Switzerland	Cairo	1914–1926
	Shanghai.	1921
	Kobe	1914–1925
	Nagasaki.	1916–1925
	Port Said	1920–1926
	Bangkok	1916–1932
Turkey	Malta	1914–1929
	Madras	1914–1923
Venezuela	Mexico City	1923–1933
	Georgetown	1923

APPENDIX IV

Belligerent Interests Protected by the United States in World War II

(Based on a tabulation prepared in May 1941 in the Special War Problems Division of the Department of State)

1. AMERICAN EMBASSY, Berlin (Covering Germany and German-occupied Poland, Bohemia, and Moravia):
   - (*a*) Great Britain, including India, overseas possessions, and mandated territories
   - (*b*) Australia
   - (*c*) New Zealand
   - (*d*) Canada
   - (*e*) France
   - (*f*) Belgium
   - (*g*) Luxembourg
   - (*h*) Union of South Africa

2. AMERICAN CONSULAR OFFICES IN BELGIUM:
   - (*a*) Great Britain, including overseas possessions
   - (*b*) Union of South Africa
   - (*c*) France
   - (*d*) Australia
   - (*e*) Canada
   - (*f*) Luxembourg
   - (*g*) New Zealand

3. AMERICAN CONSULAR OFFICES IN THE NETHERLANDS:
   - (*a*) Great Britain, including overseas possessions
   - (*b*) Australia
   - (*c*) Union of South Africa
   - (*d*) France
   - (*e*) Belgium
   - (*f*) Egypt
   - (*g*) Canada
   - (*h*) New Zealand

4. AMERICAN LEGATION, Copenhagen:
   - (a) Great Britain, including overseas possessions
   - (b) Australia
   - (c) Canada
   - (d) Union of South Africa
   - (e) France
   - (f) Belgium
   - (g) New Zealand

5. AMERICAN CONSULAR OFFICES IN NORWAY:
   - (a) Great Britain, including overseas possessions
   - (b) Australia
   - (c) Canada
   - (d) Union of South Africa
   - (e) France
   - (f) Belgium
   - (g) New Zealand

6. AMERICAN CONSULATE, Luxembourg:
   - (a) Belgium
   - (b) France
   - (c) Great Britain, including overseas possessions
   - (d) Canada
   - (e) New Zealand
   - (f) Union of South Africa
   - (g) Australia

7. OFFICE OF AMERICAN EMBASSY, Paris (for occupied France):
   - (a) Australia
   - (b) Belgium
   - (c) Great Britain, including overseas possessions
   - (d) Canada
   - (e) Luxembourg
   - (f) New Zealand
   - (g) Union of South Africa

8. AMERICAN EMBASSY, VICHY (for unoccupied France and Monaco):
   - (a) Australia
   - (b) Great Britain, including overseas possessions
   - (c) Canada
   - (d) New Zealand
   - (e) Belgium
   - (f) Luxembourg

9. AMERICAN EMBASSY, Rome:
   (a) Australia
   (b) Belgium
   (c) Great Britain, including overseas possessions
   (d) Canada
   (e) Egypt
   (f) France
   (g) New Zealand
   (h) Norway
   (i) Union of South Africa

10. AMERICAN CONSULATE, Lagos:
   (a) Italy

11. AMERICAN CONSULATE GENERAL, Casablanca:
   (a) Great Britain, including overseas possessions
   (b) Canada
   (c) New Zealand
   (d) Belgium
   (e) Australia

12. AMERICAN CONSULATE GENERAL, Algiers:
   (a) Great Britain, including overseas possessions
   (b) Canada
   (c) New Zealand
   (d) Australia
   (e) Belgium
   (f) Luxembourg

13. AMERICAN CONSULATE, Tunis:
   (a) Great Britain, including overseas possessions
   (b) Canada
   (c) New Zealand
   (d) Australia
   (e) Belgium

14. AMERICAN CONSULATE, Martinique:
   (a) Great Britain, including overseas possessions
   (b) Canada
   (c) New Zealand
   (d) Australia
   (e) Belgium

15. AMERICAN CONSULATE, Saigon:
    (a) Belgium

16. AMERICAN CONSULATE, Dakar:
    (a) Great Britain, including overseas possessions
    (b) Canada
    (c) New Zealand
    (d) Australia
    (e) Belgium

17. AMERICAN CONSULATE, Trinidad:
    (a) France

18. AMERICAN CONSULATE GENERAL, Beirut:
    (a) Belgium
    (b) Great Britain
    (c) New Zealand
    (d) Australia
    (e) Canada
    (f) Netherlands

19. AMERICAN LEGATION, Bucharest:
    (a) Great Britain, including overseas possessions
    (b) Canada
    (c) New Zealand
    (d) Australia
    (e) Union of South Africa
    (f) Belgium
    (g) Yugoslavia

20. AMERICAN LEGATION, Sofia:
    (a) Great Britain, including overseas possessions
    (b) Canada
    (c) New Zealand
    (d) Australia
    (e) Union of South Africa
    (f) Belgium
    (g) Netherlands
    (h) Yugoslavia
    (i) Greece
    (j) Luxembourg

21. AMERICAN LEGATION, Budapest:
   (a) Great Britain
   (b) Australia
   (c) Canada
   (d) Union of South Africa
   (e) Belgium
   (f) New Zealand
   (g) Yugoslavia

22. AMERICAN LEGATION, Athens:
   (a) Great Britain
   (b) Australia
   (c) Canada
   (d) Union of South Africa
   (e) Belgium
   (f) Egypt (provisionally)

23. AMERICAN CONSULATE, Salonika:
   (a) Great Britain
   (b) Australia
   (c) Canada
   (d) Union of South Africa
   (e) Yugoslavia
   (f) New Zealand

24. AMERICAN LEGATION, Belgrade:
   (a) Great Britain
   (b) New Zealand
   (c) Australia
   (d) Canada
   (e) Union of South Africa
   (f) France
   (g) Belgium
   (h) Egypt (provisionally)
   (i) Greece (provisionally)

25. AMERICAN EMBASSY, Moscow:
   (a) Belgium

APPENDIX V

Foreign Interests Relinquished by the United States to Switzerland in December 1941

(Based on Department of State press release no. 649, December 18, 1941)

AMERICAN LEGATION, Sofia:

(*a*) Great Britain, including overseas possessions
(*b*) Canada
(*c*) New Zealand
(*d*) Australia
(*e*) Union of South Africa
(*f*) Belgium
(*g*) Netherlands
(*h*) Yugoslavia
(*i*) Greece
(*j*) Luxembourg

AMERICAN EMBASSY, Berlin

(Covering Germany and German-occupied Poland, Bohemia, Moravia, Belgium, Netherlands, Norway, Luxembourg, Paris (for occupied France), Salonika, Belgrade):

(*a*) Great Britain, including India, overseas possessions, and mandated territories
(*b*) Australia
(*c*) New Zealand
(*d*) Canada
(*e*) France
(*f*) Belgium
(*g*) Luxembourg
(*h*) Union of South Africa
(*i*) Egypt
(*j*) Panama (at Brussels)
(*k*) Haiti
(*l*) Costa Rica

AMERICAN LEGATION, Budapest:
- (a) Great Britain
- (b) Australia
- (c) Canada
- (d) Union of South Africa
- (e) Belgium
- (f) New Zealand
- (g) Yugoslavia
- (h) Greece (custody of property only)

AMERICAN EMBASSY, Rome
(Covering Athens):
- (a) Australia
- (b) Belgium
- (c) Great Britain, including overseas possessions
- (d) Canada
- (e) Egypt
- (f) France
- (g) New Zealand
- (h) Union of South Africa
- (i) Norway
- (j) Haiti
- (k) Luxembourg

AMERICAN LEGATION, Bucharest:
- (a) Great Britain, including overseas possessions
- (b) Canada
- (c) New Zealand
- (d) Australia
- (e) Union of South Africa
- (f) Belgium
- (g) Yugoslavia
- (h) Greece
- (i) China (informal)

AMERICAN CONSULATE, Saigon:
- (a) Belgium
- (b) Yugoslavia
- (c) China
- (d) Cuba
- (e) Portugal

AMERICAN CONSULATE, Hanoi:
  (*a*) Belgium
  (*b*) Yugoslavia
  (*c*) China

AMERICAN LEGATION, Bangkok:
  (*a*) Cuba

AMERICAN CONSULATE, Chefoo:
  (*a*) Panama

AMERICAN CONSULATE, Dairen:
  (*a*) Panama

AMERICAN CONSULATE GENERAL, Shanghai:
  (*a*) Panama

AMERICAN CONSULATE GENERAL, Tientsin:
  (*a*) Panama

AMERICAN CONSULATE, Lagos:
  (*a*) Italy

APPENDIX VI

Foreign Interests Protected by the United States as of January 1944

(From the Department of State Bulletin, *March 18, 1944, pp. 268–269)*

A. DIPLOMATIC AND CONSULAR REPRESENTATION:
> Of Australian interests in—
>> Finland
>> French Guiana
>> Martinique and Guadeloupe
> Of Belgian interests in—
>> Finland
>> French Guiana
>> Martinique and Guadeloupe
> Of Brazilian interests in—
>> International Zone of Tangier
> Of British interests in—
>> Finland
>> French Guiana
>> Martinique and Guadeloupe
> Of Canadian interests in—
>> Finland
>> French Guiana
>> Martinique and Guadeloupe
> Of Costa Rican interests in—
>> Sweden (consular services not performed in connection with such representation since Costa Rica maintains consular offices in Sweden)
> Of Cuban interests in—
>> International zone of Tangier
> Of Haitian interests in—
>> Finland
>> Great Britain
>> Ireland
>> Portugal

A. DIPLOMATIC AND CONSULAR REPRESENTATION—Continued

Of Haitian interests in—Continued

    Spain

    Sweden

    Turkey (not yet definitive)

Of New Zealand interests in—

    Finland

    French Guiana

    Martinique and Guadeloupe

Of South African interests in—

    Finland

Of Swiss interests at—

    Barbados, West Indies

    Hamilton, Bermuda

    Nassau, Bahamas

Of Yugoslav interests in—

    Aden, Arabia (consular district of)

    Finland

    French Guiana

    Martinique and Guadeloupe

B. PERFORMANCE OF CONSULAR SERVICES ONLY:

For Cuba at—

    Algiers, Algeria

    Tehran, Iran

    Baghdad, Iraq

    Monrovia, Liberia

    Wellington, New Zealand

For Haiti in—

    Kingston, Jamaica (consular district of)

For Panama at—

    Algiers, Algeria

    Belize, British Honduras

    Colombo, Ceylon

    Alexandria, Egypt

    Port Said, Egypt

    Suez, Egypt

    Bombay, India

    Calcutta, India

    Karachi, India

    Tehran, Iran

    Belfast, Northern Ireland

B. PERFORMANCE OF CONSULAR SERVICES ONLY—Continued

> For Panama at—Continued
>> Jerusalem, Palestine
>> Istanbul, Turkey
>> Johannesburg, Union of South Africa
>
> For Peru at—
>> Corumbá, Brazil

C. EXTENSION OF GOOD OFFICES:

> For China in—
>> Colombia
>> Dominican Republic
>> Ecuador
>> Haiti
>> Honduras
>> Venezuela
>
> For Colombia at—
>> Istanbul, Turkey (occasional services for Colombian nationals when requested by Colombian Government through Department)
>
> For Iceland at—
>> Algiers, Algeria ⎫ occasional services for Icelandic na-
>> Chungking, China ⎬ tionals when requested by Icelandic
>> Tehran, Iran ⎭ Government through Department
>
> For the Netherlands at—
>> Cartagena, Colombia (issuance of bills of health to ships proceeding to certain Netherlands ports)
>> Cayenne, French Guiana
>
> For Switzerland in—
>> Tahiti (occasional services for Swiss nationals when requested by Swiss Legation, Washington, through Department)
>> Afghanistan (Swiss nationals may, if they so desire, apply to American Legation, Kabul, for protection)

D. CHANNEL OF COMMUNICATION WITH SWISS GOVERNMENT IN CONNECTION WITH REPRESENTATION BY SWITZERLAND OF THE INTERESTS IN ENEMY TERRITORY OF:

> Costa Rica
> El Salvador
> Guatemala
> Honduras
> Nicaragua

APPENDIX VII

Powers Protecting Enemy Interests in the United States During World War II

Belligerent	Protecting power	Belligerent	Protecting power
Bulgaria	Switzerland	Japan (in American Samoa).	Switzerland
Germany	Switzerland		
Hungary	Sweden	Japan (in Territory of Hawaii).	Sweden
Italy	Switzerland		
Japan (in continental United States)		Rumania	Sweden
Until March 1945	Spain		
After June 1945.	Switzerland		

APPENDIX VIII

Foreign Interests Protected by Switzerland as of December 1942

(From the Rapport du Conseil Fédéral sur sa gestion en 1942, *pp. 18–19)*

GERMANY:

In the United States of America, the British Empire [with the exception of the Union of South Africa, Rhodesia and Palestine], Haiti, the Netherlands West Indies, Iraq, Syria and Lebanon.

UNITED STATES OF AMERICA:

In Germany, Bulgaria, Denmark, Hungary, Indo-China, Italy, Japan and occupied China, Rumania, Thailand, France.

BRAZIL:

In Denmark.

BULGARIA:

In the United States of America, Egypt, the British Empire.

COLOMBIA:

In Germany, France, Italy, Japan.

COSTA RICA:

In Germany.

CUBA:

In Germany, France, Italy, Japan.

DOMINICAN REPUBLIC:

In Germany, Italy, Japan.

EGYPT:

In Germany, Bulgaria, Finland, France, Hungary, Italy, Japan, Rumania.

BRITISH EMPIRE:

In Germany, Bulgaria, occupied China, France, Hungary, Indo-China, Italy, Japan, Rumania, Thailand.

ECUADOR:

In Germany, Italy.

FRANCE:
In South Africa, the United States of America, Egypt, Iran.

GUATEMALA:
In Germany, France, Italy, Japan.

HAITI:
In Germany, France, Italy.

IRAN:
In Germany, France, Italy.

ITALY:
In the United States of America, Brazil, Egypt, the British Empire [with the exception of Canada, British India, Somaliland and the Sudan], Haiti, Iran, Mexico, Nicaragua, Syria and Lebanon, Venezuela.

JAPAN:
In Egypt, Great Britain, the following British colonies: the Fiji Islands and other Possessions in the Western Pacific, Kenya, Uganda, Tanganyika and Zanzibar. In the Dominions of Australia and New Zealand. In the Dutch West Indies. In the American Possessions in the Pacific.

NICARAGUA:
In Germany, Italy, Japan.

PANAMA:
In Germany, Italy, Japan and occupied China.

NETHERLANDS:
In occupied China.

PERU:
In Germany, Italy.

RUMANIA:
In Egypt.

EL SALVADOR:
In Germany, Italy.

THAILAND:
In the British Empire, the Dutch West Indies.

URUGUAY:
In Germany, Hungary, Italy.

VENEZUELA:
In Germany, Italy, Japan.

APPENDIX IX

Foreign Interests Protected by Sweden as of June 1944

(Based on an official tabulation in the Department of State)

Interests of	Protected in	Interests of	Protected in
Argentina	Japan	Japan—Con.	Hawaii
	Germany		Union of South
Belgium	Japan		Africa
	Thailand	China	Denmark
Bolivia	Japan	Mexico	Germany
Bulgaria	Iran		Italy
Denmark	Union of Soviet		Japan
	Socialist Re-	Netherlands	Denmark
	publics		Germany
Finland	Union of Soviet		Italy
	Socialist Re-		France (unoc-
	publics		cupied)
	Great Britain		Rumania
	Egypt		Hungary
Greece	Germany		Finland
Honduras	Japan		Japan
Iran	Bulgaria		Thailand
	Rumania	Norway	Denmark
	Hungary		France (unoc-
Iceland	Germany		cupied)
	Italy		Thailand
Japan	India	Rumania	Great Britain
	Ceylon		United States
	Burma		Brazil

Interests of	Protected in	Interests of	Protected in
Slovakia	Union of Soviet Socialist Republics Iran	Germany	France (colonies and mandates except Morocco)
Union of Soviet Socialist Republics	Germany Hungary Slovakia Denmark Finland Rumania Italy France (unoccupied)		Egypt Iceland Iran Mexico
		Hungary	Great Britain Iran United States Egypt Brazil Paraguay Uruguay

APPENDIX X

Foreign Interests Protected by Spain
as of June 1944

(Based on an official tabulation in the Department of State)

Interests of	Protected in	Interests of	Protected in
Germany	Bolivia	Japan—Con.	El Salvador
	Brazil		Venezuela
	Colombia		Bolivia
	Costa Rica		Paraguay
	Cuba		Brazil
	Dominican Republic		Peru
		Rumania	Palestine
	Ecuador	France	Palestine
	Guatemala	Italy	Algeria
	Honduras		Bolivia
	Nigeria		Morocco (Casablanca)
	Palestine		
	Panama		Gibraltar
	Paraguay		India
	Peru		Palestine
	El Salvador		Paraguay
	Union of South Africa		Peru
			Uruguay
	Uruguay		Ecuador
	Venezuela		Costa Rica
Japan	Canada		Cuba
	Colombia		Guatemala
	Cuba		Panama
	Ecuador		El Salvador
	United States		French West Africa (Dakar)
	Panama		

APPENDIX XI

Payment of Financial Assistance to American Nationals Through Swiss Representatives in World War II

(Enclosure to the Circular Instruction from the Secretary of State to all American Diplomatic and Consular Officers, Foreign Service Serial no. 109, dated January 22, 1944, MS., file 340.1115A/3344B)

1. To lighten the burden of work and the expense involved in making individual payments, whether from official relief or pension funds or from private funds, to American nationals in territories where the interests of the United States are represented by Switzerland, the United States Government proposes that Swiss representatives charged with such representation make no distinction between the several kinds of payments in advancing funds to American nationals found to be in need. All such American nationals able to qualify for financial assistance in accordance with the rules hereinafter stated will be entitled to receive from the Swiss representatives monthly payments corresponding to their established needs up to the maxima hereinafter set forth in a tentatively established scale. From time to time, the scale will be revised upward or downward upon the basis of such recommendations as may be made by Swiss representatives charged with the representation of the interests of the United States. It would be of great assistance to the Department if upon recommending increases in the maxima, the Swiss representatives would furnish cost of living statistics (current market prices) showing in each instance the rise in the cost of staples in comparison with a previous period. All recipients, with the exceptions specified below, will be limited to the maximum monthly payments for their place of residence, regardless of their ability to repay to this Government amounts greater than the sums advanced. Furthermore, the financial assistance herein authorized is intended entirely to supplant the transfer of any other funds to the American nationals concerned. It is realized that a limitation upon the amount that American nations may expend in enemy territory, even from their own resources, will entail some hard-

ship. The conservation of foreign exchange, however, is an essential factor in the present economic policy of the United States and it is expected that Americans everywhere will willingly share with those in the armed forces the sacrifices that must be made in winning the war.

2. The maxima may be exceeded to meet such extraordinary expenditures as may be essential to the health or safety of American nationals for medical, surgical, or dental care, for hospitalization, for reasonable legal defense against political or criminal charges, or for a decent though modest burial where such is not provided by friends or relatives nor by the local authorities. This paragraph may be interpreted to cover also reasonable rental charges for graves, burial niches, or other repositories of the ashes or remains of American nationals in enemy territory, provided that the payment of such charges is essential to the undisturbed tenure of such places of burial. Payment should be made only after submission of each case for approval by the Department, which will notify the nearest of kin if names and addresses are furnished and will authorize payment if the necessary funds are deposited with the Department. Subject likewise to the approval of the Department in each instance, such charges may be paid to protect the places of burial of stateless persons closely related to American nationals able to establish that they have previously paid such charges.

3. Payments should be made against receipts in quadruplicate embodying promises to repay without interest the sums advanced. With respect to mentally deficient American nationals, it is presumed that their guardians or members of their families will usually be able to execute the receipt forms. It is desirable that the receipts, of which a specimen is transmitted herewith, be plainly marked, "Original", "Duplicate", "Triplicate", and "Quadruplicate". The original and duplicate should be forwarded to the Department, the triplicate retained by the Legation, and the quadruplicate retained by the Swiss Government or its representatives, as the Swiss Government may determine. It is suggested that receipt forms be printed in small type and on lightweight paper. Their cost is a proper charge against the funds of the United States Government. It is assumed that the Swiss Government will have such forms printed in Switzerland, but they may also be printed locally, wherever it may prove impracticable for Swiss representatives to procure the forms from Switzerland.

4. Receipts should indicate the evidence of American nationality borne by recipients of payments and the names and addresses of per-

sons, firms, or organizations, if any, to whom the United States Government may look for reimbursement of the sums advanced. Recipients of payments may attach to the original receipt, checks, or other negotiable instruments payable to the Treasurer of the United States, in amounts that cover partially or fully the sums received, upon the understanding that the obligation to repay such sums will not be discharged until the Treasurer of the United States actually receives full repayment in legal tender of the United States.

5. The Department will inform interested persons in the United States of its willingness to accept private deposits to be used either to reimburse the Government for sums advanced to American nationals in territories where the interests of the United States are represented by Switzerland, or to be held as a reserve against which such advances may be charged upon the receipt of evidence of payment to beneficiaries. Such deposits will be held by the Department until the receipts of the beneficiaries are received in the Department. The receipts (and the promissory notes embodied in them) will thereupon be canceled and forwarded to the depositors of the funds, and sums corresponding to the amounts shown by the receipts to have been advanced will at the same time be transferred from the special deposits to the credit of the Treasurer of the United States. If any private deposit is insufficient to discharge in full the obligation of a beneficiary in whose behalf the deposit is made it will be applied against the indebtedness, the promissory note will be appropriately endorsed, and the depositor so informed. Notes accompanied by negotiable instruments will be canceled upon the receipt by the Treasurer of the United States in legal tender of the United States of full repayment of the sums advanced and will then be held in the Department's files at the disposition of the payer. Notes not redeemed in any of the above-mentioned ways will be held until eventually repaid by the actual recipients of the sums advanced.

6. Swiss representatives charged with the representation of the interests of the United States may explain to the recipients that the financial assistance herein provided should not be considered as public bounty but as loans from public funds to American nationals finding themselves in an abnormal position by reason of the war. It is accordingly expected, as already indicated, that all sums advanced will eventually be repaid. However, the ability to repay is not an indispensable condition to financial assistance and American nationals able to qualify therefor in accordance with the rules hereinafter stated should in no event be refused payments simply because they cannot foresee a time when

they will be able to repay the sums advanced. When a recipient of financial assistance offers to reimburse the United States Government in foreign currency for sums previously advanced in accordance with this instruction it is requested that a report be forwarded to the Department covering the following points: (a) The Swiss representative should indicate in his report the source from which the formerly destitute American national has received the foreign currency, in order that the Department may consider whether the funds have been acquired legitimately; (b) The obligation being payable to the United States Government in legal tender of the United States, each advance of funds in foreign currency should be listed to show the United States dollar equivalent at the accounting rate of exchange prevailing as of the date on which the funds were advanced (that is, the rate prevailing for the accounting purposes of the Swiss representative concerned; usually the rate at which the Swiss representative purchased the foreign exchange for the account of the representation of the interests of the United States) and the sum of all such equivalents will represent the total obligation in United States dollars; (c) It would be appreciated if the Swiss representative would indicate whether in connection with the representation of the interests of the United States he could reasonably expect to expend within a brief period the foreign currency so offered; (d) The report should also indicate whether the Swiss representative will be permitted by the authorities of the country in which he is stationed so to expend foreign currency received in reimbursement of previous advances of financial assistance; (e) The rate of exchange prevailing as of the date when reimbursement is offered should also be shown, as well as the total amount of foreign currency offered in reimbursement (whether partial or full reimbursement is contemplated); and (f) since the person offering such reimbursement and members of his household become ineligible to receive further financial assistance, unless resumption of payments is specifically authorized by the Department, the report should indicate that financial assistance has terminated. Upon the receipt of such a report, the Department will ascertain from its records whether the obligation has already been discharged in the United States either partially or in full and, in appropriate instances, will authorize the Swiss representative to accept reimbursement in foreign currency to such extent as the obligation remains undischarged.

7. Territories where the interests of the United States are represented by Switzerland are hereby divided into ten classes and the basic maxi-

mum monthly payment for an adult is hereby established tentatively for each class as follows:

Class I	$60	Class VI	$90
Class II	65	Class VII	100
Class III	70	Class VIII	110
Class IV	75	Class IX	120
Class V	80	Class X	$90

8. In a single household with more than one adult member of the family, only one adult may receive the basic maximum monthly payment. For each additional adult member of the same family entitled to receive payments the monthly payment to the family may be increased by seventy-five per cent (75 per cent) of the basic maximum, provided that the total maximum monthly payment for all of the adult members of the same family entitled to receive payments shall not exceed two hundred fifty per cent (250 per cent) of the basic rate. The monthly payment for the family may be further increased by twenty-five per cent (25 per cent) of the basic maximum for each minor member of the family entitled to receive payments, provided that the total maximum monthly payment for the minor members of the same family entitled to receive payments shall not exceed seventy-five per cent (75 per cent) of the basic maximum. The maximum monthly payment for a single family in one household shall not exceed three hundred and twenty-five per cent (325 per cent) of the basic maximum, unless in special cases, such as extraordinarily large families, the Swiss representative recommends to the Legation at Bern and receives specific exceptional authority to pay a larger percentage of the basic maximum. A minor entitled to receive payments may, if not living with an adult entitled to receive payments, receive up to the basic maximum monthly payment prescribed for an adult, provided that only one minor in a household shall receive such treatment; in any such case, younger brothers or sisters residing with such a minor shall be considered as minor members of the family. It is emphasized that the rates of payment authorized above are maxima. It is expected that whenever possible the actual sums advanced will be less than the permitted maxima, and such advances should in no event be more than enough to provide for minimum essential needs. Whenever a payment to any individual exceeds the basic maximum, the receipt should indicate in detail the method of calculating the sum advanced, whether the excess is attributable to the fact that the payment includes authorized financial assistance for additional

members of the family, or to extraordinary expenditures authorized by paragraph two. Monthly payments may not be increased to discharge indebtedness.

9. Territories are hereby classified tentatively as follows:

Baltic States	Class II	Luxembourg	Class III
Belgium	Class III	Manchuria	Class II
Bulgaria	Class VIII	Monaco	Class VIII
Burma	Class III	Netherlands	Class III
China	Class II	Netherlands In-	
Czechoslovakia	Class V	dies	Class I
Denmark	Class V	Norway	Class V
France	Class VIII	Philippine	
French Indo-		Islands	Class III
china	Class III	Poland	Class II
Germany	Class III	Rumania	Class VIII
Greece	Class V	Straits Settle-	Class III
Hong Kong	Class I	ments	
Hungary	Class VIII	Thailand	Class III
Italy	Class VI	Yugoslavia	Class III
Japan	Class III		

10. Except upon the specific authorization of the American Legation at Bern, payments may be made only to persons who, upon the date of the severance of diplomatic relations (which for the purpose of this instruction is considered to be December 7, 1941), were in possession of valid American passports, valid American certificates of registration, or letters from American diplomatic or consular officers informing them that their applications for registration had been approved by the Department for a period extending beyond December 7, 1941. Seamen's certificates issued by the Insular Collector of Customs and the United States High Commissioner at Manila are also acceptable as establishing Philippine citizenship. Eligibility to financial assistance is dependent upon paragraphs ten and eleven of this instruction and not upon the current validity of the applicant's *schutzpass* or similar documentation. Once established, eligibility to financial assistance continues unless the beneficiary performs a known act of expatriation or some other adverse reason for termination of financial assistance is known to the Swiss representative, the Legation at Bern, or the Department. A refusal of an application for renewal of a *schutzpass* or registration would of course terminate financial assistance. The Department has also decided to ter-

minate financial assistance to those American nationals who when given an opportunity to do so fail to return to the United States, except in those rare cases in which the Swiss representatives inform the Department that in their opinion the individuals offered repatriation are physically unable to undertake the voyage to the United States. In cases where the Swiss representative is not satisfied that an applicant is actually physically unable to travel, the burden of proof rests with the applicant who may, if he or she so desires, present a medical certificate obtained at his or her own expense, for the consideration of the Swiss representative. For that purpose the Swiss representative may prepare a list of reputable and competent physicians to whom such applicants may apply for examination and the necessary certificates. Refusal of repatriation prior to the severance of relations is not to be considered as a criterion in determining eligibility to receive financial assistance, except so far as such refusal may have jeopardized the right to protection or may have indicated an absence of ties with the United States (see numbered paragraph eleven). In view of the Department's decision to defer repatriation from the Far East of families of mixed status until the final exchange and to avoid unnecessary separation of families, bona fide American nationals who expect to be accompanied by alien members of the family qualified for exchange [that is: (a) alien spouses; (b) alien unmarried minor children; (c) alien parents where presence of parent is essential for the welfare of the child; (d) alien medical attendant or nurse (with certain exceptions) where the presence of such an employee is certified by a responsible medical authority as essential to the health of the traveler] may defer their departure until the final exchange without being considered to have refused an opportunity for repatriation, provided that in each instance (A) both American and alien members of the family signify a definite intention to proceed to the United States by the final exchange vessel and (B) the Swiss representative is satisfied that the intention is genuine. The Department wishes to emphasize that it is always of paramount importance, and especially so at a time when our country is at war, to make sure not only that applicants for financial assistance are technically entitled to protection and assistance, but that their loyalty to the United States is beyond doubt. The Department does not wish Swiss representatives to render any assistance to persons claiming American nationality to enable them to engage in work in industry which might prove helpful to the war effort of enemy countries and the Department desires to be informed of the names of any Americans who seek such assistance with a statement of the circumstances of each case. This applies to any activity on the part of American nationals which contributes either directly or indirectly to the enemy war effort. The convention relative to the treatment of prisoners of war, signed at Geneva on July 27, 1929, governs the labor of prisoners of war and, by extension so far as it is adaptable to civilians, the labor of civilian internees. The United States Government will interpose no objection if civilian internees voluntarily accept offers of employment so long as the labor performed is not of a type prohibited by Articles 31 and 32 of the Convention. It is not possible for the Department to determine in advance the various occupations or industries that might, under "total mobilization", contribute to the enemy's war effort. The Department accordingly wishes to receive reports of decisions taken in actual cases for its consideration and will notify the Legation in the event that it takes exception to the decision in any case submitted.

11. Applications for payments desired by persons unable under the terms of the preceding paragraph to establish their claims to American nationality should be referred to the American Legation at Bern, which may, at its discretion, approve or disapprove them. In reaching its decisions, the Legation should be guided by the criteria established by the Department's circular instruction of August 12, 1941, diplomatic serial no. 3382, concerning advances of Government funds for repatriation purposes. In each instance, the Legation should report its decision and the facts of the case to the Department by air mail. If, upon receiving such a report, the Department wishes to reverse the Legation's decision (be it approval or disapproval of an application), it will so inform the Legation, which will then communicate the revised decision to the Swiss Government for the guidance of the appropriate Swiss representative. In reviewing the decisions submitted by the Legation the Department may find it appropriate in certain cases to authorize the use of private funds deposited with the Department on behalf of an applicant whose claim to citizenship is merely circumstantial and who is therefore not eligible to advances from Government funds. In such cases the Legation will be directed, if it perceives no objection, to request the Swiss Government to authorize its appropriate representative to make subsistence funds available to the applicant, within the prescribed maxima for Government funds and in accordance with the procedure applicable thereto, to the extent only that private funds are on deposit on the applicant's behalf with the Department.

12. Applications referred to the Legation at Bern should be transmitted by mail if mail communications are reasonably expeditious.

Otherwise they may be transmitted by telegraph at the expense of the United States Government, in which event, to effect an economy, several applications should be grouped in one telegram stating only such essential facts as the name and the place and date of birth of each applicant and a brief description of the evidence of nationality in each applicant's possession. Such telegraphic applications should be followed as soon as feasible by a properly documented application transmitted by mail. Approval of a telegraphic application should be considered provisional, pending a decision upon the application transmitted by mail. Payments should not be retroactive. In the absence of circumstances that may be found by the Department to warrant exceptional consideration, payment of financial assistance should commence as of the date of the application upon the basis of which the applicant is found to be qualified under this instruction to receive such assistance. The Department desires to have a record of each person claiming American nationality who has applied for financial assistance, whether or not any payments are made. An effort should be made, therefore, to obtain and submit the full names and last known addresses in the United States and abroad of all persons applying for financial assistance, with pertinent details concerning their alleged American nationality and the names and addresses of the next of kin or other references in the United States.

13. Aliens, including alien spouses and alien children of American nationals, cannot qualify for payments from funds of the United States Government except as hereafter indicated in this paragraph and in paragraph 15. The following procedure is authorized as a purely temporary expedient in the Far East pending the completion of the exchanges: Notwithstanding the provisions of this paragraph, alien members of a family qualified for inclusion in an exchange (see paragraph 10) may, if in need and not otherwise provided for, receive monthly payments in amounts to which they would be entitled under this instruction if they were American nationals, provided that in each instance: (a) the alien member of the family signifies or has signified a definite intention to proceed to the United States by the final exchange vessel, accompanying the American members of the family; (b) the Swiss representative is satisfied that the intention is genuine; and (c) the American member of the family is eligible to receive financial assistance. Receipts embodying promises to repay should be executed in such cases by the American member of the family, if possible; otherwise by the beneficiary. All doubtful cases should be referred to the Legation at Bern. Reports analogous to those requested in the last sentence of paragraph 12 should

be submitted in each instance, whether financial assistance is granted or refused.

14. It is recognized that the Swiss representatives charged with the representation of the interests of the United States may find it necessary to make payments by mail to American nationals residing in regions remote from the offices of the Swiss representatives. It is suggested that receipts might be obtained by mail and payments effected by money orders. Receipts not signed in the presence of a Swiss representative should if possible be signed in the presence of another American national and should in any event bear the right thumbprint of the person signing the receipt.

15. Since prisoners of war and interned civilians are supported by the detaining Power, it is expected that payments made to them will generally not exceed a sum sufficient to provide spending money for miscellaneous personal needs not supplied by the detaining Power. (The American Red Cross is studying the possibility of supplying such comforts free of charge.) It is thought that a maximum monthly payment of ten per cent (10%) of the basic maximum rate will usually be sufficient for that purpose. If it is established that the needs of internees exceed ten per cent of the basic maximum, the monthly payments to them may be increased. If it becomes necessary to use a form of group receipt for such payments, it is hoped that the form may be drawn up in such a way as to include the essentials of the enclosed standard individual receipt form previously mentioned. No payments will be made to officers or to persons of equivalent status held as prisoners of war, who receive pay under the convention relative to the treatment of prisoners of war, signed at Geneva on July 27, 1929. Paragraphs 10 to 13 inclusive do not apply to prisoners of war. If in need any member of the United States Army, Navy, Marine Corps or Coast Guard detained as a prisoner of war and not of officer or equivalent status may receive small payments of spending money authorized by this paragraph. Vouchers covering payments to prisoners of war under this paragraph should bear the notation that the amount is to be charged to the War Department or the Navy Department, whichever is appropriate. The Department has also authorized provisionally the granting of financial assistance to interned merchant seamen (including aliens having the status of American seamen) on the same basis as it is granted to prisoners of war.

16. In view of previous inquiries, Swiss representatives may be informed that, for the purposes of this instruction, citizens of the Commonwealth of the Philippines are considered to be American nationals.

However, unless such nationals are able to qualify for payments under numbered paragraph ten, their applications should be referred to the Legation at Bern.   Except in the case of a Filipino who is a citizen of the United States, the receipt should be clearly marked, "Philippine Citizen".

17. You are requested to communicate to the Swiss Foreign Office the substance of this instruction and to express this Government's hope that the appropriate Swiss representatives will be informed of it as soon as possible by mail, wherever that would be reasonably expeditious, or by telegraph, as will doubtless be considered desirable with respect to its transmission to the Far East.   Emergency relief payments shall cease as soon as the foregoing wishes of this Government are communicated to the Swiss representatives charged with the representation of the interests of the United States, with the exception that the Swiss representatives, for a further period of two months, may at their discretion continue to extend emergency relief in worthy cases of nationals unable to qualify for immediate payments under numbered paragraph ten pending the receipt of decisions from the Legation at Bern on applications referred to it under numbered paragraph eleven.   In particular, sympathetic consideration might be given to such cases as involve nationals able from resources in the United States to reimburse the sums advanced during that period.

18. From such credits as the Department will from time to time establish for the representation by Switzerland of the interests of the United States, you are authorized and requested to make block allotments to the Swiss Government in the amounts estimated to be necessary for expenditures attributable to such representation, including payments herein authorized.   It is assumed that such funds will in turn be allotted by the Swiss Foreign Office in the manner indicated in numbered paragraph eight of your telegram no. 221 of January 22.

19. At such time as this Government's policy may be determined with respect to any special categories of payments not authorized by this instruction, further instructions will be issued.

INDEX

INDEX

Accounts, expense of protection, rendered to Department of State, 91, 168, 169–170, 278.

Adee, A. A., Assistant Secretary of State, on good offices for Venezuela (1906), 83.

Administrative procedures, international uniformity, 154.

Agent:
Definition, 46 n.
Historical usage, 45, 137–138.

Alien Property Custodian, control of property of enemy aliens, 200, 206.

Aliens:
Employment in U.S. Foreign Service, U.S. Minister to Turkey (1894, quoted), 17.
International standards of treatment, 144–145.
Local power, responsibility for, 143–146.
Relief and pensions for, limitations, 218, 284, 286–287.

Aliens, enemy:
Employed by protecting power, 174.
Expulsion from F r a n c e in Franco - Prussian W a r, 41–44.

American Academy, custody in war, 192.

American churches in Europe, custody in war, 192.

American republics:
Sovereignty not impaired by protection, 121.
Swiss protection of, in World War II, 211.
U.S. good offices for Chinese in, 124, 152.
U.S. instruction to Foreign Service officers, and requests for British aid in protection of persons, 121.

American School at Tokyo, custody in war, 193.

Anderson, Chandler P., Legal Adviser to American Embassy at London, efforts for prisoners of war, 95–98.

Anglican Church at Trieste, custody in war, 191, 193.

Archives:
British:
Custody in Brazil and Bolivia, 29, 75.
Violation by Turkey and by Germany, 93, 186.
Custodianship, *Foreign Service Regulations* (q u o t e d), 181–182.
Custody in war, 28, 29, 90–91, 181, 186, 188.
French:
U.S. custody in Mexico and Venezuela, 31, 32, 80.
Violation by Turkish officials, 93.